Inspired by Jerry Hopkins' biograp*Here Gets Out Alive*, and a stint on lead kazoo for bedroom band The Rulers, Jeff Apter has written more than 30 books about Australian music and musicians. His subjects include Bon Scott, Daniel Johns, AC/DC's Young brothers, Marc Hunter, Keith Urban, Johnny O'Keefe, Jon English and many others. As a ghostwriter and/or co-writer, Jeff has worked with Kasey Chambers, Richard Clapton and Mark Evans, formerly of AC/DC, and was on staff at *Rolling Stone* for several years. Jeff lives on the NSW South Coast with his wife and two children, and enough pets to fill a small zoo.

www.jeffapter.com.au

Praise for *Keith Urban*

'Keith Urban has done just about everything in country music that anyone could ever imagine. This biography by Jeff Apter reveals the highlights and struggles in getting there.'
—Ricky Skaggs, 15-time Grammy Award–winning musician

'A celebratory portrait of Urban's life and career. Informed, engagingly written, this is one for Urban fans—and there's a lot of them out there.'
—*The Sydney Morning Herald*

Praise for *Bad Boy Boogie*

'An utterly fascinating read.'
—*Weekend Australian*

'A must-read for Scott's following.'
—*The Herald Sun*

'A not insignificant number of books have been published on Bon Scott . . . Jeff Apter has written the cream of this crop.'
—*Glam Adelaide*

Praise for *Friday on My Mind*

'A great book for Australian music buffs . . . offering plenty of nostalgia and great stories.'
—*Canberra Weekly*

'Jeff Apter shows his usual insightful feel for Aussie rock as he takes us on a fabulous journey.'
—*Daily Telegraph*

'Engaging . . . a portrait of an artist who eschewed the hype and constantly refined his craft.'
—*Sydney Morning Herald/The Age*

'Filled with surprises for both the knowing and uninitiated . . . a moving, heartfelt summary of a life that will live on forever in The Great Australian Songbook.'
—*Glam Adelaide*

'Upbeat . . . an entertaining read for fans of early Aussie rock.'
—*The Herald Sun*

Praise for *Malcolm Young*

'In Apter's hands it is a story as spellbinding as one of Young's guitar riffs.'

—Helen Pitt, author of *The House*

'A ripping yarn about a legendary musician . . . Jeff Apter's book delivers in spades, with plenty of nuggets of gold and interesting new snippets for the AC/DC fan.'

—*The Canberra Times*

'A fascinating ride . . . Apter's book is more than a biography, it's a tribute to a talented and canny man.'

—*100% Rock Magazine*

Don't Dream It's Over

THE REMARKABLE LIFE OF
NEIL FINN

JEFF APTER

SYDNEY·MELBOURNE·AUCKLAND·LONDON

First published in 2023

Copyright © Jeff Apter 2023

All rights reserved. No part of this book may be reproduced or transmitted in any form or by any means, electronic or mechanical, including photocopying, recording or by any information storage and retrieval system, without prior permission in writing from the publisher. The Australian *Copyright Act 1968* (the Act) allows a maximum of one chapter or 10 per cent of this book, whichever is the greater, to be photocopied by any educational institution for its educational purposes provided that the educational institution (or body that administers it) has given a remuneration notice to the Copyright Agency (Australia) under the Act.

Allen & Unwin
Cammeraygal Country
83 Alexander Street
Crows Nest NSW 2065
Australia
Phone: (61 2) 8425 0100
Email: info@allenandunwin.com
Web: www.allenandunwin.com

Allen & Unwin acknowledges the Traditional Owners of the Country on which we live and work. We pay our respects to all Aboriginal and Torres Strait Islander Elders, past and present.

A catalogue record for this book is available from the National Library of Australia

ISBN 978 1 76106 8089

Internal design by Julian Mole, Post Pre-press Group, Australia
Set in 13/17 pt Adobe Garamond Pro by Post Pre-press Group, Australia
Printed and bound in Australia by the Opus Group

10 9 8 7 6 5 4 3 2 1

The paper in this book is FSC® certified. FSC® promotes environmentally responsible, socially beneficial and economically viable management of the world's forests.

Another one for me

Contents

Prologue	1
1 'I wanted to carve my own track'	3
2 'I was transfixed and transformed and transported. All of the trans'	18
3 'There's a lot of go in this Te Awamutu youngster'	30
4 'Wow! It's a hit!'	45
5 'Career? Who wants a career?'	57
6 'Paul and I had a plan'	73
7 'It is a cause of concern if you start to become known as clowns'	87
8 'You can fart and they'd clap, mate'	101
9 'We weren't used to having another strong personality on stage'	115
10 'Karekare brought out a lot of extremes'	126
11 'It was emotional as hell'	136
12 'It feels more like a celebration than a funeral'	148
13 'No one knew what the fuck was going on'	160
14 'A lot of things I've been worrying about weren't important at all'	171
15 'I would hope that a genuine musical exchange takes place'	184
16 'I am deeply saddened by the loss of a close friend'	198
17 'One of the most extraordinary musical experiences of my life'	212
18 'I don't like cards, so we decided to go and make a noise'	224

19 'Is it a flock of Finns? A festoon of Finns?'	238
20 'Yes, I've joined Fleetwood Mac'	251
Coda	269
Acknowledgements	273
Neil Finn: Ten musical moments	275
Selected Neil Finn discography	277
Selected bibliography	284

Prologue

April 1977

Neil Finn wasn't home when the phone rang. His brother Tim was on the line, calling from London. Neil's mother Mary answered.

'Can you ask Neil to call me?' Tim asked. 'It's important.'

A few hours later, Neil, who was eighteen, got his big brother, who was almost six years older, on the phone.

'What's going on?' Neil asked.

'Um,' Tim said, taking a deep breath. 'Do you want to join the band? Do you want to join Split Enz?'

Neil didn't respond immediately.

'I need to think it over,' he told Tim. 'Let me call you back.'

Tim was gobsmacked. How could it be possible that Neil didn't want to join the band? Neil was, without doubt, their biggest fan. He knew their songs; he understood their humour, their ethos, their *weirdness*. He'd been in the audience at their first show, in Auckland in 1972, and had since seen them play dozens of times. Neil had written the group's name on his school pencil case—he'd even sat in on band writing sessions. And he probably even knew how to slap on the greasepaint that the band wore on stage. Surely the idea of joining Split Enz, who had made records and had a cult following overseas, would be irresistible?

How could he not want to join?

An hour passed before Neil called Tim back.

'Yeah, alright,' he said down the line. 'I'm in.'

Tim was hugely relieved. Many years later, looking back on this fateful day—for Neil, for Tim and for Split Enz—he admitted that while a bit stunned, he was quietly impressed by Neil's response, his cheeky decision to make his older brother play the waiting game. 'I think that's the coolest thing he's ever done.'

So what if Neil couldn't actually play the electric guitar, the role for which he was being hired? (Founding member and guitarist Phil Judd had just jumped ship, after coming to blows with Tim in Atlanta, Georgia, near the end of a rough six-week US tour.) Oh, and there was the matter of Neil's own band, After Hours, who were about to undertake their first recording session, and who'd just been praised in the local press. How should Neil break the news to them? And what exactly should Neil tell his parents? He was just a kid from New Zealand who'd only ever travelled as far as the Gold Coast in Australia.

But none of this mattered to Neil Finn right now. The stars had just aligned for him; surely he could sort out all this stuff in due course. Within days, Neil was on a flight to London, and his world would never be the same.

1

'I wanted to carve my own track'

Music was always a feature of the life of Neil Mullane Finn. It seemed to be present virtually from the time he was born on 27 May 1958, at the Wharenoho Maternity Home in Te Awamutu, the fourth and final child of Richard and Mary. Carolyn was the oldest, followed by Brian (soon to be known as Tim), Judy and now Neil. Mary was 36 when Neil was born, as was Richard, who was known as Dick to pretty much everybody.

Music could always be heard in the Finn household. And with it came a lot of joy; some of Neil's earliest and fondest childhood memories were music related. 'A good tune is hard to come by,' Mary Finn told her children, and Neil took that to mean that a great song, one that brought people together, should be treasured. Even the daggy songs, the sugary ballads—and especially the ones that tugged at your heartstrings.

Most Friday nights, after Dick had finished work at his

accountancy firm, Finn & Partners, in Te Awamutu—a sleepy community about 150 kilometres south of Auckland, on New Zealand's North Island—the Finns staged singalongs at 78 Teasdale Street, their modest but comfortable home.

Family friend Colin O'Brien typically led these singsongs, which were held around the piano in the Finns' lounge room. Dick and Mary were the perfect hosts, keeping Colin stocked with beer and ciggies as he and everyone else sang late into the night. 'He didn't live a long life,' Neil said of O'Brien in 2014, 'but he was responsible for a lot of joy at those events.' At some point in the evening, Neil's uncle George would clear his throat and launch into his signature tune, 'Shake Hands with a Millionaire', a standard from the 1930s, while another family friend, Peggy Dawson, charm bracelets rattling on her wrist, would belt out a very serviceable 'Stormy Weather'. (Tim likened her to an 'Irish Ethel Merman'.)

As for Neil's parents, while Mary relished the songs of Irishman Patrick O'Hagan—she had deep Irish roots—Dick loved jazz more than anything; his musical hero was American trumpeter Bunny Berigan. But after a couple of whiskies Dick could be persuaded to tackle Ray Charles's 'You Don't Know Me'. It was his favourite song, hands down, and a popular Friday-night number, even if Dick wasn't the world's greatest singer. ('Tone deaf' was the usual assessment. But he could whistle up a storm.)

Everyone had their own big moment. And that included Neil, who had barely started school when he made his first singalong performance alongside Tim. The boys took it all very seriously; when they knew 'their time' was approaching, they'd get together in the hallway, out of sight, nervously figuring out their harmonies. The song everyone loved to hear the boys sing was 'Jamaica Farewell', made famous by American actor and recording star Harry Belafonte. As maudlin ballads went, it was hard to top, but they sang it as if Caribbean folk music could be found in the DNA of two young boys who'd rarely left Te Awamutu.

Neil wasn't an especially sombre kid, but he did develop a fondness for what he called 'the slow, sad songs . . . that had a bit of melancholy attached to them', such as 'Jamaica Farewell'. Looking back, he'd call it the 'Danny Boy' concept, 'drawing joy out of misery'. As Neil understood it, he was learning a crucial lesson: 'Empathy is the biggest factor in music. Full stop.' And he quickly grasped how to play to the crowd—Neil would never suffer from stage fright.

Friday nights at the Finns could get pretty rowdy, but in the main, Dick and Mary were a sensible, conservative, middle-class Kiwi couple who raised their children accordingly. Te Awamutu may not have got wise to the 'Swinging Sixties'—Neil summed up its sleepiness when he said you'd walk miles just to see 'an old man's collection of twigs'—but the country town, and his family, provided Neil with solid roots. 'I had great, loving parents,' Neil said. 'Te Awamutu was a cool place to grow up. Small town, big dreams.'

An annual event staged at Te Awamutu was the Agricultural & Pastoral Show (known simply as the A&P). Throughout Neil's life he retained a vivid memory of a day spent aboard the 'War and Peace' float, which his father filmed on his Super 8 camera. The children on one side of the float, who represented peace, were dressed in white tunics, smiling and waving to the crowd, but not Neil, who was on the 'war' side of the float. He wore camouflage gear and held a small plastic rifle, a grim look on his face. 'I stood there and I was so serious,' he recalled. That memory sparked a song that Neil wrote many years later, which he called 'Turn and Run'. 'You know where I stand,' he sang, 'holding my plastic gun.'

Certain subjects remained taboo for the close-knit Finns. Sex, for instance, was never mentioned at home. In 1970, when Neil was twelve, the family went to the cinema to see *Ryan's Daughter*, the mildly racy tale of an affair between an Irish girl and a British soldier. Not long into the movie, when Mary became aware of the subject matter—one kissing scene was one too many, as far as she was concerned—she insisted that they leave immediately. As Neil remembered, Dick was disappointed: 'He seemed to be quite enjoying it.'

Neil found plenty of less controversial diversions when he wasn't attending St Patrick's School, where he was enrolled in 1963, or singing the hits of Harry Belafonte around the family piano. He and his mates would jump on their push-bikes and set out on the seven-mile (eleven-kilometre) trip up nearby Mount Pirongia. At the top they'd take a break and, in Neil's words, 'have a couple of bottles of fizzy drinks, some chocolate and then cycle back'. Neil also enjoyed racing his go-kart down College Hill in Te Awamutu, although one time he took a corner too quickly and came off, hitting a car and flying through the air. While his injuries weren't too severe, the crash stuck in his memory. One day he'd revisit his spill in a song called 'Go Kart', which he'd record with his wife Sharon.

Neil also formed a band, of sorts, with his friends: they donned Beatles wigs, and substituted tennis racquets for guitars and a cardboard box for a drum kit. They called themselves The Cavemen. Surprisingly, they didn't make it to the New Zealand Music Hall of Fame.

Neil also had more solitary pursuits. At the rear of the family home in Teasdale Street was an orchard, where he liked to spend quiet time by himself. He'd document the experience in Crowded House's 'Private Universe'. 'Highest branch on the apple tree,' Neil sang, 'it was my favourite place to be.'

Family holidays were also full of music. The Finns usually spent their vacations at Mount Maunganui, a resort town on the east coast about 100 kilometres from Te Awamutu with striking views. After a day spent in the water—the Finns were keen swimmers—the clan would get together with two Scottish brothers, Jesuit priests Matt and Peter Durning, family friends who loved to sing. 'They both had very fine voices,' Neil said in 1996, when discussing the Durnings, 'and sang in beautiful harmony.'

One of the songs the Durnings introduced Neil and Tim to was 'Terry', a ten-tissue weepie that had been a big hit in the UK during 1964 for doe-eyed singer Lynn Ripley, known simply as Twinkle. When it came to motorcycle crash songs, 'Terry' gave The Shangri-Las' 'Leader of the Pack' a run for its money: 'Please wait at the gate of heaven for me, Terry.' Neil and Tim would sing it, probably not fully grasping the tragic nature of the lyric. Another teary tune the Durnings introduced to the boys was 'Poor Little Lambs', a western-styled ballad, also known as 'The Whiffenpoof Song', that was best summed up by its central lyric: 'I'm a poor little lamb/Who's lost its way.' Neil liked it even more than 'Terry'.

★

The mid-1960s was a great era for rock and pop music. It was the time of The Rolling Stones' '(I Can't Get No) Satisfaction' and 'Get Off of My Cloud'—one of the first records Neil owned—as well as The Beatles' 'Help!' and 'Ticket to Ride', and Bob Dylan's 'Like a Rolling Stone'. Gerry and the Pacemakers rode the 'Ferry Cross the Mersey', while the King, Elvis Presley, was 'Crying in the Chapel'. Groups such as The Kinks and The Move and The Who were changing pop music forever.

A few of these great songs did find their way onto the New Zealand airwaves and the Top 40—what was known as the Lever Hit Parade—although, as Neil once stated with a rueful chuckle, 'New Zealand got the '60s about five years later than the rest of the world'. You were more likely to hear Engelbert Humperdinck on the radio than the Rolling Stones.

But for seven-year-old Neil, this period was more important for another reason. The family had been to see the hit film *Doctor Zhivago*, and Tim, who was then thirteen, had learned how to play 'Somewhere My Love (Lara's Theme)', a feature of the soundtrack, on the piano. That was all the motivation Neil needed to tackle the piano himself. He took lessons with a teacher named Connie Nicholson, who he'd never forget; he thanked her publicly some 40-odd years later at the opening of a Split Enz exhibition in Te Awamutu.

Neil always seemed reluctant to admit it, but he did try to emulate Tim's efforts—and sometimes even outperform his brother. 'I was very competitive,' he conceded in 2014. 'That's what got me started.' When Tim won the lead role in a school production called *My Fair Laddy*, it was the first of many times that Neil looked on from the audience while his brother stepped into the spotlight. That provided even more motivation for Neil to pursue music—he then started playing the guitar, too.

St Patrick's staged an annual talent quest and one year Neil stepped forward and sang 'You Are My Sunshine'. He was declared the winner, hands down, and gleefully pocketed the ten shillings prize money. But big brother Tim was the family's golden child, a high achiever academically and a strong performer on the sporting field. The only downside for Dick was that Tim preferred rugby and tennis to cricket, much to his father's disappointment. Dick once took Tim to a father-and-son game, but Tim was cracked on the skull by the ball and never played cricket again. (Neil found good use for his tennis racquet one day at St Patrick's when he used it to whack a kid who'd been beating up Tim.)

When Tim won a scholarship, he left Te Awamutu in late January 1966 to become a boarder at Sacred Heart College in Auckland. Tim was about to meet a group of budding artists and musicians whose influence on him—and, by association, on Neil—would be monumental.

★

One of Tim's new friends was fellow boarder and Auckland native Jonathan Michael 'Mike' Chunn—he was known as 'Chang', while Tim was 'Fang'—who'd had a musical awakening after a viewing of The Beatles' hit movie *A Hard Day's Night*. Tim, meanwhile, had seen British tourists The Dave Clark Five—of 'Glad All Over' renown—at the Founders Theatre in Hamilton; his sister Carolyn was with him at the gig, screaming her heart out. Chang and Fang quickly discovered that they shared a love of the amazing new music coming out of the UK.

Chunn accompanied Tim on a trip home from Sacred Heart, which was when Neil first met him. Neil slapped away at some makeshift drums while Tim and Chunn strummed guitars, and the trio bashed out a serviceable rendition of some Beatles songs. But Neil was much more impressed—and inspired—when, during September 1967, some eighteen months into Tim's time as a boarder, he sent home a musical care package. It was a reel-to-reel recording made at Sacred Heart of 'Fang and Chang' singing a few songs from The Beatles and Bee Gees. As far as Neil was concerned, this was the real deal. He'd had no idea that big brother Tim could sing that well; his voice was high and pure. 'It just sounded so good,' Neil later remembered. 'I couldn't believe it.'

Neil, who'd been learning the basics on a guitar that Tim had left behind, became even more determined to master the instrument. Piano was all good and well, but The Beatles played guitars. And The Beatles were, as Tim advised Neil, 'gods that walked the earth'. To help him understand how godlike they were, Tim gave Neil a Beatles Fan Club magazine subscription.

Every year since 1936, Sacred Heart had hosted the Walter Kirby Music Competition, named for one of the college's old boys who'd become a highly regarded musician. In 1968, Tim and Chunn placed second in the event, singing—you guessed it—a Beatles song, in this instance 'Yesterday'. In December of that year, just after The Beatles' White Album—a sprawling two-LP set that included such classics as 'Revolution 1' and 'While My Guitar Gently Weeps', plus John Lennon's creepy experimental piece

'Revolution 9'—was released, Neil looked on as Tim, Chunn and a few others got together and listened with reverence to the music that was spread across the two LPs. They devoured 'every word, every song', remembered Neil. They were obsessed.

Neil, too, grew incredibly fond of the 'Fabs'—'Let it Be' was the first release of theirs that he bought with his own money. But his all-time favourite song didn't typically appear on most 'Top 10 Beatles Songs' lists. It was 'Across the Universe', John Lennon's heartfelt ode to peace, love and transcendental meditation that appeared on the *Let It Be* album. The mesmerising opening line, 'Words are flowing out like endless rain into a paper cup', would stick with Neil; he'd revisit the paper cup image in his most popular song, 'Don't Dream It's Over'.

Neil was like a sponge, soaking up all this music. Whenever Tim visited his family at Te Awamutu, he'd find Neil in his bedroom, banging away at the piano. Tim was struck by how determined his brother was. Neil's nickname as a kid was 'The Ant' because of his desire to get things done, to solve problems. In that way, he was a lot like his mother, as Tim related in 2004. '[My mother] wouldn't even pause if something went wrong; she'd be straight onto it—and that's Neil.'

Neil felt he was ready to take the next step and write a song of his own. But he employed a unique method for his first stab at songwriting—he teamed a melody of his own with words cribbed directly from the back cover of a Donovan record, 1968's 'Hurdy Gurdy Man'. Neil, clearly, wasn't yet familiar with the complicated world of copyright. He was pretty pleased with his handiwork at the time, but over the years he adopted a more pragmatic opinion of his first song. 'It's pretty appalling, actually,' he said in 1998.

★

A big social event during the Finns' annual vacation at Mount Maunganui was the Soundshell Talent Quest. In 1970, when Neil was twelve, he entered and sang a very presentable version of Arlo Guthrie's 'Coming Into Los Angeles', accompanying himself on acoustic guitar. Neil's main competition was a Hamilton cabaret singer crooning the bossa nova hit 'Quando Quando Quando', an easy-listening favourite. Surely a drug ballad like 'Los Angeles', originally sung by the son of American dustbowl legend Woody Guthrie, was a better choice? Apparently not, at least according to the judges at the Soundshell. Neil placed second.

It was a given that Neil, just like Tim, would enrol at Sacred Heart, and he started classes there in 1971. Tim, meanwhile, readied himself for the University of Auckland, where he planned to study philosophy and politics. But Neil didn't take to boarding school, even though he excelled in Latin, French, maths and music during his first year. By his own admission, he was 'a little shit', a stirrer egged on, in part, by his older brother, who'd given him a copy of *The Little Red Schoolbook*—a highly controversial tome written by two Danish schoolteachers that, among its many topics, tackled the thorny issues of sex and drugs. Although written as a guide for schoolkids of Neil's age, in conservative New Zealand it had been labelled 'communist propaganda'. Neil devoured the book; he'd recall that it offered 'quite practical advice . . . it said it was okay to masturbate'.

The closest that teenager Neil came to an authentic sexual experience, however, was a close encounter with a girl named Denise Beatty, at a time when he was hospitalised after breaking his arm in a game of rugby. 'No tongues,' Neil clarified in 2008.

Neil's nemesis at Sacred Heart was a brother who caned him vigorously for some misdemeanour. 'He left four impressive welts on my buttocks which became black and blue bruises over the course of a week,' Neil remembered. The caning, if not the bruises, stayed with him for years.

Neil spent much of his time in the school's music room. There he befriended fellow student Bernard McHardy. They bonded over the songs of Elton John, who they saw play at the Western Springs Stadium in Auckland in October 1971. It was Neil's first big concert—'very exciting' was his assessment of seeing the Rocket Man in action. Neil quickly mastered John's hit 'Your Song' on the piano.

Neil and McHardy entered the 1971 Walter Kirby, singing James Taylor's 'Carolina in My Mind'. Neil went one step better than Tim had done three years earlier and won the event. Neil and McHardy were so chuffed they committed the song to tape; it was Neil's first recording. Forty years later, Neil was speaking at an event in Sydney called Song Summit when McHardy, who was in the audience, re-introduced himself. 'I could tell at fourteen he was going to be big,' said the Sacred Heart old boy, who'd hung onto the tape.

Neil also won the next Soundshell event when he and his family returned to Mount Maunganui. He sang Carole King's 'You've Got a Friend' and pocketed $100. It was Neil's first big payday.

★

Big brother Tim, meanwhile, had begun his university experience in late February 1971, along with Mike Chunn. Tim had no defined career path; he'd later joke that he was probably destined to become 'some jaded alcoholic lecturer in English'. However, there was an overachieving gene in the Finn family: one uncle was a psychiatrist, while two cousins living in the US, Miles and Margot, were on their way to significant careers as a nuclear physicist and a history professor, respectively. Dick ran a successful accountancy firm. And he and Mary hoped that Tim, and possibly Neil, too, would achieve great things—ideally in a 'sensible' career. But Tim's world was about to be flipped upside down.

Tim found himself drawn to a hostel on campus simply known as Room 129. It was there that he met a collection of 'freaks' who were studying at the University of Auckland's highly rated Elam School of Fine Arts. Rob Gillies was part of the group, as was Geoffrey Noel Crombie, a lanky eccentric, who Tim came to understand had a 'particularly Wellingtonian bent on life'. Philip Judd also resided in Room 129; he was a Hastings native, 'a talented painter and musical savant', said Neil. By comparison, Tim was a bit provincial, a country boy out of his depth. But he quickly adapted to life among the art-school set. 'There were girls, there were drugs,' he recalled. And music—loads of music. Tim drank it all in and also began singing with some of his new pals in an outfit they named Qwunt.

During 1971, Neil and his family set out for their first visit to the uni in Auckland to check in with Tim, to see how he was getting on. They stayed at the Waterfront Hotel, which was close to the university campus, all of them sharing one room. His parents—and Neil—were shocked when they saw Tim. He'd grown his hair, loosened up and seemed to have embraced a whole new way of life. 'He became a bit of a freak, hanging out with art-school people and making amazing music,' said Neil. 'I was absolutely entranced by it and wanted to do it, too.'

*

After Tim's final exams for the year, he tried California Sunshine, a form of LSD. Word got back to Dick and Mary that their son had been 'dabbling with hallucinogenics' and they decided to travel to Auckland to stage an intervention. Neil, in a commendable gesture of sibling loyalty, dashed to a nearby phone booth to tip him off. Tim, unfortunately, wasn't there and his parents went through with their surprise sit-down.

Neil seemed to make a habit of helping out his siblings. Another time, his sister Judy left some pot in the house, and Neil and his buddy Dean Taylor had to 'rescue it', as Taylor described, before Neil's mother found the stash.

Tim moved off campus and into a house owned by his parents in Mission Bay, sharing with Rob Gillies, for the princely rent of $5 a week. Neil made a habit of dropping in most Sundays to play music and drink beer, his copy of *The Little Red Schoolbook* in his pocket. It was all quite a shock for the very conservative neighbourhood—a bunch of long-hairs hanging out and having a high old time.

In July 1972, English band Jethro Tull, whose albums *Aqualung* and *Thick as a Brick* were on high rotation among Tim and his friends, played a show at Auckland Town Hall.

Neil had a ticket for the gig, as did Tim, Noel Crombie—who dressed in an African-style linen suit, accessorised with two neckties—and a few others from Tim's lively uni crowd. When Tim collected Neil, he seemed anxious.

'What's up?' Neil asked.

'We're going to go and smoke some pot,' Tim whispered. 'I hope that's okay.'

'That's no problem,' Neil told him. 'I've already tried it.'

Tim was taken aback. In some things, it seemed, Neil was already one step ahead.

Despite their 'acid intervention', Neil's parents were tolerant. According to his friend Dean Taylor, Dick and Mary saw their sons' musical obsession, and everything that came with it, as a phase from which they'd eventually move on. 'They did seem pretty cool about it and didn't seem to get in the way of their sons' ambitions. But they never stopped being protective.'

Dick and Mary were stunned, however, when Tim told them he was dropping out of university to form a band with Phil Judd, who'd also dropped out. They decided to name the band Split Ends. Their immediate goal was to snare a slot on the upcoming Great Ngaruawahia Music Festival, New Zealand's first big outdoor rock festival, to be staged in January 1973.

Neil had a bombshell of his own to drop when the last school term of 1972 rolled around. He told his parents that he was leaving Sacred Heart and had enrolled at Te Awamutu College, a public school. As much as he admired Tim, Neil was tired of living in his shadow, and the longer he stayed at Sacred Heart, the more annoying it became. Teachers seemed to revel in reminding him of

Tim's many achievements. 'The brothers were relating to me as Tim's little brother,' said Neil, 'and I wanted to carve my own track.' He'd had enough.

Not for the last time in his life, Neil was going home.

2

'I was transfixed and transformed and transported. All of the trans'

Inspired by the American folk boom of the 1950s and early '60s, and the music of such leading lights as Joan Baez, Bob Dylan, and Peter, Paul & Mary, folk clubs had become increasingly popular in New Zealand. And as soon as music-obsessive Neil returned to Te Awamutu in 1972, he joined a folk club called All'n'Some. It was run by Felicity Saxby, who, Neil quickly learned, was 'a worldly and wise Englishwoman' with a strong sense of social justice. She'd emigrated to New Zealand in 1966 with her doctor husband John—Felicity worked closely with him in the trailblazing field of psychodrama therapy—and their four children. Her daughters Fritha and Blithe sang with Felicity at All'n'Some events, which occasionally took them to different folk clubs in the region, Neil travelling with the other members in the Saxbys' Bedford van. Saxby also organised one-off concerts, where Neil performed at the Plunket Society—an organisation for mothers and babies—and for patients at the Tokanui Psychiatric Hospital, which was managed by Saxby's husband.

As much as he enjoyed the folk club, Neil's decision to join was born of pragmatism: there weren't many other places to play music in Te Awamutu. He also had a markedly different understanding of folk music than most of the older members of the club. As far as Neil was concerned, folk music was the domain of the singer/songwriter and breakout stars like James Taylor, Carole King and Cat Stevens. He was bingeing on such records as David Bowie's *Hunky Dory*—while still known as David Jones, Bowie had sung in London folk clubs—and Neil Young's *After the Gold Rush*. (He admired Young's 'wilfulness, his determination to do his own thing', qualities that Neil would one day share.) But as Neil discovered, when he played any contemporary songs at All'n'Some, the true 'folkies' in the group would furrow their brows and respond with something old and mysterious that came from another time and place altogether. Neil soon learned that there was more to folk music than 'You've Got a Friend'.

It was at All'n'Some that Neil first heard the music of Sandy Denny, the Brit with the sad and beautiful voice who, after achieving great things with the Fairport Convention, had just released her second solo album, *Sandy*. (She would die, tragically, in 1978, aged just 31.) Denny's 'Who Knows Where the Time Goes?' was a Brit-folk classic, a towering song. Interestingly, Denny's musical career had begun in a folk club not unlike All'n'Some, operating out of the Troubadour, a coffee house in London's Earls Court (one of about 400 folk clubs running in the UK at the time). Neil became a rusted-on fan, so much so that almost 50 years after first hearing Denny's music, Neil covered her 'Quiet Joys of Brotherhood' while on tour in 2020 with his son Liam.

Neil made some good friends, and formed strong bonds, during his time with All'n'Some. It was through the club that he met Rod Murdoch, his first real musical mentor; they were introduced by Felicity Saxby at an event at the Kon Tiki Folk Club in Hamilton. Murdoch was a quietly spoken man ten years older than Neil. They'd jam at Murdoch's home in Ngaruawahia, Neil playing keyboards and guitar, sometimes even trying his hand at mandolin. Murdoch also played mandolin as well as a twelve-string Spanish instrument called the bandurria. Soon after meeting they co-wrote a song called 'Lady Laura Lee'. 'It was [my] first sense of getting in the zone and really communicating with another musician,' explained Neil.

*

On 10 December 1972, a very underage Neil—'I was still a pimply schoolboy'—sat with his sisters Carolyn and Judy in an Auckland venue called the Wynyard Tavern. He was about to witness the debut performance of Split Ends, which comprised Tim, Mike Chunn, Phil Judd, a violinist named Miles Golding and flautist Mike Howard. Chunn's brother Geoff sat in on drums. Apart from knowing that Tim 'looked a little freaky' at the time, Neil really had no idea what to expect. As the gig progressed, however, it became clear to Neil that there was some magic at work, even though it was hard to describe exactly what he was hearing. 'I was transfixed and transformed and transported,' Neil said in 2014. 'All of the trans.'

Neil was now even more determined to make his own music—maybe even forge a career in music. And he loved the band; he began quoting lyrics from Split Ends songs whenever he sat down to play with Rod Murdoch.

'We could see he was pretty determined to follow in his brother's footsteps,' said Neil's friend and classmate Dean Taylor. 'Not only did he have a big brother who played in bands, but he could play and sing. Neil was definitely cool.'

Neil would visit the band's rehearsal space at Malmsbury Villa, a rickety old house in the Auckland suburb of Kohimarama that actually leaned to one side and seemed about to fall into the sea. Tim and Judd lived in the leaning house of Malmsbury. 'It's a real little killer/Here at Malmsbury Villa,' Tim would sing.

Neil had taken on a part-time job at Martin's Electrical Store in Te Awamutu. On Friday nights he'd play the organ on the footpath outside the store, entertaining shoppers as they walked past (and hoping someone might stop and actually buy one). Sometimes, Neil cheekily ordered a guitar for the store, just to have one handy, because they weren't the store's biggest sellers. It was around this time that he wrote his first 'proper' song, based on a piece of music of Murdoch's called 'Late in Rome'. Neil retitled the piano ballad 'Serge'. 'The basic storyline was mine,' Murdoch recalled, 'but Neil's music was more complex than anything I was doing.'

'Remember those late nights,' sang a very earnest Neil, still very much a virgin, 'with ladies on my arm, nights of passion.' Looking back in 1994, when he played the song during a Crowded House show in Nashville, Neil admitted that 'Serge' still left him puzzled. 'I don't know what a fifteen-year-old boy from Te Awamutu was doing writing about ageing dancers in Rome. It's still a big, big mystery to me,' he told the crowd. Neil wondered if someone 'slipped some acid into my school milk'.

With their sights still firmly set on the upcoming Great Ngaruawahia Music Festival, Split Ends, meanwhile, played more shows at such Auckland venues as the Levi's Saloon. Neil, of course, found a way to catch each and every gig. 'The shows were like nothing else I'd ever seen,' he said. 'They suggested a whole other universe, really.' But even though the band did score a slot on the festival, thanks to the support of co-promoter Barry Coburn (who'd soon manage the band), their set was a disaster. Neil, along with Taylor and some other schoolfriends, was among the 18,000 punters looking on when the band, dressed in homemade outfits, took the stage in the early evening. But this was not an art-rock audience; they'd come for the guitar rampage of local hero Kevin Borich. The heckling began during their opening number and didn't let up.

After a few songs, the festival MC, poet Adrian Rawlins, fearing for the band's safety, came onstage and whispered something in Tim's ear. 'We've just been told we have to get off,' Tim told the audience. 'Do you want us to go?' It's likely that Neil was the only member of the audience to reply in the negative. Later that night, heavy metal headliners Black Sabbath burst eardrums while, as they played, a cross on a nearby hillside burst into flames. The crowd went nuts.

★

Split Ends' festival failure hurt Neil almost as deeply as it hurt the band; Phil Judd was so distraught that he considered chucking it in. But thanks to the continuing support (and money) of Barry Coburn, come April 1973 Neil was holding in his hands a prized item: the group's first recording, a song called 'For You'. 'Split Ends', their theme song of sorts, was on the B-side. It was released during the same week that The Sweet's 'Block Buster!' was top of the New Zealand pop charts. 'For You', which was released on the small Vertigo label, sounded nothing like the glam-rock stomp of Sweet, but that didn't matter to Neil, who played it for an entire day nonstop. As far as he was concerned, it was a masterpiece: 'It blew my mind.' Neil was now even more determined, if that was possible, to become a musician. Perhaps he'd form a band of his own.

A budding muso needed cash, and Neil took on other part-time jobs, punching the clock as an orderly at the Tokanui Psychiatric Hospital, where he was once required to push a corpse across the hospital's lawn on a gurney. As an adult, Neil came to understand that the reason he held no fear of hospitals or doctors was because of his time at Tokanui.

As for Split Ends—they were yet to tweak their name—they decided to 'go electric' and were soon joined by a gun keyboardist named Eddie 'The Prof' Rayner, who'd played in a local band named Orb. By May they'd cut another single, '129', a valentine to the Auckland uni hostel where much of the band had first met. On release, it was the 'For You' situation all over again: a handful of fans, most notably Neil, loved it to death, while the listening public paid no attention. They were too preoccupied with The Carpenters' 'Top of the World', the current national number 1. The new Ends' song didn't bother the charts.

On the night of 18 November, Neil, sat with his parents at home as Split Ends appeared on a heat of *New Faces*, a hugely popular TV show. The band performed '129' and, despite looking like they'd been beamed down from another planet—they'd started dressing more outrageously and camping it up on stage—the group went over well and made it through to the finals. But then came another letdown; after performing an original called 'The Sweet Talkin' Spoon Song', one judge told the band they were 'too clever' to succeed. They ran second last. Neil couldn't believe it. 'To me it seemed so obvious,' he said, that Split Ends were 'so much better than anything on the show'.

But the band continued writing and playing live—and getting better. That Christmas, Neil eavesdropped as Tim told his parents that he intended to make music his calling. This was no whim. Dick and Mary told Tim that he had their support, but in a 1979 interview, Mary Finn said she was 'in shock for about a month' after Tim broke the news.

*

It was a given that any New Zealand act with a whiff of ambition would try their luck 'across the ditch' in Australia. Some, such as rockers Johnny Devlin, spruiked as 'New Zealand's answer to Elvis Presley', and Ray Columbus, who had a number 1 hit in Oz with 'She's a Mod', as well as jazz singer Ricky May, had made a mark. But Split Enz, as they were now known, seemed destined to be square pegs in a tough local scene dominated by such reprobates as Billy Thorpe and AC/DC, who plied their trade in the country's hefty concrete beer barns.

Regardless, the band said their goodbyes and reached Sydney in mid-March 1975. Oddly enough, Split Enz played their first gig at Sydney's premier beer barn, the Bondi Lifesaver. They didn't go over very well.

Split Enz may not have rocked hard, and they looked much like what they were—middle-class art-school dropouts—but they entered a music scene full of possibility. In Sydney, anything-goes radio station 2JJ had just started broadcasting, while *RAM* (*Rock Australia Magazine*) had been covering the local scene for several issues. ABC TV's *Countdown*, operating out of Ripponlea in Melbourne, was beginning to make a splash. Host Ian 'Molly' Meldrum played the hits, but he also gave acts on the rise the chance to play in front of a large national audience. *Countdown* might have been cheesy, but its reach was huge.

Not long after arriving, Split Enz had a stroke of dumb luck. Keyboardist Eddie Rayner had a habit of sometimes opening his mouth before engaging his brain; he once stated that he'd 'rather be a hot tool than a cold chisel'. Rayner told a reporter that Skyhooks, whose debut LP *Living in the 70's* was on its way to selling a staggering 300,000 copies, were no big deal. A rock band wearing make-up? 'We were doing that five years ago,' Rayner sniffed. His comment made its way to Red Symons, the band's guitarist, and Michael Gudinski, the head of Mushroom, Skyhooks' record label. They were both intrigued and went to one of the Enz's shows.

Rather than be offended, Gudinski recognised that they had something going on and offered the band a record deal, while he also signed Tim and Phil Judd to publishing contracts. In a flash they were being billed as 'New Zealand's answer to Skyhooks' and were on the line-up of a huge

Anzac Day show at Melbourne's Festival Hall, opening for Skyhooks and AC/DC.

By the time Neil reconnected with his big brother in winter 1975, when the band returned to New Zealand for some shows, Split Enz had recorded a debut album, which they named *Mental Notes*, and made some influential fans. Their manager Barry Coburn bumped into Neil at a show in Auckland, and he told him that the much-fancied English group Roxy Music was 'blown away' by Split Enz. They were set to record with Roxy's guitarist Phil Manzanera. In London, no less.

Neil had continued playing with Rod Murdoch, and together they opened some Split Enz shows during the group's Black & White tour of New Zealand, which ran from 22 June to 12 July. Tim made a point of watching Neil perform and was struck by his fearlessness. 'Neil always felt that being on stage was a natural place to inhabit,' recalled Tim, who tried his best to cloak his own stage fright with quirky audience banter. 'This is Tim/Full of vim/To the brim/And nimble at that', he'd declare in a mock vaudevillian tone, which suited the band's increasingly oddball performances. But Neil didn't bother with such small talk.

Chris Ampleford, a rep for Pye Records, the home of New Zealand cabaret star John Rowles, caught a set of Neil's when he opened for Split Enz and asked him to record some songs onto a reel-to-reel tape. Ampleford could sense right away that Neil was the real deal. He met with Dick and Mary, who asked him if he thought that Neil was talented. 'Neil is the most gifted entertainer I have ever met,' Ampleford replied, without a moment's hesitation. A deal with Pye, however, was not forthcoming. As disappointed as Neil was, it was the label that lost out in the long run. 'He had his head screwed on,' said Ampleford. 'This wasn't going to be a major setback.'

Clearly motivated by Tim's good fortune in Oz, Neil decided that he wasn't going to enrol at university in the new year, even though, admittedly, it had never really been on his radar. Instead, Neil told his parents—who'd had their share of shocks in recent times—that he was moving to Auckland and getting his own band together.

Neil had befriended Mark Hough, an aspiring muso who'd attended the Elam School of Fine Arts soon after Judd, Crombie and co. Neil had first met Hough at Malmsbury Villa, where he was part of the crowd hanging out with Split Enz. 'I liked Neil a lot right from day one,' said Hough. 'It felt like family.'

Hough, who'd soon rename himself Buster Stiggs, had intended to go to teachers' college but instead decided to move to Auckland with Neil. 'In the back of my mind I knew I would do something creative musically with him,' said Hough. He could see that the time was right for Neil to set out on his own. 'He needed to live his own life and escape his loving parents.'

Neil and Hough lived in a variety of houses in suburban Auckland, first setting up camp in Park Avenue in Grafton, where they house-shared with Paul Pattie, a schoolfriend of Tim and Phil Judd. But soon they shifted to Remuera—'a fabulous two-storey home' as Hough recalled. It was owned by the family of his future wife, Miranda Joel, who had gone abroad for six months. Joel's father was a flautist who had given recitals in his well-appointed lounge room, so the house was perfect for making music. Neil, meanwhile, found some part-time work in a record warehouse, and they settled in.

As Neil and Hough started writing songs, with Hough playing rudimentary mandolin and accordion, Geoff Chunn came in to help out on guitar, along with Gary Nichol, an art-school buddy of Hough's, who played sax. Neil sang, played piano and acoustic guitar.

Neil's original idea was to name the band The Easy Keys, as he spelled out in a letter to Tim. 'The name doesn't work,' Tim wrote back, 'but how about getting some songs down on tape?' So the unnamed ensemble set up their gear, including some basic recording equipment, in the Joels' roomy house, and got to work.

'Serge/Late in Rome' was one of the songs they committed to tape, along with such other originals as 'Symphony Sid', and 'Swallowing Swords', which was a vocal and mandolin duet from Neil and Hough. 'There were no set roles,' said Hough, 'although Neil had some prior recording experience—so I think he set the record levels.'

★

'This is Neil Sagittarius Finn, a hippie from a Hokonui commune.'

It was 19 February 1976, and Split Enz had returned to New Zealand for their Enz of the Earth tour (proving just how useful that change of consonant was). Neil was again opening for the band, this time at Auckland Town Hall, and Mike Chunn introduced him with quite a flourish—and a few biographical embellishments. The curtains opened and Neil stepped forward, playing solo, switching between piano, guitar and mandolin, performing the songs he'd recorded with Hough and the others. He also added a couple of Beatles numbers, including 'Blackbird'. Neil went over very well, as usual.

Ten days later, the tour rolled into Christchurch, where they played at the Theatre Royal. Looking on as Neil performed was Jude Fahey, a writer from *The Press*. 'I would like to get it on record now,' she wrote of the show, 'that Neil Finn is a singer of great potential . . . Barely out of school, [his] writing and use of voice is already quite sophisticated and sensitive.' Neil had found a true believer in the media; Fahey would be the first of many.

After shows in Wellington, Palmerston North, Hamilton and again in Auckland, in April 1976 Tim and the band were gone, first back to Oz and then on to London for their recording sessions with Phil Manzanera. Neil would see very little of Tim over the next twelve months.

3

'There's a lot of go in this Te Awamutu youngster'

On 7 April 1977, After Hours, comprising Neil, Hough, Alan Brown on bass and Brent Eccles on drums, played the Maidment Theatre, a 2500-seater on the grounds of the University of Auckland. The stage was decorated with pot plants and an armchair, which added a touch of homeliness. Neil, proving that the Split Enz influence was more than just musical, walked on stage wearing 'wacky' horn-rimmed glasses, and he began their set with one of many originals, a slow ballad named 'Fall Out With the Lads'. After Hours had just come from a pair of shows opening for the more established Auckland band Waves—and they'd blown them off the stage. 'Delicious exotic entrée precedes fish and chips,' read a review of the After Hours/Waves double-header.

'We had quite a full sound,' said Alan Brown, 'and we found we could really power up when we needed to.' Brown broke out in goosebumps when Neil played 'Serge/Late in Rome': 'It was truly lovely.' On the strength of their Maidment show, After Hours was offered a tour of New Zealand uni campuses. They also had a recording session lined up. 'I felt that we were about to take off,' said Brown.

Looking on at the Maidment show was Mike Chunn, who taped the concert and intended to send the recording to Tim in London. Chunn had returned days earlier from Split Enz's first American tour. He'd also just left the band due to debilitating agoraphobia, the fear of being unable to return to a safe place, an untenable condition for a touring musician. The US tour had been a rollercoaster: the group, who'd been signed to Chrysalis Records, had been collected by a limo when they arrived at LAX, and were put up at the Los Angeles Hyatt, the notorious 'Riot House' that had seen some major rock-and-roll debauchery. They were living the high life. But over the next six weeks things went rapidly downhill. Phil Judd, a new father, was conflicted about spending so much time away from his family, while Tim felt let down by American audiences. Judd turned his back while he played; Tim rarely left his hotel room. Their sophomore album, *Second Thoughts*, didn't sell.

It all fell apart in late February in Atlanta, where the band played several shows at the Great Southeast Music Hall. Judd had taken to wandering off stage mid-set and Tim—who was wired on LSD—saw red, confronting Judd in the dressing room afterwards and throwing a punch. It wasn't much of a fight, but it couldn't have been any clearer that the relationship between these close friends and collaborators had broken down. They didn't speak again for the rest of the tour. After a final show in Chicago, Judd left the band. Mike Chunn followed him. Split Enz, now based in the UK, were in a mess.

Back at the Maidment, Chunn, while deeply impressed with the younger Finn, hadn't thought about Neil as a possible replacement for Judd. After Hours were making great progress; why get in the way of a good thing? Instead, Chunn reached out to Alastair Riddell, a much-admired Auckland guitarist who'd played with Eddie Rayner in Orb. Did he want to join Split Enz? When Riddell said thanks but no thanks, Chunn got in contact with Tim and the band placed a 'help wanted' ad in the UK music press.

That's when the notion hit Chunn: why not recruit Neil? He was a massive fan of the Enz, knew their music inside out, knew the guys in the band—and he was young and ambitious. So what if he didn't know how to play the electric guitar? Neil just might be the right guy.

*

Twenty contenders showed up to audition as Split Enz's new guitarist. That's when Chunn called Tim. 'What about Neil?' he asked.

Tim was currently writing new material with Rayner and floated the idea with the keyboardist. Soon after that conversation, Tim made the call that would change Neil's life. Dick and Mary were excited for their son, but they were also concerned: wasn't 18-year-old Neil a bit young to be disappearing overseas? At least his older sibling would be there to keep an eye out, so they chose not to get in his way.

'The only reason I ever hesitated on the brink of joining Split Enz was because I thought [After Hours] might become something,' Neil said later. But the offer was simply impossible to refuse: 'The idea of going to London . . . was too compelling.' Neil's bandmate Hough, while disappointed, was thrilled for his friend. 'I was really happy for Neil when he was asked to join. It was inevitable.'

Alan Brown felt exactly the same. 'We were all, understandably, extremely disappointed, but happy for Neil.'

Neil did choose to go through with After Hours' one and only recording session, which took place at Auckland's Mandrill Studios on 7 April. But the mood in the studio was, understandably, not especially upbeat; after all, it was the end of the band. One of Neil's songs they recorded was titled 'Platform 3'—'a strange song about a guy who falls in love with a train conductor', in the words of its creator. Dancers in Rome, train conductors—Neil's early songs didn't exactly draw from personal experience, but all that would change when, after one more show with After Hours at the Maidment, he left for London.

Neil landed at Heathrow within days of Sid Vicious making his debut with the Sex Pistols, and just as ABBA's 'Knowing Me, Knowing You' took up residency at the top of the pop charts. He had only a few weeks to settle in before Split Enz's next gig, at St Albans Civic Hall just outside London, on 29 April.

*

Almost as soon as he arrived, Neil addressed the one issue that had been troubling him and bought his first electric guitar, a Yamaha. 'I'd never played electric guitar in my life,' Neil said. 'But they knew I got the ethic, got the humour . . . My youth and naivete was probably refreshing for the other guys.'

Neil quickly set about learning how to master his electric guitar, with the help of Roxy Music's Phil Manzanera, who was a formidable player. 'He was an acoustic guitar player,' Manzanera said on the *Word in Your Ear* podcast in 2022. 'So he wasn't used to playing electric guitar. He came to my house and we went through a few things.' When Neil arrived for his first Split Enz rehearsal at Chalk Farm, the only other person there was Englishman Nigel Griggs, the band's freshly recruited bassist. Though anxious, Neil felt a little better knowing he wasn't the sole nervous newbie in the group.

And while Neil may have been a fair shade of green, he knew his English music history. London venue The Marquee was a surprisingly small room, and more like a sauna when it was packed, but the place reeked of rock-and-roll legend. The Who had made their mark there, as had Jimi Hendrix and, more recently, AC/DC, who set new house records at the Wardour Street club. Neil had barely unpacked when he decided to check out The Marquee—and found that it also reeked of something else altogether. 'I went in there with romantic visions of what it would be like,' he said, 'but the place was just a stench of beer and urine—a bit tawdry, at the end of the day—so that cured me.'

Something similar could be said of his first-ever sexual encounter, which also happened in London soon after arriving. Neil was expecting romance and fireworks, but just before he and his partner got into bed, she sprayed herself with insecticide. Apparently, she had a bug problem at her flat. 'And that was about the most romantic thing that happened all night,' laughed Neil many years later, when asked about his 'first time'.

Back at Chalk Farm, Neil was making some progress with

his new Yamaha guitar, as the band readied themselves for a month-long tour of clubs and campuses. But Neil learned quickly that being by far the youngest of the new boys—Griggs was 27—meant he had an additional role. During a break in rehearsals, Rayner enquired if anyone was hungry, and all eyes turned to Neil. 'I was the guy sent down to get the sandwiches,' he said. Tim hadn't mentioned *that* when he'd asked him to join.

On the night of Neil's debut gig, he walked on stage at St Albans to discover that the band's crew had set him up on the far side of the stage. That seemed a bit odd. And from what he could gather when they launched into their first song, they hadn't exactly cranked up his amp, which was set at an angle away from the others. Neil figured it was so the band 'wouldn't have to listen to me', in case his guitar playing was painful. Even though, as Neil would readily admit, 'it was a golden time for me', he also admitted that he 'felt like Linda McCartney'. He was Split Enz's intern, learning how to play, gig by gig. And he had to get the sandwiches.

One thing Neil did have under control was how to behave on stage. The band had a very physical stage act, sometimes crashing into each other as they played, which, when combined with their wild coiffures and outrageous costumes—Noel Crombie creations both—made it hard for punters to look away. Neil slotted in perfectly: he cut his hair in jagged shapes, slapped on the Max Factor (which gave him acne), pulled demented faces and jumped around in his corner of the stage as though he was possessed. 'You've never seen anyone more zany than I was,' he insisted.

On 2 May, the band played the University of Liverpool and as Split Enz made their entrance—they never simply strolled on stage—Neil observed what he described as 'a punkish looking audience'. This was a new phenomenon for Neil, but he'd arrived during the summer of punk, as such headline-grabbing acts as the Sex Pistols, The Clash and The Stranglers gained massive media exposure and secured major record deals—the Sex Pistols with Virgin (after a few false starts), The Clash with CBS and The Stranglers with United Artists. (Tim would accompany Linda McCartney's daughter, Heather, to a Stranglers gig in London.)

Dozens of other hopefuls donned bondage gear, pierced their cheeks with safety pins and gave themselves 'punk' names like Rat Scabies or Poly Styrene. The music itself was simple; it was a world away from the trickiness of Yes, Genesis and Emerson, Lake & Palmer, the prog rockers that had dominated the early 1970s. All hopeful punks needed was a couple of chords, a decent snarl and an evil-sounding name—and they were good to go.

But was Split Enz a punk band? Neil knew that they were more musically advanced than a lot of these groups who 'were just getting up there and having a bash'. But, as Tim said in a later interview, 'When punk came along, the battle lines were drawn—you either were punk or you weren't. And Split Enz were like somewhere else altogether . . . but it was a brilliant time to be in London.' One day, while exploring King's Road, Tim and Noel Crombie wandered into the notorious SEX boutique and exchanged glares with Johnny Rotten and Sid Vicious. It was as though the two Sex Pistols were sizing up these peculiar-looking Kiwis.

It wasn't long after that Liverpool gig that Neil overheard a conversation between some punks—was it okay to like Split Enz? Did they fit with the ethos of punk? Were they part of the movement? They weren't the only ones curious about the band—Siouxsie Sioux, of prominent London punk act Siouxsie and the Banshees, would sit on the lip of the stage at many of their shows, taking in the action. She was particularly fascinated by the gangly Crombie, the oddest member of a band of oddballs, who looked like a man who had wandered on stage by accident. He would entertain himself—and mask his natural awkwardness—by staring into the middle distance while tapping away at a tambourine or taking the odd spoon solo. Crombie and Neil quickly became good friends.

*

In the northern winter of 1977, Neil and the band repaired to AIR Studios in London to record a new album, co-produced with Brit Geoff Emerick who'd worked with The Beatles at the famed Abbey Road Studios. On day one, Neil had a chance encounter with Beatles producer George Martin, who ran the studio. 'Before I played a note,' said Neil, 'there was George Martin, a deity.'

They named the record *Dizrythmia* after the official term for jet lag, and the album was released at the end of August 1977. Neil, who sang, and played mandolin and guitar on the record, didn't score a single writing credit; Tim wrote the bulk of the songs, either alone or with Eddie Rayner.

'My Mistake' was the standout track on the record and its lead single. The video, featuring the band playing in some sort of nightmare cabaret, showed how smoothly Neil had adapted—decked out in a garish red-and-white jacket, his cheeks red with rouge and wearing his 'zany' glasses, Neil pulled an interesting array of quirky faces while strumming his Yamaha, looking very much at home. The song was a hit in Australia, reaching number 15. But despite some positive UK press—they were likened to both The Beatles and Roxy Music in a *Sounds* review—the record sold poorly outside of Australia (number 18) and New Zealand (number 3). The subsequent single, 'Bold as Brass', tanked, selling fewer than 500 copies in Australia. They were heavily in debt to their label Chrysalis.

Neil's first homecoming as a member of Split Enz took place in early September as the band toured New Zealand and then Australia until 9 October. In the press material for the tour, Neil was described as 'the youngest and most recent member of the band . . . there's a lot of go in this Te Awamutu youngster and he should do well'.

After a show at the Auckland Town Hall in mid-September, Neil was introduced to nineteen-year-old Sharon Dawn Johnson, a striking, dark-haired native of Palmerston North and one of the diehard 'Frenz of the Enz'. One of the many things that Neil liked about Sharon was that she owned a shiny new Gibson SG guitar. When they became a couple, she'd pawn her cherished Gibson to help keep Neil's career afloat.

While in Auckland, Neil and Tim travelled to Te Awamutu. Their parents were elsewhere, so the brothers took the chance to work on a song together in the family home, their first co-write. They named it 'Best Friend'.

Upon reflection, it would have made economic sense for Split Enz to base themselves in Melbourne at the end of the tour and take on the world from there. It was the home of their Australian label Mushroom Records, for one thing, and rent was cheap. And their records sold in Australia—*Dizrythmia* shifted nearly 26,000 copies, also going gold in New Zealand—while they could fill good-sized rooms and earn decent money. But London was simply too seductive. By mid-October they were back in the UK, and soon enough, as Neil and Tim wrote in 'Best Friend', they'd be stuck 'in limbo, bollocks akimbo'.

★

The band had been booked to appear on a BBC program called *Sight & Sound in Concert* on 21 October, sharing the bill with American guitarist Leo Kottke. The show, which was to be filmed at the Golders Green Hippodrome in London, was in its second season and had hosted live sets from such breakout acts as Rory Gallagher, Graham Parker & the Rumour, and Finn faves Jethro Tull, which were broadcast to big TV audiences.

But it wasn't a stellar night for Split Enz. Neil's guitar didn't work when they began playing their opener, 'Bold as Brass', the first of several hiccups. The band had alienated the unionised BBC crew by operating their own lights and not opting to use the in-house stylist, and it appeared that the crew had retaliated by sabotaging their gear. When Tim asked the crowd to clap along, they all but sat on their hands. It was a disaster.

Things went from bad to weird when Phil Judd, who'd left after their disastrous American tour, briefly rejoined the band. Judd said that he and his family 'were living in England and starving', so he desperately needed the work. Weirder still, Judd roomed with Neil, who'd been brought in to replace him. They bonded, in their own peculiar way. Judd thought it a great laugh, after cooking a meal, to knock on Tim's door and tell him how tasty it was, without offering to share any of his food. Neil found this hilarious. 'I . . . bought into it,' he confessed, 'being young and stupid.'

Chrysalis demanded that the band record a single before they would agree to finance the next record, and when the band decided that wasn't such a hot idea, Chrysalis dropped them. The band also chose to fire their tour manager, John Hopkins, feeling he lacked the necessary 'pull' in the local music world. Judd then quit, for the second and final time, returning to New Zealand (where he formed a punk band called Suburban Reptiles with Neil's mate Mark Hough, now known as Buster Stiggs). Cash-strapped, label-less and without a manager, Neil, Tim and the others signed up for the dole. Not only were they out of money, but the gigs had dried up: the band didn't play live between mid-February and late September 1978.

In early 1978, the band shifted out of London, and Neil and Noel Crombie moved into a cottage at 1 Appletree Dell, Dog Kennel Lane, Chorleywood, about 50 kilometres from the centre of London. Neil may have been doing it tough—he'd never been broke before—but he'd describe the following months as 'a good life in a lovely village'.

To pass the time, Neil and Crombie would set up their matching Sony cassette recorders and experiment with home recordings (some of which can be heard at neilfinn.com). They were able to perform some very lo-fi overdubbing by playing back what they'd recorded on one machine, then playing along while recording onto the second Sony. They'd repeat this process as many as five times, leading to such eccentric pieces as 'Outa Mongolia' and 'Snake Charm Boogie'. They adopted an anything-goes approach to instruments, banging away on pots, pans, cardboard boxes, jew's harps, guitars, even a 'pungi', the instrument used by snake charmers. Anything that made an interesting noise was good. LSD was their drug of choice, which added a psychedelic haze to some of the music they were making. These were 'crazy little recordings', according to Neil. 'Really fun.'

They christened themselves Tha Nineez. Occasionally Tim, who was also working on some new songs, would drop by and join them. The good matrons of Chorleywood would sometimes glance in the window of their cottage, en route to the shops, wondering who was making all that racket.

At three o'clock one morning, Neil had been noodling away on an acoustic guitar for an hour or so, thinking Crombie was asleep. But he was startled by Crombie's voice saying: 'That's good.' Neil called the track 'Give It a Whirl'—a very Split Enz song title—and, with some input from Tim, it would become his first song to be recorded by the band. Sketches of other future songs—'Carried Away', 'Evelyn' and 'Catherine Wheels', a track recorded in 1993 by Crowded House—were made by Neil during his interlude as one of Tha Nineez. They also recorded a rough version of 'Fraction Too Much Friction', a song that would later become Tim's first solo hit.

When not busy tinkering with tapes, Neil and Crombie would kick back at the Chorleywood Common and daydream, while students from the Chorleywood College, a school for girls with little or no sight, tapped their way along the garden path, and golfers hacked around the local nine-hole course. While it seemed a very strange place to find a

New Zealand art-rock band, Neil retained fond memories of his Chorleywood exile. He said that while 1978 was the band's 'most broke' year, it was also their most 'musically fertile'.

Of course a band can't survive on daydreaming and home recording. They were broke. In May, the Enz learned that fellow Kiwi Ray Columbus, the former pop star, was involved with the Queen Elizabeth II Arts Council of New Zealand. Tim reached out to Columbus, writing that the band had 'not a bean to live on,' and submitted an official funding request, asking for $5000 'to prepare and record a NZ work for their next album'.

Michael Volkering, Director of the Arts Council, wrote back to Tim, advising him and the band that their grant was approved, in part 'because they were a uniquely New Zealand group'. Split Enz secured $5000 and were back in business. 'Money received,' the band advised via telegram, 'we won't let you down. Many thanks, ENZ.'

★

Using the Arts Council loot, the band adjourned to Quest Studios in Luton during July 1978 to record an amazing 26 songs in three days, with the aim of shopping them around to prospective record labels. Some of these rough recordings would become known as *The Rootin Tootin Luton Tapes* when they were finally released in 2007.

From these recordings it was evident that Neil had come on as a songwriter; his contributions were strong. Among them were 'Carried Away', 'Holy Smoke' and 'Mind over Matter', a co-write with Tim. The band even recorded 'Late in Rome', the first song that Neil ever composed, and 'Best Friend', which the Finns had written on their last visit to Auckland.

'Pitching' a song to the band, however, wasn't always an easy task for Neil, who was still thought of as the Split Enz intern. Sometimes, after running through a new song with the group and feeling quietly satisfied with his work, Neil would be leaving the rehearsal room when Rayner would pipe up. '*Now* I know what song that reminds me of,' he'd say, eroding a little of Neil's self-confidence in the process. Rayner was very much the piss-taker of the band.

Split Enz had another song, 'I See Red', which they'd demoed at Quest and sounded like a sure-fire hit in waiting. It was then recorded as a one-off at Startling Studios, which was situated inside Tittenhurst Park, the stately country manor that had been John Lennon's home and was then owned by Ringo Starr. Nineteen-year-old fledgling British producer David Tickle was hired for the session. First the band tried out 'I See Red' as a slow ballad. 'No,' Tim insisted, 'it needs to be fast. Play as fast as you can.' He was only satisfied when he saw Neil's guitar pick flying out of his hand, having hit the strings so hard. 'That's it,' said Tim, finally satisfied with the tempo, while Neil searched for a new plectrum.

The group had been in touch with Michael Gudinski, their Australian label head, and he visited them in the UK. He listened to their new songs and agreed to finance their next album—and also put Neil and the entire group on a weekly retainer of $80 each. There was one caveat: they had to allow Gudinski to take 'I See Red' back to Oz and release it as a single.

In November, the band settled into The Manor, a studio in Oxfordshire, to record the *Frenzy* album. British engineer Hugh Padgham, at the start of his long association with Split Enz, gained an interesting take on Neil during the *Frenzy* sessions. 'Neil was obviously very talented,' said Padgham, 'but he was new to the band—and Tim didn't feel threatened.' Gudinski, meanwhile, released 'I See Red' on Mushroom and it became the band's first big hit, reaching number 15 in Australia in mid-January 1979 and charting for almost six months.

After finishing work on *Frenzy*—which featured Neil's 'Give It a Whirl'—they returned to their digs in London to find that their flat was awash; the pipes had burst during their absence. They read that as a sign and duly booked flights back to Australia. Neil's UK sojourn was over.

4

'Wow! It's a hit!'

Neil may have just experienced poverty, but pop stardom was something entirely new to him. Yet that was what greeted him when the band resettled in Rose Bay, in Sydney's eastern suburbs in 1979. When he and Tim walked down the street, teenagers would recognise them and start chanting the chorus of 'I See Red'. Neil enjoyed the recognition. 'It wasn't like being an art-school band,' he said. 'It was pop and fun and immediate.'

The response was even stronger in New Zealand when the band headlined the Nambassa Festival on 28 January, after promoter Peter Terry lobbied strongly to get them on the bill. He covered their airfares from Australia, two weeks' accommodation, expenses and a rehearsal space nearby. In exchange, the band agreed to play for free. The festival would also feature Australia's Little River Band and local acts Midge Marsden and Golden Harvest, amid the usual assortment of healing-arts workshops, displays and stalls. It was New Zealand's Woodstock.

There were pre-show problems, however. The band had barely disembarked from their flight when they were set upon by the police drug squad, with a TV film crew in tow. The police found nothing. (Neil would have a similar experience in the US at the height of Crowded House's fame.) Then the rehearsal space they were to use, an old hall, burned down, along with their equipment; damages amounted to a whopping $30,000. All this was forgotten by the band—well, as much as it could be—when they began their set at 8.30 p.m., playing to a crowd of more than 50,000. 'When they hit the stage,' remembered Terry, 'all this pent-up energy exploded and they went right off.' Tim was very much the master of ceremonies, imploring the huge crowd at one point to 'get funky with Noel Crombie for a while'—they did—but Neil's youthfulness and his attractiveness weren't lost on the audience. And he'd mastered the electric guitar.

Nambassa was part of their 28-date Whirlwind tour of the Shaky Isles and Australia, and while in New Zealand the band undertook some recording in Auckland (known now to collectors as the *Harlequin* demos). New songs were coming hard and fast. They were back in New Zealand during May, and this visit included two big events for Neil: he reconnected with Sharon Johnson, and he celebrated his 21st birthday on 27 May. In typical Neil fashion, he marked the occasion by playing a Split Enz gig, at the Wellington Town Hall.

A local TV crew documented the show, and Dick and Mary Finn agreed to a rare on-camera interview. Their past concerns about their sons—especially Neil—appeared to have been forgotten. It seemed that maybe there was a future in rock and roll after all. When asked how it felt to see the band perform, Dick smiled and replied, 'It's quite an experience but if I had a choice, I'd perhaps prefer Count Basie . . . but it's quite a thrill.' At his side, Mary beamed.

Neil, while he was applying his make-up backstage, was asked about turning 21. 'I haven't been given a key yet,' he replied drolly. 'Six flagons of beer and a bottle of wine, but no key.'

*

Back at Rose Bay, Neil and Tim would write in separate parts of the flat they shared: Neil was upstairs in his room, Tim downstairs. Nathan Brenner, a Gudinski protégé who now managed the group, had laid down a challenge for the Finns: 'Why don't you try and out-write each other?' And though they didn't actually write together, they did shout out potential song titles, using each other as sounding boards.

One day, Neil called down to Tim. 'What do you think about "I Got You"?' Tim agreed that it sounded like a fine title. 'And what do you think about "Nobody Takes Me Seriously"?' Tim asked. Neil, too, agreed that might work. ('That was a pretty good day,' Neil said in 2014, in a hefty understatement.)

But Neil had some problems with 'I Got You', the song that would make Split Enz—and him—famous. He thought the chorus didn't work; he felt it was 'too corny'. At the same time, however, Neil sensed that there was something special going on. 'I knew it would be a good song,' he said, and he felt that even more strongly when the band started to bang it into shape during pre-recording sessions. In the end, Neil didn't need to alter the chorus.

The new album, which would be produced in Melbourne by David Tickle, had the working title of *Take One*. The budget of $40,000 was the biggest yet for Split Enz, and a generous one given that Skyhooks, the band that had all but built Mushroom Records, were on the wane (and soon to fold), and the label was shedding some other less successful artists.

Even Molly Meldrum, a supporter of the band, spoke with label head Gudinski and pointed out that Split Enz had cost him a lot of money, which was true. Perhaps he should drop them, Meldrum suggested. Gudinski, to his credit—and eventual financial benefit—dug in and kept the band on his roster. Still, the label only pressed 6000 copies of the new record, now called *True Colours*, when it was ready to roll in late January 1980. A street campaign preceded it; the posters read 'The Enz is Now'. It couldn't have been more prophetic.

Neil, who had three of his own songs—'I Got You', 'What's the Matter with You' and 'Missing Person'—on the finished LP, was in an optimistic mood. At Christmas he had written to his friend Dean Taylor back in Te Awamutu. 'We've just finished a new album,' he reported, 'which we're pretty excited about, so we're hoping for great things with it.' But Neil couldn't have predicted how big *True Colours* would become, and how it would turn his life upside down.

*

A video was now an essential companion for every new single, particularly with the huge influence and reach of *Countdown*. But Neil was less than thrilled by the clip for 'I Got You', which was directed by Aussie Chris Löfvén, who'd done wonders for Daddy Cool and their 1971 anthem 'Eagle Rock' with a film clip that had cost $200. Neil felt that he wore far too much make-up and looked 'stiff'. He would go as far as to call 'I Got You' 'the most awful video ever'. Its attempt at some kind of pop noir was pretty clumsy, but it did make one thing abundantly clear: Neil had morphed into a pop star. Löfvén's camera zeroed in on the boyishly handsome Neil (whose eyebrows seemed to have a life of their own) for much of the clip; it couldn't get enough of him. As for the band, they spent their time in a picture frame located to the rear of Neil, playing their instruments as he 'acted out' the song's nervy, paranoid lyric. Big brother Tim, for the first time in his career, was relegated to the background.

Perhaps it was awful, but the clip—and the wonderful song, of course, Neil's first classic—did the trick. 'I See Red' had moved the band towards the mainstream, but to many they were still seen as crazy-haired art-rockers from 'across the ditch'. Now, with Neil out front, at least for the moment, they were something else altogether; they were a pop band that was helped, no end, by the rise of FM radio in Australia, a format that was tailor-made for their latest music. On 14 April 1980, 'I Got You' overtook Queen's 'Crazy Little Thing Called Love' to become the number 1 single in Australia, and it remained at the top for a staggering eight weeks. Even Freddie Mercury and the guys had only managed seven weeks at number 1. 'I Got You' became the biggest hit song in Australia that year. The song, much like 21-year-old Neil's face, was everywhere.

It was a smaller moment, though, that proved to Neil just how big it had become. He was in New Zealand, visiting Sharon's father, when he heard 'I Got You' blasting from a radio in the kitchen. *Wow!*, Neil thought to himself. *It's a hit!*

When Neil finally had the chance to see his family back in Te Awamutu, his mother surprised him by showing him how she'd mastered 'I Got You' on the piano but, as was her tendency, she never changed key as she played. Neil didn't quite know what to make of it. 'It sounded more like a swing song,' he confessed.

Back in Australia, 'I Got You' and *True Colours*—which reached number 1 and sold strongly for more than a year—were hogging the charts, while *Countdown* aired the 'I Got You' video every time they did their chart rundown. When the band performed the song live, shrieks of 'I love you Neil!' almost drowned them out. With all this exposure, Neil started to find the most mundane things incredibly challenging. He was in a Myer department store when a group of teenage girls spotted him and before Neil knew what had hit him, he was being chased up an escalator. It was like a scene out of *A Hard Day's Night*. This would become a regular occurrence whenever Neil left his house: someone would spot him and soon enough he would be swarmed by young women. Fans tagged 'I Lust for Neil's Finn' on a fence near where Neil and Sharon lived. Neil later said that all the adoration was 'fun for about five minutes' but then became 'distressing'. He really just wanted to do his shopping without being hassled.

Neil's old friend Buster Stiggs had joined Phil Judd's latest band, The Swingers, and moved to Australia. He house-shared with Neil and Sharon in Melbourne's Glen Iris—Tim remained in Sydney with his girlfriend, an English dancer named Liz Malam—and got to witness some of the madness from close range.

'Neil had a lot of adoration from fans and was becoming a public figure,' Stiggs observed, 'but he was always the singer-songwriter first.'

One night, a crowd rushed the group's vehicle after a Split Enz show, surrounding it, most of them yelling out for Neil. Stiggs, who was in the car, had never seen anything like it. 'It was a surreal, scary and mind-blowing experience, all at once,' he said. It took some time before they were finally able to make their escape.

Neil reacted to the attention by staying home more and more, only leaving to play gigs. 'I don't think it suited my personality to be that visible,' he said. (Almost 40 years later, he'd write a song called 'Recluse', proving that some things never changed.) He and Sharon played lengthy games of Monopoly to pass the time, while she surrounded herself with a reliable group of friends who looked out for her while Neil was away. And Split Enz toured a lot as *True Colours* gained traction, spending much of February 1980 in New Zealand, then playing more than 50 gigs in Australia from March right through to the end of June, when they packed Melbourne's Festival Hall. *True Colours* was on its way to selling a whopping 300,000 copies in Australia—only Pink Floyd's *The Wall* and *Glass Houses* by Billy Joel sold more copies during 1980.

On the road, the band spent their downtime indulging in seemingly endless water-pistol fights and what Neil called 'general goonery in the bus'. Tim described it as 'an idiotic and ecstatic time'.

★

When he was a child, Neil had a bizarre dream about famous American musician Herb Alpert, leader of Herb Alpert & The Tijuana Brass and best known for the 1966 instrumental hit 'Spanish Flea'. In the dream, Alpert was on his deathbed and he handed his trumpet to Neil, who was standing nearby. 'You'll have to carry on,' Alpert told him, as his life seeped away. So it must have struck Neil as more than a little weird that A&M, the label owned by the still-very-much-alive Alpert, signed Split Enz in the wake of the success of *True Colours*. The band would tour the US in November 1980. (They remained on Mushroom in Australia.)

But prior to that, Split Enz had returned to the UK. When they played 'I Got You' on *Top of the Pops* on 11 September—introduced by Robin and Maurice Gibb and the notorious Jimmy Savile—Neil, sans guitar, stepped out in a sharp powder-blue suit, emoting wildly as he sang, the camera following him like a stalker. Tim, a vision in red, stood to his right, playing guitar and chiming in on the chorus. The song swiftly hit a record UK high for the band, peaking at number 12. It was a huge thrill for Neil, particularly given that less than three years earlier he'd been adrift in Chorleywood, living on the dole, freaking out the locals. Next stop was Canada, where *True Colours* breached the Top 10 and was fast-tracking its way to 200,000 sales.

It was a lot for Neil to absorb when he returned to Sydney in mid-December and settled in to speak with raccoon-eyed TV host Donnie Sutherland. 'It's a real buzz to be back, as they say,' said a smiling Neil.

By this time, as Neil revealed, 'I Got You' had even hit the Top 10 in Israel, where a record's popularity was boosted by fans sending in postcards to radio stations, insisting that they play the song. As for the US, the vastness of the market was a bit overwhelming for Neil, although that didn't prevent *True Colours* climbing to number 40 on the *Billboard* album chart. 'It means we have to keep going back and consolidating that,' Neil figured.

Sutherland made it known to Neil, who was with Noel Crombie, that *True Colours* was the biggest-selling Australian album for 1980. It was the perfect ending to a crazy twelve months. Neil was just as thrilled by the fact that he was about to spend Christmas in New Zealand, the first time he'd done so since joining the band.

'It's been great,' Neil said, neatly summing up the best year of his life.

★

Momentum was everything for a band coming off a huge hit, and Split Enz had already begun work on the follow-up to *True Colours*. But first priority for Tim was his wedding to Liz Malam, which took place at Claudelands in Hamilton, not far from Te Awamutu. Neil and his parents looked on proudly as Tim recited his vows. But then it was back to work for the brothers Finn, because Split Enz had a huge show on 24 January at Sweetwaters '81, a festival staged on a farm in Ngaruawahia. The headliner was none other than Roxy Music, the band who'd helped initiate Split Enz's UK odyssey.

A taste of the next Enz album, in the shape of Neil's songs 'One Step Ahead' and 'History Never Repeats'—the latter featured another of his twitchy, anxious lyrics—were swiftly released and both reached the Australian and New

Zealand Top 5, 'One Step Ahead' in December and 'History Never Repeats' in April. Also charting highly at the time of 'History' was the even twitchier 'Counting the Beat', a surprise number 1 for The Swingers, the band of Phil Judd and Buster Stiggs (and bassist Bones Hillman). It would be their only big hit.

During the 'History' video, in a repeat of 'I Got You', Neil was separated from the band; it was only during the latter part of the clip that they actually appeared together. No further proof was required: Neil, the former intern/sandwich boy, had become the face of Split Enz. This might have explained why Tim, when asked by *RAM* about his current role in the band that he formed, huffed, 'I mainly do just vocals.' (Not quite true; he had written five songs for the new album, one more than Neil had.)

Neil was in much better spirits than his brother when he spoke about the complicated title of their new record with *Nightmoves'* Lee Simons. In Australia, it would be called *Corroboree*, a word from the Aboriginal Dharug language, while in the rest of the world it would be known as *Waiata*, a Māori word for 'song'. The original idea had been to name the album using a native language of each country in which it was to be released, which meant it could have had as many as a dozen different titles. As admirable as the scheme was, it proved unworkable.

Neil explained to Simons that they'd also considered calling the record *Jamboree*, but Mushroom proved resistant. 'I think they thought it sounded like a Dolly Parton album,' he grinned.

★

The Finns' homeland became quite the talking point when the band began an American sortie in California on 8 May 1981. It was the first of two month-long US visits during a year in which they played almost 100 shows and spent six months on the road.

US TV talking head Tom Snyder interviewed Neil and Tim. Tim gave Snyder a Māori tiki, telling him it was 'for good luck'. The topic quickly turned to New Zealand—what was it really like? 'It's a fantastic place to grow up as a kid,' said Neil, before adding, 'and it's also a great place to retire.' It was the in-between bits that were tricky, Neil explained. 'I think it's the only country in the Western world that has a declining population,' added Tim.

They had a similar conversation with the ageless Dick Clark, when Split Enz appeared on *American Bandstand*. Clark asked Neil why so many young people left New Zealand.

'Well, it's basically the worst place in the world to be if you've got any ambition, certainly as far as being a rock band,' explained Neil. 'But it's a wonderful place to have a nice quiet time, relax, play sport, go outdoors, climb mountains, ford rivers'—at this moment Tim burst into an impromptu rendition of 'Climb Ev'ry Mountain' from *The Sound of Music*.

Clark asked if they'd one day return to make a home in New Zealand, a question that proved to be prophetic for both the Finns. 'Well,' replied Neil, 'I think we all want to be buried there.' Behind him, his bandmates suppressed their laughter.

They may have been in an irreverent mood, but there were darker forces at work during 1981. Tim was stalked by a mother and daughter when the band toured Canada. Eddie Rayner and manager Nathan Brenner got into a skirmish that left Brenner with a concussion. Even the normally calm Neil argued with hotel staff during one stop. The label's choice of Neil's 'Iris', meanwhile, as the lead single in North America proved to be a big mistake; the record failed to chart. (Neil confessed that he'd never met anyone called Iris; he simply woke up one day, the name popped into his head 'and the song came with it'.) And not shooting a video for the song was also another massive clunker, especially for a band as visual as Split Enz, in an era when an attention-grabbing video could turn an okay song into a hit.

Most critically, Tim's marriage was falling apart after less than a year as a result of all the time he'd spent on tour. By the time they returned to Australia, for another big festival show at Tanelorn, in northern New South Wales, on 4 October, Tim was in a precarious mental shape and suffering panic attacks. (He was 'suicidal', according to Brenner.) It was younger brother Neil who came to his rescue.

After the Tanelorn show, their last of the year, Neil and Tim travelled to Phillip Island, off the Victorian coast, home to the smallest penguins in the world. They had planned to write some songs, but instead spent most of their time hiking, climbing and soaking up the scenery, just like they'd done on holiday in Mount Maunganui when they were kids.

It was a key moment in their sibling relationship, a genuine turning point. As Neil recalled, 'I suddenly found myself in an unfamiliar position of being there for Tim and offering support when he was feeling quite fragile.'

Typically, some great music emerged from this difficult time, including a song that would become Neil's first great co-write with his brother.

5

'Career? Who wants a career?'

The song that Neil and Tim wrote during their time together in the wild was titled 'Dirty Creature'. Bassist Nigel Griggs also helped with the music. The lyrics painted a vivid and at times grotesque picture, with striking images of death and darkness, and also namechecked Taniwha, a deadly creature in Māori mythology that lurked in bodies of water. When teamed with a melody that was anxious, insistent and surprisingly funky, 'Dirty Creature' came on like the sound of a nervous breakdown—*Tim's* nervous breakdown.

The video for 'Dirty Creature' was also heavy going, but it was one of Neil's favourite Split Enz clips. In keeping with the song's watery theme, the band dived—fully clothed—to the bottom of the pool at the Channel 9 studios in Melbourne and did their best to play to the camera, quite literally, in the case of Neil, who tried to strum an acoustic guitar while submerged in the murky depths. The band suffered for their art. 'We froze,' said Neil.

The 'Dirty Creature' video ended with Tim alone, afloat in a small boat, an unintended visual metaphor for what lay ahead.

Tim's marriage may have failed, but this didn't deter Neil, now 23, from tying the knot with Sharon on 13 February 1982, on a scorching-hot summer's day in Melbourne. Neil, surrounded by his family and his bandmates (his *other* family), was swept up in the moment and celebrated a little too much after the ceremony, which necessitated a brief lie-down. But he recovered sufficiently to join their guests at the piano for the obligatory Finn singalong. It was just like Friday nights when he was a kid back in Te Awamutu.

'Both Sharon and Neil are very down to earth and anti-rock star,' said wedding guest Buster Stiggs. 'I so respect Neil and Sharon for staying together through times that would kill any relationship.' As the ensuing 40 years would prove, theirs was a union built to last.

Parent album to 'Dirty Creature', *Time and Tide*, released in April, was the last great Split Enz release. Apart from 'Dirty Creature'—which reached number 6 in Australia during April 1982—the album's other hit was perhaps pop music's first sea shanty. 'Six Months in a Leaky Boat' was credited to Tim 'and Split Enz', and was obviously inspired, again, by Tim's recent troubles. When he sang, 'I just spent six months in a leaky boat/Lucky just to keep afloat', it seemed unlikely Tim was singing about a voyage on the *Oriana*. (He had been reading *The Tyranny of Distance*, a book by historian Geoffrey Blainey, which was also an inspiration.)

The track's video, which opened with images of a sailing boat cutting through the waves, went to town on the song's nautical theme, offering up Tim dressed as a ship's captain and the band decked out as crew, dancing a hornpipe—and when Neil joined Tim on the rousing chorus, it all came beautifully alive. As with 'Dirty Creature', there was a lyrical nod to New Zealand, as Tim sang 'Aotearoa', the Māori name for New Zealand.

While 'Six Months' was climbing to number 2 in Australia, big news came in from overseas—the song was receiving radio airplay in the UK, particularly in Manchester. But then disaster struck from a seemingly unrelated event, the brief but bloody war in 1982 between the UK and Argentina over the disputed (and largely unknown) Falkland Islands. This led to an on-air banning of songs with lyrics that BBC censors considered 'problematic', among them 'Don't Cry for me Argentina', and, unfortunately, 'Six Months in a Leaky Boat'. The song was effectively scuppered, as was any chance of Split Enz scoring another UK hit. 'Leaky Boat Ban Over Falklands', one scribe dryly observed.

Despite the setback, the band was locked into what had become a gruelling annual routine—new album, new videos, big tour. They played just over 100 shows during 1982, throughout Australia, New Zealand, Canada (where *Time and Tide* was a hit) and the US. While playing the Palladium in LA, Neil said he was 'taken aback by the level of hysteria in the crowd', much of it directed at him. But after a final show in early September in Auckland, the band simply stopped.

It had been a hectic few years in the wake of 'I Got You'-mania and everyone needed to recharge. Especially Neil; early in 1983 he learned that Sharon was pregnant. It felt like the right time to put up the shutters.

★

It was in March 1983 when Neil quietly resurfaced, in the most unlikely of places—a North Queensland beach, as he and Tim were filmed by a crew from Channel 7's *Sounds*. Over the past six months, apart from two well-paid festival shows in New Zealand in the new year, Split Enz had been silent.

It was unusual to see Neil dressed so casually; he was wearing white shorts and a cream shirt, a green towel slung over his shoulder, a straw hat in his hand, every inch the holidaymaker. Tim looked pretty comfortable too as he reclined in a catamaran, chuckling about 'how rough' it was to be on vacation, basking in the sunshine. When *Sounds* host Donnie Sutherland insisted that they talk shop, a very relaxed Neil shot back: 'Career? Who wants a career?'

Sutherland did finally entice the Finns to speak, and Neil admitted that it wasn't a smart financial move to be off the road, but he knew it was good for the group: 'we'd rather have the spirit of the band remain intact'. Neil also mentioned for the first time publicly that he'd been busy 'being an expectant father', with the baby due in September. 'Beaten them all to it,' Neil smiled, pointing at Tim, but also thinking of the rest of the band. Most of the guys were married but none were yet parents. Neil was ahead of the pack, yet again.

Tim, too, was an expectant parent—of his first solo album, *Escapade*, which was due out in June. Tim pointed out that no one from Split Enz was involved; it was very much a solo effort. Tim explained that it was quite different in sound and style to Split Enz.

'Neil's heard it,' he said when asked about the record. 'Ask him.'

Neil laughed and rather than answer the question he said, 'He missed us, you know.'

'Sibling rivalry,' a smiling Tim said slightly off camera.

Talk then returned to the band. There were plans for another lap of the globe, beginning in October. 'When we swing back hopefully it will be in a big way,' said Neil. 'People will forgive us our absence.'

That didn't turn out to be the case. What none of them knew was that Tim's solo album would, quite unintentionally, drive a stake right through the heart of the group—and also help launch the next phase of Neil's career.

*

Upon its release in June, Tim's Escapade was a surprise hit. The lead single, 'Fraction Too Much Friction', set the tone. This was far breezier than 'Dirty Creature', even if the subject matter—boy meets girl, then 'sit back and watch everything slide', as Tim sang—was very familiar. The song reached number 8 in Australia and charted for twenty weeks.

Part of the success of 'Friction'—and subsequent releases 'Staring at the Embers' and 'Through the Years'—was a series of cutting-edge videos directed by Richard Lowenstein. During 'Friction', Tim strutted the streets of Melbourne, a boom box perched on his shoulder, with American expat Venetta Fields, who sang on the album, locked in step beside him. It was vibrant and fun—and so what if Tim was singing about trouble in loveland?

Art director on 'Friction' and 'Embers' was 24-year-old Benalla-born Nick Seymour, the younger brother of Hunters & Collectors singer Mark Seymour. (They also had two sisters, Hilary and Helen.) Like the Finns, the Seymours were a musical family; Nick's mother Paula, an Irish music buff, had taught her children 'harmony and round' and they'd frequently sing at family gatherings. After studying at the Victorian College of the Arts, majoring in printmaking, Nick had been employed as location art director at Crawford Productions, the legendary TV production house that had created hit shows *Homicide*, *Division 4* and *The Sullivans*. Nick also played bass in a number of Melbourne bands, among them The Glory Boys and Scratch Record Scratch.

Neil first met Seymour around this time, and these were encounters he never forgot. 'He was a real smart-arse,' said Neil. When invited to Neil's house, Seymour would pick up random items and announce, 'Oh, look, a rock star's toaster', simply because Neil was in Split Enz. Seymour may have been a smart-arse but, as Neil pointed out, he was a wise guy 'with a smile on his face'.

While *Escapade* dominated the charts, and was declared Best Album at the *Countdown* Music & Video Awards, Neil, too, had hit a purple patch. He and Sharon were now living at Osborne Street in South Yarra (number 11, to be precise). Neil would record demos in the front room of the house, using a Yamaha drum machine, in a room he was convinced was haunted. It was there he wrote one of his best Split Enz songs, 'Message To My Girl'. Clearly inspired by his married life, with a baby on the way, the original title was 'I Love You' and the finished song, a heartfelt ballad with a deceptively simple melody, was one of his most candid. It was also the last hit for Split Enz, reaching number 12 in January 1984. The disappointing parent album, *Conflicting Emotions*, didn't sell anywhere near Tim's *Escapade*, which eventually shifted more than 200,000 copies and charted for a year. *Escapade* became one of the top twenty bestselling albums of 1983 in Australia.

Neil featured almost exclusively for the first two minutes on the 'Message' video, which became one of the band's best-known clips. Neil now looked far more comfortable in front of the camera, as he walked and sang and eventually joined up with his bandmates. There was none of the awkwardness (or eyebrows) of 'I Got You'. Directed by Noel Crombie and Melbourne-born video-maker Ray Argall, the clip, which was shot in a warehouse, was famous for being completed in one take. The camera was mounted on tracks, which made it easier to follow Neil. It actually required two takes, but its simplicity was a masterstroke.

While at work on *Conflicting Emotions*, Neil had a brief encounter with Simon Le Bon of Duran Duran, who'd opened for Split Enz in mid-1982 at some US shows. Split Enz had started recording *Conflicting Emotions* at Sydney's Paradise Studios, but a flood forced a move to Studios 301, where Duran Duran were recording their album *Seven and the Ragged Tiger*. One day, Neil was walking down the hallway when he spotted Le Bon, who was hunched over a notepad, scribbling lyrics and muttering obscenities—clearly, a deadline was looming. Neil smiled at Le Bon as he passed him and, and as he later confessed, was tempted to say, 'Well, at least I've got *my* lyrics done.' What Neil didn't know was that Duran Duran's Nick Rhodes and John Taylor had seen Split Enz play at Birmingham back in May 1977 and were big fans.

Conflicting Emotions, however, was a troubled record. Neil wrote six of the ten songs; Tim contributed the other four, none of which were highlights. It was clear that Tim's solo success had pulled him away from the band—the album's title pretty much said everything about the situation. *Countdown*'s Molly Meldrum exacerbated the problem when he announced on air that he preferred Tim's new music to that of Split Enz. Clearly, time was running out for the band. 'At the heart of *Conflicting Emotions* was the fact we weren't a very settled band,' Neil said later. 'The balance had shifted and it wasn't a comfortable feeling.'

Brit Hugh Padgham, who produced the album, also sensed that something wasn't quite right. 'I didn't have problems with the band,' he said, 'but they did with each other.'

In the midst of all this tension came something good when Neil's son was born at Melbourne's Royal Women's Hospital on 24 September. The new parents named their son Liam Mullane—Mullane being Neil's middle name. Neil reported that Liam had 'long, piano-playing fingers'—which he would put to good use, in due course—'and lots of hair'. Liam was very much his father's son. And it wouldn't be long before baby Liam was part of the Split Enz entourage. The smell of backstages and tour buses would become very familiar to him.

*

Noel Crombie had been playing drums with the band for a couple of years, but only as a fill-in until they recruited a permanent timekeeper. Enter Paul Newell Hester, an effervescent, highly likeable Melburnian with a sharp wit and a virtuoso talent on the skins. His mother, Anne, had played drums in jazz ensembles, and she'd taught her son how to play. The Hesters—Paul had a sister named Carolyn, and his father was known as 'Mulga Mike'—lived in the Dandenongs. Paul shared his birth date, 8 January, with two legends: Elvis Presley and David Bowie.

Mad for music and footy, Hester was a high-school dropout who played in various bands before achieving some success with an outfit named Deckchairs Overboard. He'd also been in a relationship with Deborah Conway, from the band Do-Ré-Mi. Rob Hirst, the drummer for Midnight Oil, was an advocate of Hester's, describing him as 'a natural, gifted comic and brilliant drummer'. In short, he was just the guy that Split Enz needed. Hirst informed Hester that the band was on the lookout for a new drummer.

Neil spoke with Hester and asked him to audition. But even though Hester—who was 24, a year younger than Neil—felt he'd done well enough to get the nod, he was asked to sit in with the band a couple more times, still without confirmation that he was hired. On what was essentially his fourth audition, Hester brought a small cassette recorder into the rehearsal space. He had a plan. As their jam ended, he asked, 'I must be in now, right?' and recorded each member saying, 'Yes.' It was a very Paul Hester thing to do. If he hadn't been such a fine drummer, he could have been a stand-up comic.

Hester had been living in Sydney but shifted south in early 1984 and moved in with Tim Finn, who had a house in Caulfield. It turned out that not only was Hester the right man for Split Enz, but he was also just the person that Tim needed in his life—Hester's larrikin streak never ceased to lift Tim's spirits. And he kept their house in good order: Hester loved to serve tea in a pot with a cosy, a tea towel draped over his shoulder.

Neil would also grow close to Hester, appreciating what he brought to a band that had started to lose its sense of humour—which had been such an essential part of Split Enz. 'We feel like a new band again, with Paul on drums,' he said. 'There's much more power.'

That rejuvenation, however, was short-lived. Tim, still high on the success of *Escapade*, had become romantically involved with the striking, sophisticated UK-based actress Greta Scacchi. They met on the set of the Australian movie *The Coca-Cola Kid*, in which she starred and Tim featured on the soundtrack. Tim made a cameo in the film as Phillip, a bandleader and jingle writer, appearing in a musical scene with Hester, who grinned and flashed a peace sign from behind his drum kit. It was while shooting this scene that Tim met Scacchi—and the sparks flew.

Tim was at Scacchi's side when she returned to the UK after the shoot, putting a geographical barrier between himself and the band. When asked about Scacchi, Tim said she was 'the image of perfect beauty'. He was lovestruck. The rest of the group, meanwhile, played a few 'secret' shows at Melbourne venue The Club in late May under the moniker While the Cat's Away, the Enz will Play. Neil was now effectively the band's leader.

In June 1984, Tim returned to Melbourne and called Neil, asking him to come over to his house in Caulfield. It was important that they speak.

'I'm going to leave the band,' Tim informed his brother. Neil wasn't surprised. He knew that everything was changing for Tim, personally and professionally. It was time for him to move on from the group that had been his world for the past dozen years. Neil understood that.

Tim also had some advice for Neil. 'You should form your own band with Paul. You shouldn't have to deal with this myth, this saga, that is Split Enz.'

'I left in the end due to two things,' Tim explained in 1996. 'One, I'd fallen in love and wanted to drop everything and be with this person who didn't live in my part of the world, and B, I'd done a solo record which was surprisingly successful.' Tim likened recording *Escapade* to having an extramarital affair. 'In a way it did break some of the bond that did exist between us.'

As for Neil, he was in a quandary. The band had been talking about making another record, an EP, and they intended to get back on the road. Neil had been in the group for seven years—his entire adult life to date, pretty much—and had grown tight with the other guys. 'It was such a close bond,' he said. 'It seemed like a huge chunk of my life.'

Neil had to plan his own future, and he wasn't quite sure if he was ready to quit Split Enz. For one thing, it was the only way he knew how to make a living, and he now had a child to provide for. But he also knew that Split Enz was Tim's band, and always would be.

Tim's decision to quit Split Enz was made public on 16 June 1984. *The New Zealand Herald* took the news so seriously that they ran a mock obituary, mourning the death of the band. Neil, meanwhile, had come to the realisation that he simply couldn't continue with the group either. 'I just had this weird feeling about being the frontman of a band my brother had formed,' he said. He too was done.

A band meeting was called at the home of Nathan Brenner, their manager, and Neil told the others of his decision. Paul Hester was mortified; he'd only just joined the group. The rest of the band—Rayner, Crombie and bassist Nigel Griggs—said very little. But the dream was undeniably over.

Neil mumbled goodbye and got into his car to drive home. Not long into his journey he was sideswiped by another motorist, sending his car into a spin. Neil pulled over; he was stunned—and his car was a write-off—but he wasn't hurt. As he waited for help, Neil watched his three bandmates drive by him, in slow succession. No one noticed that Neil was there, or that he'd been in a wreck.

Two tram drivers walked over and asked if he was okay.

'Oh, there's my friend ... there's my friend ... there's my friend,' mumbled Neil, as Crombie, Griggs and Rayner drove past. The tram drivers 'were convinced I was delirious', Neil reported later. 'There was something very symbolic about that.'

*

Neil's next item of business was to advise the band's many devotees of his decision. 'This is not a farewell letter, nor is it a message of gloom,' he wrote for the Frenz of the Enz Fanclub newsletter. 'Yes, the band is calling it a day; there comes a time in everyone's life when a change is for the best. Such is the case for us.' As part of their farewell, there'd be a new record and one final tour, titled, inevitably, Enz with a Bang.

Neil, Crombie, Rayner and Griggs assembled for a press conference at Melbourne's Hilton Hotel on 25 July. Tim, who was in Italy with Scacchi, was represented by a cardboard cut-out; clearly, the band hadn't lost their sense of humour. 'It's as amicable a split as can possibly be,' Neil told the reporters. 'There were a few tensions but nothing beyond the normal group.'

'We thought it a good time to finish while we were still friends and there was still music left in us,' Neil said in a subsequent interview. He admitted to not being a big fan of bands that hang about after their peak, struggling for relevance, which is how Split Enz may well have ended up. Some could argue it had been that way since the runaway success of *True Colours*; brilliance had only come sporadically for the band since 1980.

During a *Good Morning Australia* interview with host Gordon Elliott, Neil jokingly blamed Paul Hester for the band's demise. Was it really his fault?

'I think I just kept a bad band together for another year,' Hester joked.

As this showed, the rapport between Neil and Hester was easy and natural. They could even squeeze a laugh out of a situation that many people found devastating.

Neil and the band had been persuaded to stretch their planned EP into a full-length album, which they recorded in just under five weeks at AAV studio in Melbourne. The record was titled *See Ya 'Round* and emerged in late November 1984. Neil wrote the bulk of the album, including their final charting single, 'I Walk Away', another strong pop-rock track and a very clearly stated farewell, which stalled at number 45 in the Oz charts. (Neil liked the song enough to later re-record it and add it to the Australian edition of the first Crowded House LP.) A subsequent single, Neil's 'One Mouth is Fed', sank without a trace. The rest of the band had been invited to contribute songs to *See Ya 'Round*: Hester wrote 'This is Massive', Rayner provided 'The Lost Cat' while Crombie contributed 'Ninnie Knees Up', a flashback to his time living with Neil in Chorleywood. Tim didn't have a song on the finished album, a record that felt rushed and lacked a single Split Enz classic.

Neil came to concede that *See Ya 'Round* was 'a bit half conceived'. In his haste to get it finished, he reached into his past, re-recording 'Late in Rome', now known as 'Serge', and 'Fall Out With the Lads', now called 'Voices', both from his time with After Hours. Only 'Voices' made the finished record. It's likely he was already thinking beyond the album and farewell tour, planning what he would do next. He did have some ideas; yes, he wanted to continue with Hester, and he also wanted to be part of something more streamlined, more pared back. Neil joked—half joked, perhaps—that he craved a band that could fit comfortably into a hire car.

Neil also wanted to start a band—*his* band—from scratch.

★

The Enz with a Bang tour started with a show at Canberra on 30 September 1984, and every venue was packed. Baby Liam travelled with Neil and Sharon for much of the journey, lightening the mood backstage. Greta Scacchi joined the entourage for part of the tour as well.

The band played as though they'd been reborn, bouncing around the stage like human pinballs as they fired off one classic after another: 'One Step Ahead', 'Message To My Girl', 'Dirty Creature', 'I See Red', 'History Never Repeats' and, of course, 'I Got You'. Their set list had grown into a greatest hits.

During the last show of a three-night stand at Festival Hall in Melbourne, Neil was so taken by the occasion that he stage dived into the huge crowd. Unfortunately, the audience didn't quite know how to respond and they parted, which resulted in Neil crashing to the floor. 'Neil,' Tim called from the stage. 'Come back. We need you.' Neil recovered sufficiently to finish the gig but was inconsolable afterwards as he sat in the dressing room, sobbing. The reality of what was happening—the end of the Enz—had hit him like a sledgehammer, as had the many tequilas that he drank after the rapturously received concert. Crashing into the Festival Hall floor didn't help, either.

Nick Seymour was at the after-show party at the Tropicana Club in Richmond. He spotted Neil, who was nauseous, and said he'd drive him home. During the drive, in between dry heaves, Neil told Seymour that he intended to start a new band. Seymour may have struck Neil as a bit of a smart-arse, but he was also canny. He badly wanted to work with him. All he had to do now was work out how to become part of whatever Neil did next.

The closing New Zealand leg of the tour began with a show at Wellington on 12 November and continued for almost four weeks. During that run of dates, a function was held for the band, their families and the crew. Neil and Tim took the stage inside the marquee and sang a rough-and-ready version of the Bee Gees' 'Words'.

'This is the sort of thing we used to sing at talent quests at Mount Maunganui,' Tim told the gathering, a claim that was absolutely true.

Neil spoke with a film crew and reflected on what he believed the band had achieved. 'What we did in 1980 is really significant,' he said. 'I think we opened a lot of doors for bands like Men at Work. Just because we weren't in the Top 10 didn't mean we didn't attract a lot of attention.' He mentioned that the band had been receiving a lot of fan mail from the US, with enthusiasts hoping the band would undertake a farewell tour of the States. That, sadly, didn't eventuate. 'Riding on waves is probably not as much fun as trying to make them, I reckon,' Neil said, before rejoining the gathering.

Prior to their final show, at Auckland's 3000-capacity Logan Campbell Centre, the members of the band got ready in Crombie's hotel room and travelled to the show together, just as they'd done twelve years earlier. There was no entourage, no security, simply the musicians. 'It was just the six of us, like the old days,' said Tim. 'It was brilliant.' Their transport—a rental car—was fancier than their 1972 ride, a loaned Morris 1800, but the shared sentiment was much the same as that first show at the Wynyard Tavern: they were excited and nervous. But they were also feeling melancholic. Everyone believed they'd never play together again.

It was a long concert, 22 songs in all. The audience simply didn't want them to finish and demanded they play several encores. But after a final, rousing 'History Never Repeats', that was it; the show, and Split Enz, were done.

6

'Paul and I had a plan'

In typical Neil Finn fashion, he didn't take long to get back to work. Come February 1985 and he was recording demos with Paul Hester—heeding Tim's advice—in Melbourne; among them was a track named 'That's What I Call Love'. A few weeks prior, on 27 January, Neil and Hester had performed at the EAT Appeal benefit concert staged at the Myer Music Bowl. EAT stood for 'East African Tragedy'; it was a large-scale fundraiser for famine-ravaged Ethiopia, taking place almost six months before Live Aid, whose kingpin, Bob Geldof, had been involved with the Melbourne concert. The EAT Appeal show raised a million dollars, which was donated to the Red Cross. Helped out by members of Midnight Oil and Divinyls, Neil and Paul performed the Split Enz song 'One Mouth is Fed'. It was very fitting given the theme of the day.

Neil had learned some valuable lessons while in Split Enz and had a clear business plan for his as-yet-unnamed outfit. He intended to shop his demos directly to US record labels, rather than sign with an Australian label and then hope to get an American deal. It was a bold plan, and also a smart one. Neil had made some strong business connections with such people as LA-based attorney Gary Stamler and Aussie manager Grant Thomas, who'd both play big parts in bringing his plan to fruition. He'd managed to stash away some money from the final Split Enz tour, too, which would finance the trip.

But what he and Hester needed right now was a bass player. Neil came up with a unique way of auditioning players—he'd give them tapes of the songs he was working on with Hester and ask them to add their own bass parts. Nick Seymour was the third of these contenders, and he returned to the rehearsal studio with a distinctly funky version of 'That's What I Call Love' that clicked with Neil. He also liked Seymour's energy—he was dancing around the space as he played, and Neil found that infectious. 'It felt fresh,' he said. And fresh was exactly what Neil was looking for.

As far as Neil was concerned, Seymour 'was very confident and outgoing and we thought, *What the hell*,' he said during a segment on *The J Files*. It also helped that Seymour expressed interest in working on the band's image: their visuals, their costumes, record design and so on, all the aspects of being in a group that didn't appeal to Neil. Seymour would be the band's very own Noel Crombie, the concepts guy. And, just as importantly, Seymour meshed well with Neil and Hester. 'We fed each other lines and we were quite an engaging group of people; there was a lot of front there, and that doesn't hurt for a band,' Neil figured.

Seymour was hired but was kept on ice while Neil and Hester went overseas to try and secure a record deal. They first travelled to London and then LA, meeting with half a dozen Artist & Repertoire people at different labels, mostly on the strength of their Split Enz connections. 'We talked to a lot of people who probably wouldn't [have been] interested otherwise,' as Neil understood it. Among them was Tom Whalley from Capitol Records—when he met with Neil and Hester, he'd been in his job for just days, in a junior role at the prestigious label, the American home of The Beatles. Whalley very much liked what he heard and kept in touch with the pair when they returned to Melbourne in early March.

Neil was a big fan of synth-pop band The Reels, the biggest act to ever emerge from regional Dubbo, and he enlisted Craig Hooper, a former member of the band, to play guitar for his new group. On 13 March, the quartet got together in a South Melbourne rehearsal space. Hooper, like so many others who encountered Paul Hester, thought that he was one of the funniest people he'd ever met—there were nonstop laughs when they rehearsed. After one early session, Neil dropped Hooper at his girlfriend's place. Hooper was hunched over, his eyes red and watering. When his girlfriend opened the door, she was concerned—was he okay?

'I'm fine,' Hooper told her. 'I've just been laughing nonstop for hours and my ribs are a bit sore.'

About two weeks in, the four musicians bumped into another group who was using the same space, who said they were about to play their first gig.

'That's great,' said Neil. 'How long have you guys been rehearsing?'

'Two years,' he was told.

Neil spoke with the others in his band. There was no way they were going to rehearse for two years. 'Right,' Neil said, 'we're not going to do that. We should book a tour as soon as possible.' Hooper, Seymour and Hester all agreed.

A 24-date Australian tour, which would run to the middle of June 1985, was quickly organised. But Neil had a problem. 'Guys,' he told the others, 'the agency called. They need a band name to put on the posters and in gig listings.' It was agreed to name the band The Mullanes—clearly, what was good for Neil's son was good enough for his new outfit. But it was strictly for this one tour. 'The Mullanes was only ever going to be a temporary name,' said Craig Hooper. 'We just wanted to force ourselves to get out in front of people because a week of playing gigs will improve a band more than three months in a rehearsal room.'

Neil wasn't totally sold on the name anyway. He feared that cynical journalists—and there was no shortage of them in the music business—might rename them 'The Malaise' or 'The Mundanes'. Neil was also concerned that Americans might think they were some sort of Irish folk group. 'That's how paranoid we were,' he chuckled in a 1995 interview. But the tag would do for the time being. And, frankly, no one could think of anything better.

When The Mullanes played their first gig, their set list was a mixed bag. They combined crowd favourites such as songs Neil wrote for Split Enz, including 'One Step Ahead' with Enz obscurities ('Hello Sandy Allen', Neil's ode to the tallest woman in the world) and newer songs in development—including 'Now We're Getting Somewhere' and 'Love You 'Til the Day I Die'—as well as a cover of The Reels' song 'Return'. Hester stepped out from behind his drum kit to sing 'This is Massive', which had appeared on the final Split Enz album, and they even had a crack at the Buddy Holly classic 'Not Fade Away'. Just like their set list, the band, too, was a work in progress. Their sound was tougher than Split Enz, more guitar heavy.

In late May, four gigs into the 'Coaster to Coaster' tour, Neil and Nick settled onto the couch of a Brisbane TV show called *Clipz* to speak with host Rod Lockington. They were about to play their next gig, at the Homestead Inn in Brisbane. Neil, who'd bleached the tips of his hair gold, was asked about the band's name. Was he concerned that it might be shortened to 'The Mulls'?

'Well, I certainly hope not,' he replied with a knowing chuckle, 'but we'd be very popular up the east coast.'

Neil had smoked his share of grass and understood the drug culture. They'd just come from Byron Bay, the hippie capital of Australia, where they played at the Piggery Arts Factory.

And what about big brother Tim? Neil was asked. Where was he at the moment?

Tim was in the UK, reported Neil. (He'd been signed to Virgin Records, the label of famous entrepreneur Richard Branson.) And he'd just been to the Cannes film festival. 'Times are pretty hard for Tim,' Neil said with a grin.

And what about Tim and Greta Scacchi? Were they happy?

'Absolutely, blissfully happy,' said Neil. 'It's good that he's found love at last.'

★

In strictly financial terms, The Mullanes' tour wasn't a success. Neil was multitasking, acting as the band's tour manager, and while he was able to secure good 'guarantees'—agreed fees for the gigs—thanks to his history with Split Enz, the rooms weren't packed. 'We played to uniformly small audiences all around Australia,' he recalled. 'So we basically burned every promoter from one end of the country to another.'

At the end of each show, it was left to Neil to settle up with the owner of the venue. 'I was the guy who had to go in and count out the money over the ironing board. The guy's going, "There you go, $2000" and I had to go, "Actually, sorry, it's $4000 according to this piece of paper here." They'd get really upset with me.'

But Neil enjoyed the tour. It was a very different experience to playing with Split Enz—there were no huge expectations. Punters came to the gigs out of curiosity, wondering what Neil Finn was up to musically, rather than demanding to hear his old hits. And unlike the Enz, there was little in the way of production: the band arrived at the venue, usually a pub, in their street clothes, then set up their gear and played. It was all very much a do-it-yourself, back-to-basics operation. Neil's biggest problem, such as it was, came during interviews—sometimes he couldn't get a word in. Paul Hester was a very good talker, and funny to boot. Journalists loved him.

When speaking about The Mullanes with Sydney's Triple J, Hester had fun with his and Neil's recent past. 'We've been on a roll since we finished with'—here Hester dropped his voice to a conspiratorial whisper—*'the other band.'*

Neil taped most of the shows and was happy with what he heard. And he was also pleased by how swiftly things had come together for him in the six months since the end of Split Enz. 'Paul and I had a plan,' Neil said when he appeared musician Shayne Carter, soon to form the highly rated alt-rock band Straitjacket Fits. Carter was drunk and belligerent—he had a serious drinking problem and an attitude to match—and, as he revealed in his memoir *Dead People I Have Known*, somehow managed to stumble his way backstage. As far as Carter was concerned, The Party Boys were evidence of all that was wrong with music—for one thing, they were playing in front of a banner flogging Rheineck beer. To his mind, they were a bunch of sell-outs, corporate rockers. 'I was a junior Johnny Rotten, calling out the fakes. Of course, I challenged every one of the musicians to a fight.' Carter was swiftly turfed out of the venue.

Carter hung onto a grudge against Neil, despite admitting that he 'was always magnanimous and never confrontational'. When asked, Neil did recall the backstage run-in, but didn't think he was in any danger. 'He was slumped up against the wall and fell over,' Neil told New Zealand's *Herald on Sunday*. That was where it ended.

But Neil had another encounter on The Party Boys run that would leave a deeper impression on him—and provide great source material for a new song. When the tour reached Palmerston North, Sharon's hometown, Neil was feeling like anything but a party boy (a band name he detested, incidentally). He was sick with flu, running a temperature, and was convalescing in his room when he was given a note. It was from a diehard fan, who'd flown in from the US for the gig. 'I have to meet with you,' it read. Neil knew of the woman; she had written to him care of his parents, making it known that she was coming to New Zealand and simply had to meet him. As Neil recounted later, the woman had written that 'if she saw me out, and I snubbed her, or I was mean to her in any way, she would never get over it. She would, y'know, go and throw herself off a cliff.'

As Neil would go on to write in a lyric, 'I could not escape/A plea from the heart', and he dragged himself downstairs to say hello. After talking for a short while, and, as Neil remembered, having blown his nose '50 times or so', he excused himself and stumbled back upstairs to his room.

A little later that night, Neil returned to the bar where they'd spoken. When he spotted the woman, she didn't seem to be in dire emotional straits—in fact, she was merrily cutting it up on the dance floor with a well-known TV identity, with whom Neil believed she became very familiar as the night wore on. Despite his flu, Neil began working on a song that documented the peculiar events of the night. The opening line, 'She came all the way from America' pretty much wrote itself, and 'Mean to Me' was born. Neil even snuck in a mention of his hometown Te Awamutu, whose name, he figured, 'had a truly sacred ring' to his visitor from the US. (After 'Mean to Me' was released, the woman confronted Neil at a show, less than thrilled by the suggestion in the song that she'd slept with the TV figure.)

The Party Boys tour was a turning point, and not just for Neil. Dave Dobbyn was set to begin work on the soundtrack for the animated film *Footrot Flats*, which would include 'Slice of Heaven', the biggest hit of his career. And Neil too was about to record what many would consider his signature song, a yearning ballad he named 'Don't Dream It's Over'.

★

Neil had written 'Don't Dream It's Over' back when Tim was living in Caulfield with Hester. A few visitors had dropped by one particular day, and Neil, not feeling very sociable, disappeared to the music room, where he started playing the piano. The song—words and music—came pretty much all at once, which wasn't often the case for Neil. But, as he knew, it was 'usually a good sign' on the rare occasions it did happen. The next day he went home and recorded a demo, this time on guitar. He then added 'drums'—a matchbox for the snare and a rubbish bin for the bass drum, whatever was handy. Neil tested the demo in his usual manner, by playing it back about a dozen times—soft, loud, speeded up, slowed down. He did this, in part, to see if the song worked, but also to savour the simple joy of having created something out of nothing.

Neil liked the song's lyric, especially the line 'My possessions keep causing me suspicion/But there's no proof'. He didn't usually crowd words together in that manner. He also came to suspect that he wrote the lyric about building a 'wall between us' because he didn't want to mix with the people visiting Tim's house as he worked on the song. There was nothing too cryptic about it; he simply wanted some space. And so what if Neil may have unintentionally borrowed the 'paper cup' image from his favourite Beatles song, 'Across the Universe'? It worked beautifully.

Of course, over time, when huge crowds sang 'Don't Dream It's Over' along with him, Neil's spare lyric would come to mean something else together. It became a unifying song, an anthem. Neil would describe it as 'an affirmation of hope'.

'Don't Dream It's Over' was on a tape of demos that Neil had sent to Tom Whalley, his man at Capitol Records, before he and Hester set out for Los Angeles, where they settled into a two-bedroom townhouse at 1902 North Sycamore, in the Hollywood Hills, in November 1985. Rent was US$1800 per month. It was their base while recording their debut album at two renowned LA studios: Sunset Sound, where Brian Wilson had crafted The Beach Boys' timeless *Pet Sounds*, and the studio in the Capitol Records building, which had been used by everyone from Frank Sinatra to Michael Jackson and Paul McCartney.

Seymour soon joined them. He hadn't been to LA before, so Neil ensured that he was collected from the airport in proper style, in a limo. Seymour spent the entire ride with his head poking out of the sunroof, drinking in everything that LA had to offer, as they made their way through La La Land. Seymour's girlfriend was the only non-band member to make the trip, and the four of them settled into the house in the Hollywood Hills. Soon enough it was a drop-in centre, 'this huge dosshouse for Aussies in LA', according to Seymour, who began checking out the various warehouse parties held in and around the city. (He'd then invite many of the party-goers back to the house.)

Neil and Hester were different to Seymour; they were homebodies. When not recording, they tended to hang about the house, with a character simply known as The Rabbi delivering their pot. Purely by accident, and inspired by recent events, the band agreed on a name that was much better than The Mullanes—they were now Crowded House.

*

In the search for the right studio collaborator, Tom Whalley had sent Neil's demo tape to budding producer Mitchell

Froom, who was blown away by the songs, especially 'Don't Dream It's Over'. 'It was crazy how good it was,' said Froom in 2019, looking back. The bespectacled 32-year-old Californian keyboardist came from good musical stock; his older brother David was a highly regarded classical composer. Although Froom didn't have many production credits, Neil agreed to meet with him at his home where he had a small studio. Froom played Neil the arrangements he'd come up with for 'Something So Strong' and, crucially, 'Don't Dream It's Over', to which he'd added a gospel-flavoured organ solo, inspired by the Procul Harum classic 'A Whiter Shade of Pale'. 'Mitchell made some quite profound suggestions,' Neil told *Uncut* magazine.

That organ solo, when combined with Neil's haunting opening guitar lines—which Nick Seymour called 'the Kiwi party strum', the type of simple yet soulful playing often heard at New Zealand family get-togethers—would be the making of 'Don't Dream It's Over'.

Neil was especially won over by the R&B influences Froom had brought to his songs; they didn't sound like anything he'd recorded before. He told Froom they sounded 'exotic'. And Froom had transformed 'Something So Strong', which Neil had felt was essentially a folk song—'a little bit Greensleeves-y'—recorded with mandolin and acoustic guitar, into something else altogether: it was now a pop/rock classic in waiting. Neil had worked with some good producers before, such well-regarded people as Hugh Padgham and David Tickle, but as far as he was concerned, 'Mitchell was the first producer I've worked with who really got amongst the songs and made big suggestions.' A bond that continues some 40 years later was formed.

Work on the record continued into the new year, and on the day that 'Don't Dream It's Over' was brought to fruition, Neil felt that there was a sombre mood in the studio that seeped into the recording. 'Everyone was feeling a little bit sad . . . It has a very slow and melancholy lope to it. We found out afterwards that the tape was recording slightly slow, so it's actually a little slower than how we played it.'

American Jimmy Iovine, who'd produced huge hit records for Tom Petty and The Pretenders, happened to be in the studio on the day. 'Wow,' he said upon hearing 'Don't Dream', 'those guys have come up with a classic.' He rated it with the best of Lennon and McCartney, the highest praise Neil could have hoped for.

The only downside came when Neil, Hester and Seymour packed their bags and moved out of the house on North Sycamore and were told their $1800 bond wouldn't be returned to them. Their landlord blamed it on 'soap deposits on the shower screen', which Seymour felt was 'pretty feeble'. But the landlord owned two fierce Dobermans, and no one was prepared to argue the point.

Hotel was any indication. (They ended the night in the jacuzzi.) Through shows such as this they learned, as Neil stated, that they 'could turn a lounge room into a seething mass of people having an incredibly good time'. The band's real character was finally emerging. Over the next two weeks, the group played similar busking-style gigs at Salty's on Alki in Seattle, then at Nirvana, an Indian restaurant in New York—both were Capitol Records events—followed by two nights at Toronto's Duke of Gloucester Inn. Crowded House was unplugged a good three years before MTV claimed to have dreamt up the concept.

'Don't Dream It's Over' had been released as a single a few weeks before the gig at Yamashiro, on 20 October. It was the fourth single from the album and if it had flopped, it probably would have been all over for Crowded House and Capitol Records. By year's end, as the band played a New Year's Eve show at surfside Sydney beer barn Selina's, it had crept into the Top 100 on the *Billboard* singles chart. In mid-February, as the song's momentum built, they performed 'Don't Dream' on ABC's *Countdown*. Neil mimed Froom's organ solo on an old upright piano, raising his eyebrows at the camera as he played as if to say, 'Close enough'.

When Crowded House returned to the US to perform 'Don't Dream' on TV's *The Late Show* on 17 February, the song was on the fringes of the US Top 40—in fact it was the first song they'd heard in their limo after being collected at the airport. 'I had this shudder,' said Neil, 'of part fear and part excitement that the whole thing was gonna go all the way.' They continued touring, with shows in Seattle, Portland, Berkeley, Hollywood, Houston and then Minneapolis on 13 March, by which time the song had reached number 20.

Sharon and Liam were now on the road with Neil, as was Eddie Rayner, Neil's former Split Enz bandmate, playing keyboards.

Behind the scenes, Neil had given the okay for their American manager, Gary Stamler, to spend US$10,000 to hire four radio 'pluggers', who went out and spread the word about their latest single. The band never spoke about this; when Neil and Hester were asked what it took to 'crack America', they insisted that controversial hard rockers Guns N' Roses were their inspiration. 'I think there's a lot of parallels between Guns N' Roses and Crowded House,' said Hester, doing his best not to laugh. 'Very similar.'

Neil earnestly nodded in agreement. 'Heavily into drugs and sex and stuff.' There was no mention of radio pluggers.

And still 'Don't Dream It's Over' kept climbing. By 20 March it was at number 14, then number 9 by the end of March, by which time the video, directed by Australian filmmaker Alex Proyas, was on high rotation on MTV.

Neil, Hester and Seymour were also starting to make a splash on American TV, appearing for a second time on *The Joan Rivers Show* as 'Don't Dream' continued scaling the charts. 'Crowded House made their debut on our show in February,' Rivers said as her rowdy studio audience cheered their support, 'and the response was so incredible, so big, that we had to bring them right back.'

And though their performances of 'Something So Strong' and 'Now We're Getting Somewhere' were top notch, it was the group's form on Rivers' couch that really won over her large TV audience. Looking great in their bespoke suits, which Seymour had decorated, and clearly buoyed by their US success, they sparred playfully with their host.

When asked about their recent trip to Florida, where they'd witnessed the debaucheries of American spring break up close, Hester the Jester was in his element. 'We learned the traditional mating habit of the high-school American boy,' he revealed, grinning broadly. Talk turned to fellow guest Dame Edna Everage, who was about to join them on the set. Neil came clean and said that's why Sharon came to the show with him—to see Aussie royalty up close. 'She's broken more than a few hearts back in Australia,' Neil said of the Dame, somehow managing to keep a straight face.

When Everage made her entrance—she was a vision in sequins, sporting a stuffed cockatoo on each shoulder—Neil, Hester and Seymour dropped to their knees and bowed their heads, extending their hands for her blessing, which she duly provided. 'Aren't they lovely, Joan, Crowded House,' announced Everage. Then she turned to the band: 'I think you're going places, boys, I think you are.' As a thank you, the trio serenaded her with a quick rendition of 'Throw Your Arms Around Me'. Neil made it known that the song was written by Seymour's brother Mark, to which Nick added: 'Our family are very big fans of the Dame's in Australia, and my parents—if they get to see this . . .' With that he shook his head in mock amazement and gave Everage a squeeze, mugging for the camera.

'Crowded House,' said Rivers, as she wrapped up the show, 'You guys are just adorable.'

It was around this time that Neil reached out to big brother Tim. His follow-up to *Escapade*, an album called *Big Canoe*, didn't perform as well as his debut, while his relationship with Scacchi was faltering. And yet here was Neil riding a huge wave of American acclaim, so much so that his label, Capitol, had just floated the idea of a Crowded House TV show in the style of The Monkees, inspired by their easy rapport with such stars as Joan Rivers. (They passed.) Neil was very conscious of how Tim and his former bandmates might be feeling about his good fortune as they looked on, wondering why it hadn't happened to Split Enz. At least Eddie Rayner got to sample life at the business end of the American charts.

Neil's concerns grew even stronger when at the end of April, 'Don't Dream It's Over' reached its US chart peak of number 2. 'There was a sense of guilt . . . it took a little of the gloss off some of it,' he said. Neil had called Tim from a hotel somewhere in the US and told him that success 'doesn't feel as good as it should'.

'I think there was some guilt for Neil that it hadn't happened with Split Enz . . . Catholic guilt, it's phenomenal,' said Tim.

Tim joined Neil and the band for a show at the Storyville Jazz Hall in New Orleans during the first week of May. 'We had a couple of really good gigs where he got up with us,' said Neil. 'And I think it sort of helped him a little bit to feel like he was part of it to some degree.'

Neil, meanwhile, had to deal with something even more confronting than Catholic guilt: a near-death experience. In the air, on their way to a gig in New Mexico, a window blew out of their plane and they suddenly dropped several thousand feet. The view of the Rocky Mountains became way too close for the comfort of everyone on board. Somehow the pilot managed to regain control and land the plane, but Neil's wild ride wasn't over yet. As he stepped onto the tarmac, still recovering from the flight, armed police cornered him, demanding to see his ID. It turned out that Neil was a dead ringer for an escaped prisoner who was currently on the loose.

To Neil, the wretched events of the day were an omen: 'Don't Dream' wouldn't reach number 1. He believed it was some sort of warning from the pop gods. Unfortunately for Neil, his prophecy was spot on. The George Michael/Aretha Franklin duet 'I Knew You Were Waiting (For Me)' prevented it from reaching the top spot. Hits from Cutting Crew, Jody Watley, U2 and Madonna, meanwhile, were nipping at the heels of 'Don't Dream It's Over'.

The experience of becoming a very public figure on the back of a hit song was also something of a slap in the face for Neil. It was similar to the situation when 'I Got You' had become a huge hit, but this was the US, and the response was crazier. Neil was thrilled to hear 'Don't Dream' playing in shopping centres and supermarkets, and happy to swap stories with the likes of Dame Edna and Joan Rivers, but there was a downside. 'You find you become a bit like a politician, shaking hands and kissing babies,' Neil admitted. 'That takes a bit of the glamour off the idea of being successful.' Being mistaken for a felon on the run didn't help, either.

The madness reached a weird peak after a concert in Detroit. Hundreds of fans were gathered near the band's bus after the show, demanding something, *anything*, from them as a memento. It didn't really matter what was offered up; they just wanted a part of Crowded House to claim as their own. The band had eaten a post-show pizza and Hester opened the door of the tour bus and threw out the box. 'They just tore it apart,' Seymour told a reporter, shaking his head in amazement.

The dream run of 'Don't Dream It's Over' would continue until the end of June when the song finally dropped out of the US Top 100. By this time the band, who had returned for an extensive tour of Australia and New Zealand, were homecoming heroes. And the song's success wasn't restricted to the US; it charted highly in a dozen different countries, hitting the top of the charts in New Zealand and Canada, the Top 10 in Australia and the Netherlands and the Top 30 in Germany, Ireland and the UK. So much for it being 'too Beatles-esque'. It even made the Top 5 in Poland.

The track was seemingly everywhere; it was number 13 in the *Billboard* Hot 100 annual round-up and firmly cemented Neil's reputation as one of the best tunesmiths of his generation. *Billboard* included Neil among their Top 10 singer/songwriters of the year, while Paul McCartney made it known he was a big Finn fan. And it didn't harm the song's momentum that Neil and the band spent much of the year in motion, playing more than 150 shows, most of them in the US.

Their self-titled debut album, too, had come back to life after the success of 'Don't Dream', reaching a US peak of number 12 and eventually selling more than a million copies in America—and more than 400,000 in Australia, where it went six times platinum.

Tim's advice to Neil to start his own band had paid off handsomely, and in record time.

★

Aspects of Tim's career, meanwhile, were starting to take a similar course to those of his younger brother. After a failed stint with Virgin Records, he signed to Capitol, a deal Neil helped put in place. Tim also signed up with Gary Stamler, Crowded House's US manager. Mitchell Froom would produce Tim's first album for Capitol. It seemed that Neil had found a very practical way of dealing with the guilt he'd felt about Crowded House's success. Tim repaid the favour by helping out with backing vocals as Crowded House began recording their second album.

In February 1988, the brothers joined forces, and voices, for a session at KCRW, a college radio station that broadcast out of Santa Monica. Neil had spent the past month recording in Sunset Sound in LA and made it known that he had 'the studio tan going'. Tim had a chuckle at his brother's pallor. 'It's disgusting,' he said with a laugh. When asked about the Crowded House album-under-development, Neil suggested he might call it *Mediocre Follow-Up*, but proved that to be anything but the case when he played the ballad 'Better Be Home Soon'. It was a worthy companion piece to 'Don't Dream It's Over'. Tim also previewed a new track, 'Show a Little Mercy'.

'I bet a whole lot of people bloody bootlegged that,' Neil said after they had played their newies. 'There goes a hundred thousand sales.'

While on-air, Neil and Tim settled into an old-fashioned Kiwi singalong, working their way through some songs from the Split Enz canon—'Six Months in a Leaky Boat' and 'Charlie'—and such personal favourites as 'Throw Your Arms Around Me', the Everly Brothers' 'Bye Bye Love' and the old standard 'Goodnight Irene', the kind of tear-jerker they'd sung as kids in Te Awamutu. They even had a crack at Tim's 'Fraction Too Much Friction' but it swiftly fell apart. Tim accused his brother of live radio sabotage, but

Neil would have none of that. 'It's your bloody song,' he said, feigning exasperation. 'You should know it.'

Neil also let it slip that he and Tim were thinking about a musical collaboration sometime 'in the next couple of years', their respective careers and lives permitting. They had a very specific style in mind, too—'a two-part harmony thing that we haven't heard in some time'.

Neil, however, had more urgent matters to address. While it was a blessing to have had such a smash with 'Don't Dream It's Over' and the *Crowded House* LP, he now faced the challenge of coming up with a sequel, and the pressure was starting to weigh heavily on him. He was the band's key songwriter and its musical director; it wasn't like the best days of Split Enz, where Tim would also have a bounty of songs ready to go, and Eddie Rayner would bring in his own musical ideas. Neil also had a young family to provide for; as he told one reporter, 'I made a decision early on when I got married and had kids that I wasn't going to let anything come between that bond. But that's been very difficult at times. The music machine doesn't recognise family commitments.' Those pressures that he was feeling surfaced in some of the new material the band was recording, as the sessions continued into the early months of 1988. And, as Neil would come to do more and more often, he drew on past experiences for subject matter.

One experience had been wedged in Neil's subconscious since he was a kid. He'd shared a room with his sister Judy while she was studying for the School Certificate, a time he remembered as being 'very stressful'. She'd sometimes have awful nightmares—they were so bad that she'd scream and wake Neil. He channelled all this into a song he titled, appropriately, 'Sister Madly'. Like 'Better Be Home Soon', they'd been playing 'Sister Madly' during concerts for some time.

Musically, Neil felt that it suited the 'busking' style they used when Hester came down to the front of the stage, and future live shows would prove him right; 'Sister Madly' sometimes ran as long as twelve minutes in concert. Lanky British guitarist Richard Thompson, formerly of folk-rock legends Fairport Convention, was in the studio at the same time and Neil asked if he'd like to contribute to the record. The solo that Thompson played perfectly suited the manic theme of the song. Neil believed that the guitarist was a 'master', which was undeniable—he'd also later work with Tim, co-writing 'Persuasion', possibly the best Tim Finn solo recording. (Later on, Thompson, a convert to an obscure strand of Sufi Islam, took a strong dislike to Nick Seymour's cover art for the band's *Together Alone* album, which he felt was insulting to the prophet Mohammed. 'He told me he found me offensive,' said Seymour.)

'Into Temptation', one of several emotionally charged new songs from Neil, documented a much more recent event in his life—and it would also become one of his most misunderstood tracks. While most listeners suspected it was about infidelity—and that might well have been true—it wasn't Neil who was about to disappear 'into temptation/Safe in the wide-open arms of hell'. Not at all.

'When I'm singing "Into Temptation",' Neil explained to Triple J's Richard Kingsmill in 2001, 'I'm not singing about something that's happening to me, even though there's personal experience in there.'

The backstory was this: Neil had been on tour, in the bar of yet another hotel, when he noticed two sporting groups who were also house guests—a rugby squad and a netball team, as he learned—gradually pairing off. When Neil retired for the night, he discovered that his room was situated smack dab between the two rooms used by the rugby team, and his sleep was interrupted by frequent noises from the foyer and the other side of the walls.

'I thought they were knocking on my door,' he explained, 'and opened the door and there's a netball player disappearing into the room next door, for a night of, you know, *sports conversation*.'

The song's opening lines, 'You opened up your door/I couldn't believe my luck', was yet another intro that came to Neil straightaway, fully formed. But while he was aware the song might be misinterpreted, he hadn't expected to be quizzed by those near and dear to him. 'It is a bit uncomfortable at times when your family thinks it's all about you, that it's a direct diary.'

Another of Neil's new songs, 'When You Come', also seemed to touch on subject matter that raised a few eyebrows. His son Liam, as he grew older, couldn't bring himself to ask Neil about it, fearing that the title was meant to be taken, well, *orgasmically*. But that wasn't the case. Neil explained that the song was about 'the birth of the cosmos, when powerful things take over in your life'. While it was more about forces cosmic than orgasmic, it did leave some listeners, and not just Liam, wondering about its meaning. It sure *sounded* sexual in nature. 'It was the very first time I ever wrote a lyric as a stream-of-consciousness thing,' added Neil. 'I didn't have the song planned out. It's rare for me to write a whole set of lyrics and then set them to music.'

Songs such as these typified the mood of the second Crowded House album, which they titled *Temple of Low Men* (which *did* have a sexual allusion; it referred to cunnilingus). It was a much less playful record than their debut. Neil turned 30 in May 1988 as the album was being readied for an early July release, and he believed that this milestone, seen by many as a transition into middle age, left its mark on the finished record.

When asked to sum up the album on ABC TV's *The Factory*, Neil replied that it was 'pretty different' but 'much better'; Hester quipped that it featured 'heavy, bitchin' songs'. And it *was* a moody record, more introspective than anything they'd recorded to date, something that many reviewers and fans noted straightaway.

Village Voice critic Robert Christgau believed that by taking a more serious tangent, Neil had 'neglected the only thing he has to offer the world: perky hooks'. Neil never forgot the review, citing it as recently as 2021, during his *Fangradio* podcast. 'He claims I was wallowing in self-pity on this album, but I disagree . . . so, fuck you, Robert.' *Rolling Stone* writer Anthony DeCurtis was more generous, giving the album a four-star rating, but still acknowledged that fans of 'Don't Dream It's Over' might have trouble embracing the new Neil Finn. 'Rather than making him more expansive, or at least steeling him,' DeCurtis wrote, 'success appears to have made Finn feel more vulnerable, less sure of himself and even a tad bitter.'

Critics' barbs may have left a few scars on Neil, but it was the words of former fans that sometimes hurt the most. A punter approached Neil as he and Hester left the Prince of Wales Hotel in Melbourne after watching a gig, around the time that 'Better Be Home Soon' was released as the lead single for the album.

'Hey, Neil,' the punter said. 'C.F.G.'

'What are you talking about?' Neil replied, confused.

'You used to write good songs,' he said bluntly, before walking off. Neil figured out that he was talking about 'Better Be Home Soon' and its elementary chord progression. Did he want him to write more complex songs?

A reporter for TV's *A Current Affair* asked if Crowded House were 'the clowns of the rock industry', a reference to the band's, in particular Paul Hester's, fondness for banter and hijinks on stage and during interviews and videos. This was exactly the wrong question to ask Neil at that moment in time. 'It is a cause of concern if you start to become known as clowns,' Neil fired back, 'because obviously it undermines the fact that your music might be taken seriously.'

8

'You can fart and they'd clap, mate'

Temple of Low Men proved to be a hard sell in America, a situation not helped by their inclusion in a *Chicago Tribune* piece, 'Sophomore slump', about major-label artists struggling with their second album. But Crowded House remained a very bankable act in Australia. They spent May and June 1988 on the road in Oz, a trip that included a 4 June set at World Expo 88 on the River Stage in Brisbane. Soon after, 'Better Be Home Soon' was a hit, reaching number 2 on the Australian charts and going gold, while the album made the top spot in late July. *Low Men* would be among the Top 10 bestselling albums in Australia for the year, shifting more than 300,000 copies. (In the US it eventually went gold, selling 500,000 copies, although it climbed no higher in the charts than number 40.)

After dates in Europe during the northern summer—including a set at the prestigious Montreux Jazz Festival on 16 July, a bill they shared with Miles Davis and Carlos

Santana—they returned in August for the 'Better Be Home Late than Never' Oz tour, which concluded with five sold-out nights at Sydney's 2000-capacity State Theatre. On stage at the State on 25 August, Neil looked sharp in a tartan waistcoat, the sleeves of his white shirt rolled up to his elbows, his hair spiky, a little shorter than usual. The crowd was on their feet early on as the set opened with a thumping 'When You Come'—and they were still standing and cheering when the show ended with an impassioned 'Into Temptation', the eighteenth song of the night. Neil wisely chose to end things on a downbeat note, otherwise the audience mightn't have let them leave the building.

'This is a great place, this is a great theatre,' Neil gasped between songs, a bit out of breath. 'And by the way, when the ushers come round to tell you to sit down, you have it from me you don't have to.'

Neil was in total control—and fine voice—while delivering some of the best songs of his career. In fact, Crowded House had never sounded, or looked, better. Their fans agreed, a point made abundantly clear when Neil stepped into the spotlight during an extended 'Now We're Getting Somewhere', as Eddie Rayner vamped madly on the keyboards—plenty of screams could be heard amid the clapping of 2000 pairs of hands. The term 'sex symbol' may not have sat comfortably with Neil, but that didn't change the opinion of many of his admirers.

Neil, Hester and Seymour had also conducted their first tour of Japan, playing in Osaka and Tokyo. Early in the one-week blitz, Neil spoke with some English-speaking fans and asked what they liked about the band's music. 'The serenity,' he was told. That came as a shock. 'I've never heard anything like that in the West,' Neil said later on, adding that 'inner turmoil is a much more evocative thing to write about than "Baby, baby let's go down to the disco". Most of my songs end up being a bit bitter and twisted.' But *serenity*? That was a newie for Neil.

As was now the custom, while in Japan the band busked, playing 'Sister Madly' at a train station, Hester tapping out a rhythm on a cardboard box. Neil then stopped at a music shop and played 'World Where You Live' on an organ, to the bemusement of passing pedestrians. He hadn't done that since he was a kid working at the electrical store in Te Awamutu.

On 31 July they filmed a video for 'When You Come' at an industrial site and also in downtown Tokyo. The trio looked a little awkward as they strummed guitars while crowds of bustling Tokyoites walked around them, getting on with business. By the end of the tour, however, when the band played a show at the city's Nakano Sunplaza, Neil had been mobbed for autographs. It seemed that the 'serenity' of his music had won over a whole new army of fans.

★

The band continued touring to promote *Temple of Low Men* well into 1989, winding up with yet another run of American dates at the Arlington Theatre in Santa Barbara on 9 April. They wouldn't tour again for eight months, their longest period off the road to date.

Once back in Melbourne, Neil began working on some new songs in Melbourne's Platinum Studios, capturing ideas on an eight-track Tascam reel-to-reel recorder. But he struggled to come up with strong material for a third album. Growing increasingly frustrated, he decided to fire Nick Seymour, which came as quite a surprise to the bassist (who'd recently married American Brenda Bentleigh). It was a bizarre move, in fact, with the benefit of hindsight, and Neil handled it badly. According to Seymour, when he asked Neil for an explanation, he simply replied: 'You're just not pushing my creative buttons anymore.'

'I just didn't find that the bass was doing stuff that I wanted it to,' Neil further explained during an episode of *Great Australian Albums*. 'I was playing bass on my own demos and kinda liking what I was doing. It was classic lead-singer syndrome: you want to do everything.'

Seymour, with due justification, asked Neil exactly how he was going to find another player who was so invested in the band—in their music, their look, their image, their Crowded House-ishness. Yet Neil dug in; Seymour was out. Many close to Neil disagreed with his decision, including Sharon, the band's US manager Stamler and producer Mitchell Froom. Froom called Neil from LA and told him that he didn't think it was the right move and while Neil heard him out, he continued working on his demos with Hester, playing the bass himself.

A few weeks later Seymour called Neil. 'Look, this is ridiculous,' he said. 'The band is doing really well and I'm a really important part of it.' They met up and over several drinks, Seymour further argued his point. As Neil related, 'He put a good case forward and I said, "All right, fair enough."' With that, Seymour was back in the fold. 'It was that easy,' said Neil. 'Until you see what you're missing you don't know what you've got, essentially.'

Other moves were afoot. Eddie Rayner had joined a new outfit named Schnell Fenster, which reconnected him with some old chums: former Split Enz-ers Phil Judd, Nigel Griggs and Noel Crombie. (Rayner's place in Crowded House would be taken by American Mark Hart.) Schnell Fenster released a debut album, *The Sound of Trees*, in September 1988, and an atmospheric single named 'Whisper', which had been a moderate hit in Australia, reaching number 58. In January 1989, Crowded House had shared a twelve-date New Zealand run with Rayner's new band. They joined forces during the encore of their show in Auckland on 24 January, with Tim also taking part, playing 'Six Months in a Leaky Boat', 'Dirty Creature' and 'I See Red'. It was a Split Enz reunion in everything but name.

★

Judging by the flash rented premises in Los Angeles that Neil and the others lived in while making the new album, a large house on Woodrow Wilson Drive, his status at Capitol was still very solid. Capitol had a new president, Hale Milgrim, who'd worked with such successful acts as Linda Ronstadt, Simply Red and The Cure and was a big fan of Crowded House. Milgrim was determined to return them to the business end of the charts in the US. 'He was willing to throw as much money as it would take to get the best videos made, the best recordings possible,' said Seymour.

In mid-1989, the band set up camp in their house on Woodrow Wilson Drive. A very impressive spa was one of its many features; there was also a powerful stereo speaker set up in each room, perfect for listening to recordings after a day in A&M Studios. Every morning, Hester would join Seymour in bed and ask Neil to bring them tea. The three began greeting each other as 'Cledwyn'. Their collective mood was upbeat and positive.

Neil had a dozen new songs that they were recording; among them was 'Whispers and Moans', which, as Neil would explain to an audience, was 'for anyone who's spent a night in a hotel and had someone next door bonking that's kept them up all night'. Others included 'Fall at Your Feet' and a track called 'Anyone Can Tell'. But troubles soon arose in the studio. Neil would come to admit that there was a quality-control problem—of the twelve songs, 'only six of them were any good. We were chasing phantoms.' The band had set up easels in the studio, with the intention of dabbling in oils while making the record, but only Seymour painted anything. Neil's mind was elsewhere. 'I was too involved with agonising about the songs,' he said.

Despite the support of new Capitol boss Milgrim, the label's response to this first batch of recordings wasn't good. Neil said that a Capitol rep 'told me it was a piece of shit. How could I screw it up so badly?' Neil was understandably angry; he decided the label needed some time to really listen to the songs and, as Nick Seymour related, 'wake up to themselves'. Neil had also clashed with Froom about the production of his new songs, which was out of character. It was decided to put the record on hold while the disgruntled band returned to Melbourne. Neil had a lot on his mind beyond the rejected album: Sharon was pregnant again; the baby was due in late October.

Neil spoke with Tim about the complicated situation with Capitol. 'I was watching him railing about it,' Tim said, when interviewed for *The 100 Best Australian Albums* book, 'how he was unable to write what they wanted to hear.'

Neil was not feeling great about his writing—right or wrong, the label's criticism had dented his confidence. It was then that his mind flashed back to the KCRW radio session back in February 1988, when he and Tim had hinted at a possible Finn Brothers record. Perhaps some sessions with Tim were just the outlet he needed—while they'd written great Split Enz songs in their shared house in Rose Bay, they'd never actually written together, so it would be a first. Maybe a new sensation was exactly what Neil needed.

Neil and Tim set up in a flat Neil owned in Murchison Street, Melbourne, with views to Port Phillip Bay (and the adjacent cemetery). Neil rode his bike to the studio; this was nothing like working in stressful, traffic-clogged LA. They quickly found their favourite spots: Neil got comfortable in the kitchen, playing bass, while Tim strummed an acoustic guitar. There was a piano nearby.

They agreed to limit themselves to just a few hours a day and, to Neil's amazement, it did the trick. There was little time for hanging out and catching up; they simply walked in, settled down and got on with the work. 'We just went for it really hard,' said Neil. And songs all but fell out of them: they wrote more than an album's worth of material in the first three days. 'It was a total revelation to us,' said Neil. 'It's those moments that you do this job for.'

The first song they wrote was 'Weather With You'. Tim came into the studio with the title and the opening line, which namechecked 'Stormy Weather', the song family friend Peggy Dawson used to belt out around the piano at Teasdale Street. He and Neil free-associated on the lyrics, swapping their sister's real address (number 4 Mount Pleasant Road) for number 57, which sang much better. An absolute earworm of an acoustic guitar riff opened the track, which all came together on day one. Soon after, they wrote 'Four Seasons in One Day' (inspired by the fickle weather of both Melbourne and Auckland) and 'Chocolate Cake', a send-up of American gluttony. The lyric featured a star-studded cast that included Andy Warhol, Andrew Lloyd Webber, Elvis, Liberace, Picasso and Tammy Bakker, though some came away a bit diminished. 'Not everyone in New York would pay to see Andrew Lloyd Webber,' sang the Finns. Melbourne-based bluesman Chris Wilson would later add a swaggering harmonica solo.

Another new song was 'It's Only Natural': Tim wrote the chorus, Neil the verse. The first verse, which Neil described as 'the rubbing together of spirituality and science', had sprung from a conversation between Neil and Tim about quarks and subatomic particles, hot topics at the time that fascinated Neil. (Stephen Hawking's seminal *A Brief History of Time* had been published the year before.) It was yet another track that came together swiftly and without fuss; on the demo, all they needed were their voices, acoustic guitars and handclaps to sound just about perfect. They called their second co-write on the same theme 'Strangeness and Charm', which were the names of two quarks. A big ballad named 'All I Ask', meanwhile, was written, quite literally, in about the same time it would take to sing it on the finished record—just minutes.

As the songs took shape and his confidence returned, Neil realised that he should have ignored the psychological barriers that had earlier prevented him from writing with his brother. 'It was so obvious, stupidly obvious,' said Neil.

'We harmonise really well together.' There were other things also working to their benefit. Neil wasn't the most organised songwriter; he relied on flashes of inspiration. Tim, meanwhile, was all about structure: he'd come to each session with a pencil and a legal pad, ready to work. When Neil worked alone, he'd sometimes spend months searching through tapes for something he liked, but now, working with his more organised brother, the good stuff was much easier to access—Tim would have everything written down.

'We were good for each other,' said Neil. It was a major understatement because some of this new material was pure gold.

The songs were recorded in Tim's house in Caulfield, which he'd had converted into a studio he named Periscope. The only other person invited into the sessions was drummer Ricky Fataar, who'd worked with Tim on *Escapade*. 'We had these pure grooves going,' said Tim. 'It was fantastic.' Paul Hester helped out on a few tracks written at Murchison Street, but these songs were intended for a Finn brothers record, not for Crowded House. At least, that was the plan.

It was a magical time for Neil; not only had he regained his songwriting touch, but his second son was born on 25 October 1989. He and Sharon chose the name Elroy.

*

Neil and Tim, along with Paul Hester, were in especially high spirits when they spoke with host of TV show *Spin*—and Australian Crawl co-founder—Brad Robinson, soon after their songwriting binge. But they weren't there primarily to discuss their recent collaboration. Instead, they were speaking about their past, namely Split Enz, who were coming together for an end-of-year show—an end-of-the-decade show—at a huge event to be staged at Sydney's Darling Harbour. Naturally, the support band would be Crowded House. It would be a busy night for Neil and Paul Hester.

When Robinson asked why they had chosen to re-form, albeit briefly, Neil couldn't be any clearer with his response. 'One,' he said, 'it's the end of the decade. Two, we were all in the same place at the same time. And three, we really enjoy playing together.' Neil mentioned their brief re-formation at the end of the Crowded House/Schnell Fenster tour in Auckland the previous January. 'And that wasn't long enough.'

Neil went on to explain, very rationally, that the money being offered was great and 'anybody who can take a well-paid job over Christmas to be with his mates and his family and play some gigs would be a mug not to'. Robinson was taken aback; musicians weren't supposed to discuss 'the business'. It didn't matter to Neil, who was in a very playful mood. When the subject of the band's rusted-on fans came up, he smiled and said, 'You can fart and they'd clap, mate.'

Robinson asked about the Finns' recent songwriting burst and Tim related the incident that led to 'Chocolate Cake'. He was in a restaurant in New York when a woman at a nearby table, after scoffing a substantial meal, sat back, sighed and asked aloud, 'Should I have another piece of chocolate cake—or the cheque?' It was like a scene from *Monty Python's The Meaning of Life*—and simply too good not to use in a song. They proceeded to play it for the first time outside Periscope,

Hester tapping a rhythm on a tea chest, the Finns strumming acoustic guitars and harmonising sweetly. They were having a fine old time, ending with a cheeky jam of Andrew Lloyd Webber's 'Don't Cry for Me Argentina'.

Just prior to the New Year's Eve show, which was rapturously received—'there was little rust in the machine', noted one critic—Neil told a reporter that enough time had now passed for him to be 'really affectionate towards Split Enz'. All the complications that marred their demise—Tim's solo career, Neil's uncertainty about his own future—had faded from his memory. 'I miss Split Enz most,' he revealed, 'when I'm sitting in a studio by myself and things aren't going so well, and there's no one to have a game of snooker with or ask what they think.'

So what if Split Enz once said they'd never play again? Things had changed. 'You've got to say those sorts of things to end it,' Neil argued. 'Otherwise, it's like leaving your girlfriend and saying, "I really want to go but I might come back in a year." You have to end something before you can start it again. We did mean it at the time, though,' he added quickly.

There was another Split Enz show in Surfers Paradise, which Dick and Mary Finn would attend, and a concert at the Country Resort in Mudgee. A planned show in Newcastle on 28 December was cancelled when an earthquake hit the city, killing thirteen people—including the band's driver, who'd reached the Newcastle Workers Club, where the gig was scheduled. It cast a dark shadow over what had been a satisfying and successful reunion.

★

Working with Tim, both in the studio and on stage, had rejuvenated Neil. There was just one downside—the unresolved state of the third Crowded House album, which was still in limbo. But Neil was now convinced he had the perfect solution. In the new year, Neil took stock of the songs he had in the bank. There were maybe half a dozen good ones from the aborted 1989 LA sessions with Crowded House, and now he had a stash of great new material that he'd written with Tim. Neil started to wonder if there was some way of combining them. It had to be a smarter move than releasing two separate records.

One day, he was venting to Tim about how difficult it was for him to complete the next Crowded House record. 'He was quite emotional,' Tim recalled during a Radio New Zealand documentary. It was then that the brothers seemed to come to the same conclusion: take the best songs they'd just created and add them to the pick of the completed LA tracks. That's when another thought came to Neil: *Why not invite Tim into the band?*

Tim, whose previous two albums—*Big Canoe* and *Tim Finn*—had been commercial flops, was thinking the same. As they were mulling over the Periscope tracks, which they had decided were good enough to be finished recordings, it was agreed that Tim would join Crowded House. Tim later said he genuinely believed 'there was no way they could have done those songs without me'. Although, after a moment's pause, he did add: 'Well, they could have, but they wouldn't have been as good.' He wanted in.

Hester and Seymour received a call from Neil, who asked them to a band meeting, where he broke the news. Neil stated that the others 'were more confused by it than I was', but they did love the new songs, despite not having been part of the recordings. And, as Seymour rightly figured, 'It was going to make their mum happy.'

However, Tim's recruitment necessitated a sacking. Mark Hart had been recruited when Eddie Rayner departed in early 1989. The 35-year-old Hart, who was born in Kansas, was an in-demand all-rounder: he could play guitar and keyboards and also sing strong harmonies. Hart had toured with British pop band Supertramp, and had also worked in the studio and on the road with Tim before being brought into the fold by Gary Stamler. He'd helped out during an American tour in March 1989 and had played on the first batch of demos Neil recorded in Melbourne a few months later. (He contributed a standout melodica solo on 'Italian Plastic', the best song Paul Hester wrote for Crowded House.) But a fan club show in early December at the Prahran Town Hall would prove to be Hart's last with Crowded House. For the time being, at least.

★

The new and slightly even more Crowded House returned to LA in the northern spring of 1990 to continue the album with producer Mitchell Froom. The feature of this trip—aside from Neil being snubbed in the studio by Jon Bon Jovi and meeting a gleeful Bruce Springsteen, who'd just become a father—was the completion of 'All I Ask'. A big ballad required an equally big string arrangement, and 50-year-old Argentinian expat Jorge Calandrelli, who'd worked with Quincy Jones and Tony Bennett, was hired. Neil was a fan of those recordings of Calandrelli's; he loved what he called their 'blue notes'. Neil hoped Calandrelli could add some of that magic to his song.

The men of Crowded House had never been in a studio with an orchestra, and they felt it was appropriate to dress for the occasion. Neil, Tim, Hester and Seymour all wore their best suits and looked very sharp. Then Calandrelli and his team arrived at the studio sporting track pants and leisure wear. 'It doesn't look like an orchestra,' Neil whispered to the others. But the end result was perfect, so lush it might have been lifted straight from a Golden Age of Hollywood soundtrack. 'It could have been cheese,' said Neil, 'but it was all class.'

With the band's third album, which they named *Woodface*, finally nearing completion, a press release was prepared on 23 January 1991. It read: 'No Vacancy: Tim Finn moves into Crowded House.' Tim had actually been playing with the band since November, but now it was official. It had been a challenging couple of years for Neil—and his songs had done a lot of Frequent Flyer miles—but right now it seemed that his future, and that of the band, could not have been brighter.

9

'We weren't used to having another strong personality on stage'

Neil may have been back on the treadmill, but there was no mistaking that the prevailing mood was upbeat and fun. The 'new Crowded House', as they were introduced, sat down with Brad Robinson for a *Good Morning Australia* interview on the release of *Woodface* in July 1991. It was Hester who tackled the opening—and obvious—question as to how and why Tim joined.

Putting on his best poker face, Hester revealed, 'We've got this deal on paper and Tim's had to buy into the company. It's cost him three hundred and thirty-three bucks to buy into Crowded House Touring Inc. And he's now secretary.'

A very relaxed Tim, a streak of grey in his hair, took a slightly more serious tack, explaining that he and Neil needed to get past 'brothers' roles' to reach a point 'to just be totally open with each other'. That, he said, opened the floodgates at Periscope and resulted in the deluge of great songs they'd now committed to record. Seven of the fourteen songs on the finished record were Neil and Tim co-writes—co-sings, in fact, which gave much of the record a decidedly different sound, almost folksy in parts.

'Tim started playing with us,' added Neil, 'and it felt like a band.'

Rather than coming on too serious—they were Crowded House, after all—the interview then descended into farce. Neil bumped Seymour's drink, which spilled on his pants. Seymour jumped to his feet and, feigning anger, announced: 'Sacked! You're sacked, Neil!' and stormed off the set.

'Yeah, it's great,' laughed Hester after a beat. 'Four-piece, three-piece, two-piece, one-piece, hairpiece.'

Seymour then returned to the set in a white dressing gown, his hair wrapped in a towel. Hester had decided enough was enough; he strolled up to the camera, told the audience 'I've pooed my pants' and walked off, leaving the others in hysterics.

At the start of the *Woodface* odyssey, there was an almost tangible sense of camaraderie within the group—and it stretched beyond moments such as this. The video for 'Chocolate Cake', a surprise choice for lead single given its not-so-subtle bashing of Americans and Americana, was played strictly for laughs, even though it was their most expensive clip yet. Filmed in Melbourne by Australian director Kit Quarry, Neil, Tim and the rest of the band were cast as lounge lizards in an array of matching suits, playing the song (and pulling off some rudimentary dance moves) beneath the cheesiest of mirror balls, while drag queens, overeaters and animated bugs drifted in and out of shot.

The lounge lizards were back in action soon after on the set of *Late Night with David Letterman*, where they appeared on 12 July. While Neil had never appeared so relaxed, it was Tim who took the slicked-back look to a whole new level, with some bling draped around his neck, a handful of Brylcreem in his hair, his pants and ruffled shirt seemingly on loan from a Vegas crooner. The brothers hammed it up like never before, wiggling their hips suggestively, motioning to Letterman's bandleader, Paul Shaffer, during the 'here comes Mrs Hairy Legs' line in the song, who obligingly lifted up his trouser leg while still playing the piano. They also ad-libbed lyrics, Tim throwing in a few lines of John Denver's 'Rocky Mountain High' and Hot Chocolate's 'You Sexy Thing'. The performance was an especially big thrill for Paul Hester, who idolised Letterman.

It was clear that they had come a long way from the hand-on-the-heart emotion of 'Don't Dream It's Over', and American audiences didn't quite know what to make of the new Crowded House. Nor, it turned out, did American critics. Reviewing *Woodface* for *Rolling Stone*, Kristine McKenna questioned the choice of 'Chocolate Cake' as lead single. 'This song seems hypocritical given that Crowded House relocated to LA in order to kick its career into high gear,' she wrote. While that wasn't exactly true—they'd worked in the US but hadn't shifted base from Melbourne—and much of the review was full of praise (she described *Woodface* as 'a swinging record' and the band as 'cheerful yet sardonic, sleek, urbane and highly melodic'), her comments about 'Chocolate Cake' proved prescient. While the single charted strongly on *Billboard*'s Alternative Airplay chart, it wasn't a mainstream hit in America. It only managed to reach number 20 in Australia.

However, reaction to their new music was vastly different on the other side of the Atlantic. UK listeners had, until then, seemed to have only a passing interest in the band. The *Crowded House* LP had 'peaked' in the UK at number 99; *Temple of Low Men* hadn't even made the album chart. And while 'Chocolate Cake' was no smash, only reaching number 69, it was the subsequent releases from *Woodface* that changed the band's fortunes in the UK.

*

Before their British breakthrough, however, the band came back to Australia in late July for the Get Woodfaced tour, which was a return to smaller venues, pubs and clubs. It was more like the days of The Mullanes than a typical Crowded House tour. None of this mattered to local audiences; the 22 shows, at the Bridgeway Hotel in Adelaide and Selina's in Sydney, were packed, and *Woodface* raced to number 2 on the national album chart, quickly going platinum. It would stay on the charts for more than a year.

But by now the high spirits of the tour had started to fade. Tim was a natural-born showman, a great frontman, yet by necessity he was in a supporting role when Neil sang material that didn't emanate from their magical Melbourne sessions—and that was a good chunk of their 20-odd song set (although they did play Split Enz's 'Six Months in a Leaky Boat' and 'Shark Attack'). As Neil admitted, Tim's role was 'a musician playing a bit of keyboards and sort of hanging around a bit until there was a song he was involved in'.

Hardly surprisingly, Tim started to grow bored on stage. The pure joy he had felt in making music again with Neil was being eroded, show by show. And Neil was nobody's fool; he knew what was happening and it was beginning to bother him, too. 'We weren't used to having another strong personality on stage,' he said, 'and it upset the rhythm of the band a bit.'

On 13 August, the band played the Byron Bay Services Club in New South Wales, but what ensued between Neil and Tim had little in common with the peace, love and mung beans vibe for which the region was renowned. An onstage disagreement between them spilled into the backstage area after the show; Neil was so angry he threw a punch at his brother. ('A bogus punch,' Tim later made clear.)

After some pushing and shoving, a still fuming Neil headed out to the venue's car park and locked himself in the tour van. A local hippie had watched the situation unfold and she walked over to Neil to offer what she felt were words of wisdom. 'Let it go,' she told him from the other side of the window. 'Let it go.'

Neil was having none of it. 'Fuck off!' he roared at her.

'Those sort of places want to drag out the dark side of your nature,' Neil said of Byron Bay. But it was more than that, of course. Neil was beginning to realise that he'd made a big mistake by inviting Tim into the band.

'I feel like Stevie Nicks,' Tim grumbled to a reporter—Nicks, of course, was often relegated to banging on a tambourine and twirling about the stage when not playing her songs with Fleetwood Mac. Truth was, Tim was probably feeling more like Yoko Ono.

★

The fraternal situation had grown tricky, but there were still magical moments on tour. On 26 August they filled the Powerstation in Auckland, a 1000-capacity venue that was one of Neil's favourite places to play. 'It's just big enough to feel like a real event,' he said of the room, but at the same time 'just small enough to feel close to the action.' It was the opening show of the Get Woodfaced New Zealand leg, a thrill for local audiences who hadn't seen Neil and Tim play together since the days of Split Enz.

'This is the first glimpse of the new line-up,' a beaming Neil told the crowd after their opener, 'Sister Madly'. And the band were at their rocking best, powered by Hester's high-energy drumming, Neil's crisp guitar and Seymour's rumbling, melodic bass lines. Tim's harmonies added extra texture, while his onstage presence was undeniable; at times he danced like a madman around the others as they played. (Clearly, this was a night that Tim didn't feel much like Stevie Nicks.) They steered 'There Goes God' and 'Now We're Getting Somewhere' into totally new directions with impressive instrumental jamming—the band was loose when they chose to be, yet still tight when required. Even 'It's Only Natural', breezy on record, rocked like a hurricane.

An explosive 'When You Come' was the centrepiece of the Powerstation set. Guitar tech Paul Guthrie—nicknamed Arlo by Hester to avoid confusion with the various other Pauls in the band and crew—joined in on electric guitar while Neil wailed away on his acoustic. 'He'll be ready to join Push Push pretty soon,' Neil joked, taking a cheeky shot at a local rock band that had had some success. Neil himself might have been auditioning for a far heavier rock outfit during 'Mean to Me' when he let rip with some explosive bursts of guitar. During 'Chocolate Cake', Tim riffed on Jimi Hendrix's 'Purple Haze', yet unlike their memorable *Letterman* performance of the song, Neil left centrestage to Tim, opting instead to play keyboards.

'Good singing, Auckland,' Neil said after a rapturously received 'Weather With You'. 'You're in good voice tonight.'

It was left to Paul Hester to come up with the perfect punchline for what had been a terrific homecoming. 'It's a bit sad to see all these people coming out of the woodwork claiming to be Neil and Tim's relatives and asking for money,' he said, trying to keep a straight face. 'But apart from that you're a pretty friendly bunch over here.'

★

Enthusiasm for *Woodface* in the UK and Europe had really started to gather momentum when the band began a month-long tour with a show at London's Hammersmith Odeon on 10 October. 'Fall at Your Feet' was the second single to be released in the UK and by the first week of November it hit number 26 on the singles chart. It was an especially gratifying week for Neil Finn, songwriter, because Paul Young's cover of 'Don't Dream It's Over' was at number 22. By the following week, 'Fall at Your Feet' was at number 20, eclipsing 'Don't Dream'. It was the band's first time in the UK Top 20.

But despite their success in a new territory, the situation with Tim had already reached its unavoidable climax by then. On 1 November, on the afternoon of a show at Glasgow venue King Tut's Wah Wah Hut, a note had been slipped under Tim's hotel room door. It advised him that there was a band meeting at 5 p.m. The subject of the meeting came as no surprise to Tim—he knew he had to go. But Neil couldn't quite bring himself to utter the words, so it was left to Hester. Even then he could only manage, 'Tim, you're sacked.' Tim left after that night's show, crossing paths at the airport with his replacement, Mark Hart, the man who should never have been stood down in the first place.

Tim tried to make light of his firing from the band; he'd admit that 'I didn't know how to just be a guy in a band. And I was too tall, anyway.' It took some time for Neil to publicly acknowledge his error in hiring Tim. But Neil came to realise that what he should have done was simply include Tim on the *Woodface* album and credit the songs to 'Crowded House featuring Tim Finn', in the type of arrangement that would soon become very prevalent in pop music. He hadn't needed to add Tim to the band at all. But at the time it had seemed like a perfectly logical move to the brothers and neither Seymour nor Hester had expressed any serious concerns about the line-up change.

Of course, Tim's departure also presented some problems for Neil over the ensuing nights of the tour. 'Tim's sorry he can't be here,' he told the audience at the Olympia Theatre in Dublin on 2 November. 'He's down visiting a cousin in Cork.' Neil wasn't quite so jocular on 8 November, at the Waterfront in Norwich, when a punter called out, 'Where's Tim?' Neil stormed off the stage and left the audience without an encore.

When Neil returned to Australia, he'd barely settled onto the set of *Tonight Live with Steve Vizard* when the question was raised by the show's host: 'Where's Tim at the moment?'

'Tim's at home, actually,' Neil replied. 'He's probably on the phone if you wanted to give him a bell at any point.' Hester, as always, kept the mood light by removing a US dollar coin from his pocket, announcing that it was 'tour profits'. He went on to reveal what helped prolong the band's career: 'We have three buses now—and one driver.' Hester also confessed that while Neil was 'the hardest-working man in show business', he and Seymour were 'the laziest bastards in show business. So right there's a problem.' A quick riff on masturbation followed. It was classic Paul Hester.

The truth was that Tim *was* at home in Melbourne. One night in early 1992, he was alone in the studio when the fax machine whirred into life. It was a message from a friend, telling him that 'Weather With You', Crowded House's latest single, had just entered the UK Top 10. ('Maybe the English are just obsessed with weather,' Neil mused when he heard the news.)

Rather than feel despondent, Tim actually felt proud. 'All I needed was to know that something made in this funny little room was now in the UK Top 10,' said Tim. 'It was a blast.'

The sun-kissed video for 'Weather With You' captured the spirit of the song perfectly. Shot over two days near Queenscliff in Victoria, towards the end of summer, it played like a holiday snapshot, with images of sandcastles, kids swimming, dogs at the beach—it was so summery that Neil even dared to take off his shirt for a moment. Some locals wandered in front of the camera and joined in the shoot.

While on the Vizard show, Hester talked Australia through the video. When a tiny 1950s-era car towing an even tinier 1950s-era caravan appeared on the screen, he deadpanned: 'That's Neil's car and the family in the back there.'

Neil added that it had been a good year 'and we splashed out on a new trailer'. And the fellow on the bike who was seen in the clip? 'That's Neil's dad,' Hester clarified. A pair of Asian holiday makers, brandishing cameras, who also appeared in the video, were next up on screen. 'That's Crowded House management,' grinned Hester. 'They're the new owners of Portarlington, I might add,' noted Seymour.

★

Crowded House played 130 shows during 1991 and didn't stop for breath in the early months of 1992. Much of February and early March were spent touring the UK and Europe; this was followed by another lap of Australia and New Zealand, cheekily dubbed the 'Then There Were Three' tour, which rolled through to the end of April, and included two shows at the popular WOMADelaide festival and a winning nine-song set at the Concert for Life, which drew a huge audience to Centennial Park in Sydney. INXS, Diesel, Yothu Yindi and Richard Clapton were also on the bill, but Crowded House were the stars. By the time of their closer, 'Better Be Home Soon', most of the crowd of 70,000 were on their feet and singing along. A further million people across the country tuned in to the broadcast on Triple J.

In late June, on stage at London's Wembley Arena, Tim joined Neil for 'Weather With You', proving that their bond, both musical and fraternal, was still strong, while at the same time 'Four Seasons in One Day' became the band's third UK hit on the trot, reaching number 26. *Woodface*, meanwhile, was on its way to a remarkable total of 93 weeks on the UK charts, peaking at number 6 and selling 600,000 copies.

('It's Only Natural' made it to number 24 in the UK during September.) Five singles from *Woodface* charted in Australia. Neil and Tim were jointly crowned 1992's Songwriter of the Year by APRA and the band won the Best Live Act gong at Britain's Q Awards. Despite the drama, it had still been a golden run.

After a final *Woodface* show at an MTV Europe event in Barcelona, on 24 July, Neil took a long-overdue break. Along with Tim, their parents Dick and Mary, Sharon and the kids, Neil set out on a driving holiday of Ireland, stopping in Dublin, Galway, the Ring of Kerry, Killarney and Tralee, staying in local pubs. Most nights ended in a good old-fashioned singsong. It wasn't so much a holiday as a homecoming; after all, Mary had been born in Limerick. Tim felt so comfortable he stayed for three months; Neil and Sharon discussed relocating. 'If there was anywhere else in the world we would live, it would be Ireland,' Neil said. What he and Sharon decided on, however, was a different type of homecoming.

10

'Karekare brought out a lot of extremes'

In 1992, Dick Finn turned 70, and Neil began to think seriously about a return home to New Zealand to be closer to his parents. He hadn't spent any real time there, aside from tours and short visits, since 1977. 'My parents are getting older,' Neil said. 'I wanted to be around them a bit more and wanted my kids to grow up with them a bit.' His children, Liam and Elroy, were still young enough to not feel too disrupted by a change of country, while Sharon had her own family in New Zealand to consider as well.

The turning point for Neil occurred in early 1993, when he realised that when it came to his career there was little difference between living in Melbourne and living in New Zealand; the major music centres, the UK and the USA, were still a long way away. The situation wasn't vastly different if he lived across the Tasman. He and Sharon realised they may as well be at home, so they sold up and relocated to Parnell in Auckland, one of the most upscale suburbs of New

Zealand. They chose a property in Corunna Avenue where they would live for more than 20 years. Over time, Neil and Sharon would also buy an adjacent property. (When they finally decided to sell in 2016, the two houses were valued at around NZ$10 million.)

Neil was very wary about coming off like the returning rock star. He kept a low profile, getting around in a battered Volvo station wagon and insisting, when asked, that one of the many reasons he'd returned home was so that his kids could attend school barefoot, 'just as I did. It's a very New Zealand thing'. Many of his neighbours were older, and, as far as Neil was concerned, 'They don't care who I am, and I feel quite anonymous here.'

But the simple fact that he was Neil Finn from Crowded House was unavoidable. When an Australian journalist spent some time with Neil in Auckland, he looked on as a local spotted Neil in a café, grabbed his hand, shook it—and then, in a moment of hero worship, planted a wet, sloppy kiss on Neil's neck.

'I can still feel the guy's lips on my neck,' Neil grumbled as they drove away.

The Finn musical legacy was unavoidable in other ways, too. A TV ad for mints featured a character dressed as Tim in all his pointy-haired, heavily-made-up, late-1970s glory. And the music of Split Enz and Crowded House was everywhere: on TV, on the radio, blaring out of car radios and shopping centres.

There was something else drawing Neil back to New Zealand: his fascination with its indigenous cultures. It became a feature of the house in Parnell, which the Finns decorated with tasteful wall hangings. 'New Zealand has gone through a bit of an attitude change,' Neil said on his return. 'The Māori and Polynesian cultures feel stronger to me, and there's more of an atmosphere around town that's come from that, which I really like.' Neil's music, too, would come to reflect that influence—*Together Alone*, the next Crowded House album, would feature log drummers from the Cook Islands, as well as a Māori choir, and it would have a more distinctly New Zealand flavour than anything he'd recorded before. What was required to make that happen, as Neil explained, was for the band to 'come to the end of the world'.

That place was named Karekare.

*

Karekare Beach was only about an hour to the south-west of Auckland, but it felt very much like another planet altogether. It was remote and wild and beautiful; at night the silence was broken only by the sound of the sea and the ringing of cicadas. But Neil didn't choose it purely because of its natural beauty. He had a more practical reason in mind: 'It was about as far away from the music industry as you could get,' he explained.

Neil had made his share of records in LA and felt it was time for a big change. What he hoped for, instead, was 'an all-round sensory experience'. He wanted this new album, Crowded House's fourth, to reflect the landscape in much the same way a painter would be influenced and inspired by their surrounds. 'We wanted to create a unique experience for ourselves, something no one else had ever had,' explained Neil.

Neil, Hester and Seymour began work on their new album during Christmas 1992, not long before Neil's permanent return to New Zealand. The house they chose to use for the recording—after a month-long search—was owned by a friend of Neil's, Nigel Horrocks; he'd bought the land from Sir Edmund Hillary, the first man to scale Everest (and one of the few New Zealanders better known around the globe than Neil). It was the same house that American actor Harvey Keitel stayed in during the filming of the triple Oscar–winning film *The Piano*, which director Jane Campion had shot at Karekare. The house was way off any beaten track; they needed to carry the recording console—'a really heavy desk', stressed Neil—down a steep drive and into the house as they set up. Everything was done by hand.

When it became known that Crowded House was set to make a record at Karekare, offers started coming in from other locals to have the band also rent their houses, which they would use to house themselves and the crew. As Paul Hester would relate, 'We basically had use of the whole valley.'

Neil decided on another big change for the album: he wanted to work with someone other than Mitchell Froom, who'd produced their first three LPs. The success of *Woodface* paved the way for the band to meet and greet a number of in-demand British producers, including Steve Lillywhite, who'd worked with U2 and produced the UK chart-topping *Peter Gabriel* album; Gil Norton, who'd worked with Aussies The Triffids and equally influential Americans the Pixies; and John Leckie, who'd been trained at Abbey Road and had produced XTC's *White Music*, The Stone Roses' eponymous album and several albums by Simple Minds. But instead the band settled on 32-year-old Martin Glover, who used the pseudonym Youth. Glover had been born in Slough—a glum part of Buckinghamshire where Ricky Gervais would one day choose to set his show *The Office*—and played bass in rock act Killing Joke before working on records with acts as diverse as Alien Sex Fiend and Bananarama.

When Neil, Seymour and Hester met Youth in London, the first thing he did was roll a fat joint, which Hester read as a good sign. The three members of the band then flicked through Youth's extensive vinyl collection. Seymour admired his ability to 'wax lyrical' about any record they produced from the shelf. 'He was an incredible enthusiast.'

'He gave good reference points for what Crowded House could be like,' said Neil, who was, in part, drawn to working with Youth because he was an unknown quantity to them. Though it wasn't a big part of his nature, Neil liked the idea of taking a risk; it was part of his 'everything's different' approach to the new record. 'He was the wild card,' admitted Neil, 'the more adventurous choice.' And Youth was tight with pop-music mavericks The KLF and The Orb, which also impressed his visitors.

Youth was worldly enough, but Karekare was unlike any place he'd ever been. As Paul Hester would recall, Youth arrived with his sound engineer Greg Hunter, and they both found the seclusion a lot to get their heads around. Just days before they'd been in Brixton, which exploded with life and colour, yet here they were in Karekare, where there were no shops, very few people and not a streetlight to be found. 'They were in shock for days,' said Hester. 'Didn't know where the fuck they were.' At night, after dinner at one of their rented houses—sometimes the troupe dined with welcoming locals—everyone would slowly find their way back to the studio in the darkness, guided only by torchlight. It felt as though taking a false step could end in a one-way trip to the ocean below.

Youth was something of a late-twentieth-century hippie, with a thing for ley lines and crystals and 'shit like that', according to Neil. While seriously stoned, he buried a crystal on the beach and panicked when he couldn't find it again. In 2021, Neil would laugh about how Youth 'lost crystals and half of his mind' while working on the record. As for Neil and the band, they marked the beginning of a new record with a nude dip in the nearby waterfall. (They'd try recordings some songs in the nude, too.)

Seymour described the set-up at Karekare as 'like a cooperative campsite'. He said it was the first time he and the band had felt 'stateless . . . like we didn't belong anywhere'.

During the first week, Youth and the group, including Mark Hart, played everything pretty much live in the same room. But over time, they started to move outside and embrace their surrounds—Neil and Hart would sometimes play together on the lawn of Horrocks' house. Youth soon started to bring his own unique talents to the sessions. He'd spark up a big joint, lie down on the couch and call out to the musicians. 'Play on one string, Nick!' he'd instruct Seymour. Youth had a very different approach to Froom, who was a far more hands-on record producer.

One night, Neil was struggling with a vocal and discovered that Youth had fallen asleep on the couch while he was singing. He confronted him, demanding 'Why are you sleeping?'

'I was tired, man,' Youth replied.

Neil was angry but did find his honesty hard to argue with. Yet as the recording continued into the early months of 1993, Neil started to question whether Youth's 'vibes' were always helpful for the music they were making.

'Those magical elements in his brain didn't turn out to be particularly positive, to my mind,' said Neil. (In 2021, Neil would go as far as to refer to Youth as a 'chancer'—an opportunist who had been lucky to work with the band. 'I was pretty dark on him.') It didn't help matters that Seymour's marriage was in the process of coming undone—he'd eventually divorce—or that Neil was suffering from giardia, a parasitic infection. He lost weight and felt unwell throughout his entire stretch at Karekare.

Neil sensed that they were starting to tap into something heavy with the music they were making, but it wasn't only because of Youth's 'vibes': Karekare brought out 'a lot of extremes' in the music, he said, like 'euphoria and desperation'. While working in their makeshift studio, a mist would roll in over the sea, or the light in the sky would suddenly change—it was all very cinematic, very dramatic. Often, they'd switch to a song that they felt better suited the scene playing outside the house. If the sky turned dark, they'd switch to a moodier song, to a lighter song if the sun burst through the clouds. Karekare's impact on the music they were making was undeniable. (The finished album would actually open with a track named 'Kare Kare'.)

'Pineapple Head' was a new song of Neil's that had sprung from a fraught situation. A few years earlier, in Melbourne, Liam had come down with a fever. As Neil tended to his son with a cold compress, a delirious Liam began spouting some peculiar non sequiturs: 'pineapple head' was one of his many mutterings. Neil couldn't restrain his inner songwriter and reached for a notebook, jotting down Liam's ramblings, which he felt were just too good to ignore. (The song's opening lines, 'Detective is flat/No longer is always flat out', were direct quotes.) He then briefly left Liam, ran downstairs and wrote the song on his piano. Sharon was horrified. 'What are you doing?' she demanded.

In time, Neil came to joke about the situation: Liam was still 'hitting me up for royalties', Neil said in 2021. Liam had a knack for good lyrics; he'd also come up with the line 'Here comes Mrs Hairy Legs', which Neil had used for *Woodface*'s 'Chocolate Cake'.

The idea for 'Fingers of Love' came to Neil during the Woodface tour, when the band was taking a break in Jamaica. He was sitting on the balcony of his rented villa, smoking what he described as 'really good-quality Jamaican weed'—he'd been ripped off the day before—and sketched out the song in the golden glow of an incredible sunset, what a local described to him as 'God rays'. (Birds can be heard chirping in the background of his demo.) 'It's about blissing out on nature,' said Neil, shutting down a suggestion that there was some kind of sexual innuendo in the song.

The title of 'Nails in My Feet', meanwhile, hinted at the crucifixion of Jesus Christ, but Neil insisted that he was referring to something a little less biblical: a special pair of shoes that he wore to aerate his lawn back in Melbourne. Neil had long dreamed of building a tennis court, which he did, but was a bit surprised by the amount of maintenance required, hence his bespoke shoes.

The centrepiece of the *Together Alone* album would be the slow-burning 'Private Universe'. Neil's lyrics were partly inspired by the starlings that would gather in the palm trees outside his house every morning and early evening when he was living in Melbourne. 'They talk to me, birds talk to me,' he sang. 'They made an incredible racket,' Neil told an audience in Atlanta the next year, when introducing the song. On his website, neilfinn.com, he explained that there was also 'a midlife thing' at work in his lyric. 'It's also about your whole life and how you create your private domain.'

The creation of the album's title track was by far the biggest event for Neil and the band while at Karekare. They'd engaged the Te Waka Huia Cultural Group Choir, which comprised 60 singers, and were prepared to host a lot of people, but didn't realise they'd all bring their families to the site. About 300 people turned up on the day, including a team of log drummers from the Cook Islands who also played on the track. It was more people than Karekare had seen in years—perhaps ever.

The band opted to divvy up their responsibilities: Neil conducted the choir, while Hester gave direction to the log drummers and Hart worked with a brass band brought in for the session. (Neil had been a fan of brass bands since he was a kid; he'd watch them playing on the back of a truck every Christmas as part of a street parade in Te Awamutu.) Microphones snaked around the valley while the song was being recorded, picking up ambient sounds, including crickets, which miraculously chirped in time with the sound of the log drums.

Neil had approached Ngapo 'Bub' Wehi, a renowned Māori musician and composer, who wrote some lyrics for the song, which amplified what Neil described as the 'New Zealand experience' he wanted to capture.

The mood of the day was joyous, happily chaotic. Sharon was there, as was Noel Crombie, who added some percussion. It was a hell of a gathering, 'an incredibly emotional day', remarked Hester, clearly moved. The end result was remarkable, an inspired piece of music that felt timeless and magical, deeply infused with the spirit of the place in which it was created and those who helped bring it to life.

The idea to significantly change things up extended into the mixing of the album. Rather than working in LA, the mountain—or in this case mixer-to-the-stars Bob Clearmountain—came to Melbourne to complete the project. 'Bob is a master of organisation,' said Neil, who readily admitted that they'd left a lot of excess on the tapes ('wild sounds and weird things') that Clearmountain was left to sort through during his intense two-week stretch in Melbourne. 'He left most of them off,' Neil shrugged.

He also left off the entire song 'Convent Girls', which proved advantageous for Neil over the years. 'Playing that on stage would make me feel a little bit creepy,' he said in 2016.

'It was a memorable, amazing time,' Neil remarked of the entire project. It was apparent to everyone involved that *Together Alone* was much more than just a new Crowded House album: it captured a unique experience. What Neil didn't realise was that it would be fourteen more years before he and the band made another record.

11

'It was emotional as hell'

In August 1993, just prior to the release of *Together Alone*, the band toured South Africa for the first time, playing concerts in Cape Town, Johannesburg, Durban and Pretoria. After one of the shows, a local approached Neil and began discussing 'Weather With You'. It was apparent that the man knew the song well, because he mentioned the sample of a jew's harp that Neil had used on the track. All that was known of the sample was that the instrument had been played by an African woman—nothing more.

'You know I own the rights for that, don't you?' he said to Neil. 'I'm owed some money.'

Neil asked if he knew the whereabouts of the woman who actually played on the original.

'No, I don't. I have no idea.'

Neil understood enough about copyright to know that he had to agree to pay a royalty. 'We were happy to do it,' he said later, 'but would have been far happier if the woman herself got the money.'

Lesson learned, Neil and the band headed to Toronto to

film a video for the *Together Alone* lead single 'Distant Sun'. Admittedly the arty clip, a collection of random images and soft-focus close-ups of the band (Neil in particular) could have been shot anywhere, but the song, with its shimmering melody, was a standout from the album. It featured a lyric that many of the band's fans, especially their many female admirers, would embrace. 'I don't pretend to know what you want,' sang Neil, hand on heart, 'but I offer love.' Neil knew these were powerful words, perfectly blending pathos and honesty. He hoped it was seen as a 'universal statement'.

While that was undeniable, 'Distant Sun' didn't shine very brightly in the US upon its release in late September, despite making some inroads on minor *Billboard* charts. It reached number 26 on the Alternative Airplay list, which was peculiar, given that Crowded House wasn't a natural fit with the acts that were at the forefront of all things alternative, such as Nirvana, Pearl Jam, Beck and Smashing Pumpkins. They weren't played much on alternative or college radio. 'Bleak' wasn't a word associated with the music of Crowded House—and bleakness was very much on trend. Capitol sensed that the group's glory days in America were over, so much so that they delayed the US release of *Together Alone* until the new year. It bombed.

'Capitol thought it would get lost before Christmas,' Neil said with a rueful chuckle. 'And what happened was it got lost *after* Christmas.'

At its heart, Crowded House was a pop band. Neil's songs lifted people's spirits, which explained why their music continued to connect with an ever-expanding British following. After all, England had given the world The Beatles, and UK audiences knew a fine pop band when they heard one. *Together Alone* reached a peak of number 4 in the UK, its appearance spawning renewed interest in *Woodface*.

It said an enormous amount about the band's popularity when, early in the new year, they were declared winners of the Brit Award for Best International Group.

In a video link from St Kilda, Neil, Hester, Seymour and Hart held their trophy aloft while standing on the beach, the sun blazing. Neil grinned and thanked the 'great British public—without whom we wouldn't be here in Australia'. A few days earlier, when the award had been delivered to the band's Melbourne office, there was no accompanying note. A band associate had been using the trophy to crush walnuts when someone from the Brit Awards reached out and advised what the award was actually for.

It was a rare moment of downtime for Neil and the band; they were at the start of a year in which they'd play almost 100 shows while covering most parts of the Western music-loving world. But it was also a year when the foundations of Crowded House would begin to crumble.

*

Despite their reputation as the amiable, fun-loving court jesters of modern pop, Crowded House had its share of ugly moments. There was Neil's punch-up with Tim in Byron and the ensuing fallout, and his reckless sacking of Seymour when the songs weren't flowing. And there'd been dark moments in the studio when Neil, as the group's only writer, felt the weight of the world on his slight shoulders; sometimes he yearned for the days of Split Enz and the band's more collaborative approach to music-making.

Prior to setting out on the Together Alone tour in late 1993, Hester had spoken with Neil. As Neil related, 'He had said, "Listen, I don't think I'm going to be able to get beyond this tour. I think I'm really going to have to call it quits."'

Hester was tiring of the album/promo/tour grind that had consumed the trio's lives since 1988. But there was more to it than that. 'I think he was a little sick of [seeing] himself as a jester figure,' said Neil. 'He lost his sense of humour about it a little.' Neil also acknowledged that Hester was the laziest member of the band; a perfect day for him was a cup of tea and a spliff in front of the TV, and then a nap in the afternoon. Touring could be hard—and relentless—work. And Hester was in a relationship with a woman named Mardi Sommerfeld; she was pregnant with their first child. 'He wanted to be at home,' said his friend Brian Nankervis. 'He wanted to be with his family.'

Neil reluctantly accepted Hester's advance notice but figured at least they could get through the tour and address the problem after their final show at the end of July. However, Hester's mood darkened as the tour rolled on. Neil could see that his enthusiasm was flagging and the shows were suffering as a result.

Tempers spilled over when the *Together Alone* roadshow reached Milan in Italy. The city had never been kind to the band; Neil got a bad feeling whenever they played there. 'Something always goes wrong in Milan,' he said. Things started badly when they didn't draw a big crowd to the venue, Club Zimba, but got much worse during their set. Hester tinkered with his drums while Neil was trying to speak with the audience, drowning him out. A frustrated Neil turned and smashed his guitar into Hester's snare drum.

'Does that sound right, Paul?' he shouted, as the crowd looked on in stunned silence.

Neil stormed off stage, heading for the hotel, but Hester caught up with him and pushed him down some stairs, where he landed in a heap at the feet of a gathering of very shocked fans.

On 14 April they were scheduled to play in Atlanta, the same southern US city where Split Enz's Phil Judd had come undone back in 1977. Before the concert at the Roxy, Hester told Neil he'd had enough; this would be his last concert. He wanted to go home. The look on Hester's face, as Neil later recalled, said it all. 'I've never seen someone so unhappy.'

Neil and Hester had been all but living in each other's pockets for the past decade. They were close friends, not just bandmates, who'd ridden the Crowded House wave together. This was a huge moment in their relationship. 'It was emotional as hell,' Neil said of the situation.

The Atlanta show wasn't your typical Crowded House set, as a bootleg of the gig amply demonstrated. 'Private Universe', one of more than twenty songs on the night, ran for almost eight minutes, Hester pounding a tribal drumbeat as Hart tapped out a weird psychedelic pattern on his pedal steel guitar. Neil segued briefly into 'So This Is Love', an old Phil Judd/Split Enz obscurity, before he and the band brought 'Private Universe' home with an almighty flourish. 'Whispers and Moans', too, was heavier live, ending with a burst of guitar fire from Neil that wouldn't have been wasted on Pearl Jam, Nirvana and co. 'Fingers of Love' was thrilling, the group's harmonies pristine, while Neil's mid-song guitar solo all but exploded as he sent showers of electricity out into the night.

'Weather With You' was the first of numerous singalongs, Neil urging the crowd on from the stage. 'Okay, Atlanta, the show's yours, all yours, so let's hear it,' he announced—and the audience did as instructed, singing along lustily. Neil was clearly affected, gushing, 'Now that was a moment, Atlanta, that was a moment,' as the song ended. An epic seven-minute-long 'When You Come' followed soon after.

By the time of 'Catherine Wheels', one of many encores, the band had grown very chatty. From the stage Neil greeted his cousin Margot, a history professor based in Atlanta, who was in the crowd looking on, imagining 'her pale white New Zealand complexion going very red as I speak', while Hester took the chance to express his concerns about American health care. Then the stage mic was opened to the audience and they lined up to have their say. 'Get rid of Clinton,' stated one fan. 'Get rid of everybody but Crowded House,' insisted another. 'Morrissey for president,' said an outlier. Then this: 'If you do "I Got You" tonight, then the world will be a great place.' Neil didn't respond to the request but did say that right now he sensed a 'beautiful love vibration' in the room.

'There has to be a full moon,' Neil said while catching his breath between numbers. 'There has to be a full moon.' And there definitely was a powerful energy in the room. After Hester called out a series of encores—'I feel like listening to "World Where You Live", I'm ready for that one'—the show finally ended. Neil would rate it as one of the best gigs the band ever played.

Afterwards, Neil, Seymour, Hart and British keyboardist Jules Bowen (who was in the touring band) boarded the bus and continued on to their next show in Nashville, leaving Hester behind to organise a flight home to Melbourne.

Neil quickly arranged for Wally Ingram, drummer for opening act Sheryl Crow, to sit in for Hester until he could find a permanent replacement. Andy Kubiszewski also helped out on some shows, and Melbourne-based Brit Peter Jones, an old art-school friend of Seymour's, joined the band on 21 May.

A few days after Hester's untimely departure, Triple J reporter Lawrie Zion caught up with Neil, who tried to make the best of what was obviously a fraught situation. 'In a way it's liberating because there was such a pall hanging over the band,' Neil said, laughing at his accidental Paul/pall slip of the tongue. 'Paul's been so miserable . . . that it really cast a shadow on all of us. There's possibly a lot more unity of purpose now.'

Neil believed that Hester was relieved to have finally pulled the pin, but the truth was very different. 'I've never felt so lost and afraid as I did at that moment,' Hester would tell Channel 7's Andrew Denton on his return to Australia.

*

In June 1993, Neil and Tim had been awarded OBEs for their contribution to music. Neil did his best to downplay the honour; he believed that being a big fish in New Zealand might have made it just a bit easier for him to be acknowledged. And an OBE didn't seem to come with much in the way of benefits. He'd 'tried ringing the palace on numerous occasions', he once joked, 'and the Queen still won't take my calls.' Neil's mother, however, was thrilled by the accolade given to her sons. 'It *is* a lovely medal,' granted Neil.

But perhaps their award drew them back together after the problems of *Woodface*, and the brothers talked shop when they caught up in London in late May 1994. Neil felt that their get-together was extremely positive. 'We were both on the same wavelength, really,' he said. Neil and Tim agreed to make another record together, but this time with the benefit of the lessons they'd learned from *Woodface*.

'We both knew that was the next thing we wanted to do,' said Neil. It would be a Finn Brothers project and have absolutely nothing to do with Crowded House. In fact, Neil decided to forestall a possible fifth Crowded House album, much to the annoyance of Nick Seymour, who felt that the band was on the cusp of making the best music of their career.

Neil and Tim holidayed together on the Cook Islands and then spent a further two weeks on the island writing songs (and, in Tim's case, taking a spill from his rented motor scooter, as he'd document in the song 'Kiss the Road of Rarotonga'). During a 'secret' gig at a venue on the island called Trader Jacks, which they played with Dave Dobbyn, Tim seized the opportunity to get behind the kit. He flailed away 'like the Muppets drummer', according to Neil.

They agreed to record their new album in the new year, after a run of Crowded House shows in early 1995: first with Midnight Oil on their Breaking the Dry Australian tour, followed by a one-off with Americans REM and Grant Lee Buffalo at Western Springs in Auckland, and then their own stretch of New Zealand dates, which ended with two nights at Auckland's Powerstation in early February 1995. Crowded House wouldn't play another show for the rest of the year.

The Finn brothers chose to work at York Street Studios in Auckland. One of the people who established the site was expat Brit Jaz Coleman, who Neil had met with while considering producers for *Together Alone*. Coleman had been Youth's bandmate in Killing Joke in the early 1980s. One of the many features of York Street was a vintage 1974 EMI Neve desk, which had once been installed in the famed Abbey Road Studios. Forty-year-old Texan native Tchad Blake, who had worked closely with Mitchell Froom on the first three Crowded House albums, flew over to help with production.

Neil financed the York Street sessions; there was no record company involvement. He didn't even bother telling his label of their plans. 'We wanted to do it quickly,' Neil later recalled, 'and we didn't want to double guess or labour over anything.' What Neil wanted to make, in essence, was the opposite of a Crowded House record.

The most recent project that Tim had been involved with went by the name ALT, which was shorthand for its three members: Northern Irish singer/songwriter Andy White, Liam Ó Maonlaí (of Hothouse Flowers) and Tim. The three had bonded over a big night of clubbing in Dublin, dancing to ABBA classics and slugging cocktails. In 1994, they recorded an album they called *Altitude*, working—and living—at Tim's Periscope Studios for a time. (White slept in an office, Ó Maonlaí underneath Tim's pool table.) It was an eccentric, off-kilter collection of songs, some seemingly little more than sketches, others fully formed and memorable, and served as a useful reference point for the album Neil and Tim began recording at York Street. *Altitude* didn't sound like anything in Tim's past—and neither would the record that would be known simply as *Finn*.

While Neil and Tim did a lot of what they did so

well—singing together beautifully—they weren't hung up on hooks and melodies. This wasn't *Woodface Revisited*. One of the new songs the Finns cut at York Street, 'Suffer Never', best captured the spirit of the record they were making. Neil described it as 'dark and swampy, very unlike anything either of us has done before', which was right on the money. Another track, 'Mood Swinging Man', could best be called pop-noir, spooky and mysterious, its soundscape similar to the impossible-to-pigeonhole album that producer Tchad Blake had just made as part of the Latin Playboys (alongside Mitchell Froom, funnily enough).

'Kiss the Road of Rarotonga', meanwhile, was a brotherly rave-up, a grungy, full-throttled rocker, Tim bashing the drums with all the oomph of a 40-something Keith Moon. 'We just allowed ourselves to be boys again,' Tim said of both 'Kiss the Road' and the entire record. And not just boys—the tongue-in-cheek cover art (painted by Neil) showed two sperm cells jockeying their way into a fertilising position. It was a neat metaphor for their relationship.

It was while they were recording the *Finn* LP that Neil and Tim befriended Eddie Vedder of Pearl Jam, a musician at the vanguard of the grunge movement. The singer was renowned for risking his safety by diving into mosh pits, and was a diehard Split Enz fan, having first seen the band in San Diego when he was a teenager. (He kept a collection of rare live Split Enz recordings.) Pearl Jam were playing their first gigs in Auckland during March 1995 and Vedder contacted the Finns, inviting them to the show at the Supertop, a huge tent set up near Mount Smart. Vedder also welcomed both Neil and Tim on stage for roaring takes on 'History Never Repeats' and 'I Got You'.

Vedder was a keen surfer and the next day, Neil and Tim drove him and his bandmate Stone Gossard to Karekare. Neil's son Liam, a mad Pearl Jam fan, rode shotgun. It very nearly ended badly when Vedder got caught in a rip and needed to be rescued, but a bond had been formed. It wasn't the last Neil would see of Eddie Vedder. 'He's got a very good soul,' Neil said of his new mate.

*

The *Finn* record was scheduled for an October 1995 release, which gave Neil a chance to turn his attention back to Crowded House. Neil was sufficiently taken with York Street to ask Seymour and new(ish) drummer Peter Jones to join him there in July.

They weren't there to make an album. 'It was an attempt to try and work up some new material,' Neil clarified. Nothing more. Among these new songs-under-development were 'Anthem', 'Instinct' and 'Help Is Coming', as well as 'A Taste of Something Divine', an experimental piece recorded with local electronic musician Paddy Free (who'd go on to work with Neil on his first solo album). All would eventually be released, but not in the way the band's many fans had hoped—as part of a new studio album.

Neil, meanwhile, had asked the band's management to arrange termination of their contract with Capitol Records, despite having two records left on their deal. He'd also asked them to explore the possibility of releasing the live recording of the Atlanta show, suggesting the unfortunate title of *Paul is Dead*, a request that was rejected by the label. (It was widely bootlegged instead.)

In a 1995 interview with Triple J, Neil hinted at a life beyond Crowded House. It was clear he was growing tired of being part of a band. He spoke about how he hoped to one day gather in an exotic locale 'with twenty or thirty of our closest friends and . . . just having the desire to play music', he said. 'One thing about having a band is how rigid it becomes through people's perceptions of it . . . I'd love to make a band a less restrictive thing.'

The release of the *Finn* record in October 1995 provided Neil with some relief from the stress he was feeling towards his 'day job'. The critical response to the album was almost uniformly (and universally) positive. 'This is a mix of sweet pop and murky beasts, island-inflected melodies and scratchy and dangerous sounds', noted *Sydney Morning Herald* reporter Bernard Zuel. One critic from *The Times* in London later likened *Finn* to the sound of 'two old stoners in a toolshed' making 'homespun psychedelia', which wasn't a bad read on the album.

Even though Neil and Tim had created *Finn* purely for the chance to work together again, and it didn't contain an obvious hit, the album charted well, reaching number 14 in Australia, number 8 in New Zealand and the Top 20 in the UK. Neil had helped conjure up a successful record almost by chance—and for a fraction of the cost (and the turmoil) of a Crowded House LP.

12

'It feels more like a celebration than a funeral'

Promoting the *Finn* album had few of the demands of a Crowded House tour. This would be no epic, year-long, Frequent Flyer–points-accruing marathon; instead, the tour, named An Evening with the Finns, was short and sharp and a lot of fun. During one show, Neil mentioned the sperm cells on the *Finn* album cover. 'Have you ever wondered which one was you?' he cheekily asked his older brother. During another show, Neil and Tim launched into a rough-and-ready version of 'Release Me', a 1960s chestnut from crooner Engelbert Humperdinck.

Tim laughed off any suggestion that he and Neil were 'battling brothers' like Oasis's Noel and Liam Gallagher, who seemed to be constantly at each other's throats. Their Byron Bay punch-up was in the past. 'It's very pleasurable working with my brother,' Tim told a reporter. 'We're two songwriters who dig each other's work who happen to be brothers.' When asked if the *Finn* album was nothing more than a side project, Tim replied: 'It's the main event for us now.' Neil was just as engaged with all things *Finn* as Tim was; Crowded House was very much on hold.

Neil and Tim visited smaller theatres and clubs, starting out in Melbourne in late October 1995, then stopping in Sydney and Perth before playing dates in Europe and the UK. The first of two Finn Brothers tours ended with a show in Amsterdam on 19 November, where they combined new songs with Split Enz tracks ('Dirty Creature', 'I See Red' and 'Spellbound'), *Woodface* favourites like 'It's Only Natural' and 'Four Seasons in One Day', and their latest take on 'Throw Your Arms Around Me'. The response in Amsterdam and elsewhere was uniformly enthusiastic. Playing in a stripped-back style—just Neil and Tim with acoustic guitars, sometimes with a small band—revealed how brilliantly the songs had been constructed.

In January 1996, Neil and Tim, ostensibly in New Zealand to film a video for the song 'Angel's Heap', undertook a road trip to visit some old Te Awamutu haunts. During the drive down Highway 1 from Auckland—in an ageing Valiant Safari station wagon, no less—the brothers waxed nostalgic to a journalist who accompanied them. Neil reminisced about a girl he never dared ask out at school 'whose calves I admired for almost three years'. Tim remembered the young woman who, on their first date, let him know that she intended to be a virgin when she married, which was quite the icebreaker. They didn't date again.

Once they reached Te Awamutu they were surprised to learn that the address of their family home, 78 Teasdale Street, was now 588 Teasdale Street, and the current site of the Te Ata Rest Home. Tim spotted an undeniable irony. 'For us it was a place of fecundity and life and youth. Now it's a place for people who are winding down.' Their swimming pool, which Neil had cleaned every week, had been filled in, while the orchard that Neil so loved as a kid was now a carport. 'It's weird standing here,' said Neil, who was less than thrilled by the changes. 'They've completely fucked it.'

Inevitably—there was a journalist riding shotgun, after all—the subject turned to Crowded House. What exactly was going on there? Neil accepted that the departure of Hester had changed things considerably. 'I feel less inclined to see it as a set thing,' he said. 'Which is good.'

After their uncomfortable homecoming, the Finn Brothers tour continued, with shows in Australia and New Zealand during February and March, then dates in Canada and the US booked to follow in July. Neil, meanwhile, had been advised that Capitol had agreed to release them from their agreement to make two more studio records.

The time was nigh to make a key decision. What next for Crowded House?

*

The band returned to York Street Studios in March 1996. They recorded three songs: 'Instinct', 'Not the Girl You Think You Are' and 'Everything Is Good For You', which would wind up on a greatest hits collection, *Recurring Dream*, that was being prepared for release mid-year. But Neil didn't think these new songs sounded much like Crowded House; he sensed that the material he was writing was no longer

Top: A postcard for Neil's hometown of Te Awamutu in the Waikato region of New Zealand's North Island.
Te Awamutu Museum Collection (PA30)

Above: The site of Finn & Partners, the Te Awamutu accountancy firm run by Neil's father, Richard Finn. Te Awamutu Museum Collection (PH4239/44)

Right: A teenage Neil (right) with Mark Hough; they'd join forces in a band called After Hours.
Buster Stiggs

Neil and Tim Finn on stage with Split Enz at Melbourne's Festival Hall during their farewell Australian tour, October 1984. **Mark Goulding**

Neil lying down on the job, Wollongong, October 1984. Tony Mott

Left: Neil, Paul Hester and Nick Seymour in the ABC Studios, just prior to travelling to the USA to record 'Don't Dream It's Over', late 1985.
Peter Green

Right: Paul Hester playing pinball at Neil's house in Melbourne, 1987. **Peter Green**

Left: Nick Seymour strikes a pose backstage at the Paradiso in Amsterdam, October 1991.
Peter Green

Top: Neil backstage at the Paradiso in Amsterdam, October 1991. **Peter Green**

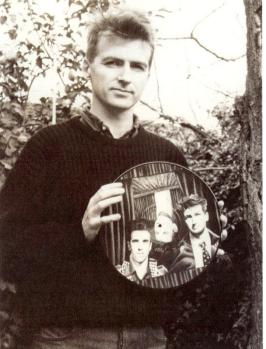

Left: Neil with the vinyl of *Temple of Low Men* in the backyard of his house in South Yarra, 1988. **Peter Green**

Paul Hester, Nick Seymour and Neil in Munich, May 1987. **DPA Picture Alliance/Alamy**

Crowded House on stage, Sydney, 1993. Tony Mott

Right: A billboard in London on the release of *Together Alone*, 1993. **Peter Green**

Below: Neil on the set of the 'Weather with You' video, Queenscliff, Victoria, 1992. **Peter Green**

Seymour, Hester, Mark Hart and Neil announce the split of Crowded House at the Elwood Beach House Café, November 1996. **Peter Green**

Hart, Hester, Neil and Seymour on the Sydney Opera House forecourt prior to their Farewell to the World show, November 1996. **Tony Mott**

Crowded House setlist, Sydney Opera House, November 1996. **Tony Mott**

Hester, Seymour and Neil say goodnight, Sydney Opera House, November 1996. **Tony Mott**

Neil greets the faithful, Sydney Opera House, November 1996. **Tony Mott**

The return of Split Enz, 2006. Left to right: Tim Finn, Noel Crombie, Eddie Rayner, Malcolm Green, Neil, Nigel Griggs. **Martin Philbey**

Neil and brother Tim on the set of *Music Max*, November 2004. **Martin Philbey**

Clockwise from bottom left: Neil, Tim and Liam Finn leave the stage at Sound Relief, Melbourne Cricket Ground, March 2009. **Martin Philbey**

Neil's Roundhead Studios on Eden Terrace in Auckland. Prosperosity/Wikimedia Commons https://commons.wikimedia.org/wiki/File:20230109_193101_Roundhead_Studios.jpg

Neil (left) with Johnny Marr (far right), Lisa Germano (rear on keyboards), Wilco's Pat Sansone (guitar) and bassist Sebastian Steinberg at the Powerstation in Auckland, January 2009. Tony Nyberg

Sean Donnelly, Neil, Sharon Finn and Alana Skyring, aka The Pajama Club, 2011.
Tony Mott

Neil and drummer Matt Sherrod in London's West End, June 2007.
Jack Ludlam/Alamy

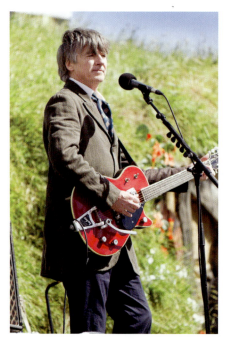

Neil performs at the world premiere of *The Hobbit: An Unexpected Journey* in Wellington, November 2012. Mike Walen/Wikimedia Commons https://commons.wikimedia.org/wiki/File:Neil_Finn.jpg

Fleetwood Mac on stage in Tulsa, Oklahoma, October 2018. Left to right: John McVie, Stevie Nicks, Christine McVie, Neil, Mick Fleetwood and Mike Campbell. Ralph_PH/Wikimedia Commons https://commons.wikimedia.org/wiki/File:FleetMacTulsa031018-79_(30294524767).jpg

Fireworks over the Sydney Opera House after a Crowded House show, November 2016. **Tony Mott**

Hart, Seymour, Neil and Matt Sherrod thank the fans at the Sydney Opera House, November 2016. **Tony Mott**

Neil Mullane Finn. Martin Philbey

suited to the band. As far as Neil was concerned, it was a clear sign—it was time to call it quits.

There were other factors at work, too. Hester's departure had permanently altered the band's chemistry. And Neil was also weighed down by his own demons. 'Big success doesn't improve people's personalities,' he said in 2021, looking back, 'and I think I had my own struggles to get through . . . I couldn't resolve in my head the dilemma on how to continue without Paul because there was something not quite good about the way we sounded.' He admitted that he could have found ways to address the problem of the band's sound, but simply found it 'too hard' and gave up.

Neil had just turned 38 and he'd been part of two groups for almost twenty years of his life. He had his own family to care for, Sharon and their two young boys, and he wanted to make his life a little less complicated. As he told *Goldmine* magazine, he 'didn't want to have the responsibility for so many people in my life. And the band didn't feel like it was really progressing'.

On 3 June, Crowded House flew to London and played a special fan club show at the Hanover Grand, a 1300-seat room near London Bridge tube station. The next day, while still in London, Neil advised the media that he was splitting up the band. After ten years, the dream was over. Interestingly, Neil had made the final calls that ended two of the Antipodes' biggest bands, Split Enz and Crowded House. He'd also written their biggest hits. It was a massive legacy.

The news came as a hell of a shock for his record label, which was busy promoting *Recurring Dream*. Most best-ofs appear when a group is about to move into a new phase of their career, but not so for Crowded House. It seemed that *Recurring Dream* was to be their musical last will and testament.

A few days later, Neil and the band made an appearance on *Later... with Jools Holland,* a TV show that had, along with its host, championed the music of Crowded House. The look on Holland's face was a mixture of surprise and dismay when he asked Neil about 'the rumours' that the group was finished.

'It's not just a rumour... it's fact,' Neil admitted. 'I sort of felt the need to kind of reinvent myself a little bit as a songwriter.'

So, asked Holland, what were Neil's fondest memories of Crowded House?

For someone who took great pride in his work, who was the songwriter's songwriter, Neil's response was surprising. It wasn't about the music at all. 'For me, undoubtedly, it's actually the times when we've jumped into the bus after an incredibly good gig and shared a space for a few hours... We got very close, about as close as four guys, four men can get—well, barring a few things,' he clarified, the audience chuckling at his accidental innuendo. 'We had a really good time.'

Yet Nick Seymour, for one, wasn't thrilled by Neil's decision. He said that both Hester and Neil were 'fools' for leaving but he came to realise that they didn't share his dream: 'They didn't want to be in the biggest band in the world.' He strongly believed that the group had at least five good years ahead of them though he did later accept that he was in the midst of his 'rock star phase', which couldn't be said of his bandmates. But there was another reason for his discontent: his future. 'I had no idea what I was going to do.'

On 24 June, Neil and the band were set to play their final show, a small-scale gig at the Horseshoe Tavern in Toronto, Canada. A journalist covering the concert noted how the atmosphere was 'more like a funeral than a wake'. Neil stuck with his line that the band was 'starting to repeat itself'; he insisted that he felt 'resolved and good' about the end. Not so Mark Hart, who seemed to bounce in and out of the group like a human pinball. 'I feel empty,' said a forlorn Hart. 'I just feel really empty.' Seymour, too, made no secret of his feelings. 'I'm disappointed.' He remained convinced that the break-up was unnecessary. Conversation over, Seymour resumed sketching in his journal.

*

For a band that had achieved as much as Crowded House, that had built such a loyal and large following, a hit-and-run farewell at the Horseshoe in Toronto seemed like a snub to their fans. *Recurring Dream* had been a huge hit, charting in Canada and Europe, and reaching number 1 in Australia, New Zealand and the UK, so interest in the band remained as strong as ever. It was such a success in Australia that it made both the 1996 *and* 1997 year-end charts for biggest selling records (at numbers 6 and 22 respectively), 'going platinum' a staggering thirteen times, selling almost one million copies in Australia alone. Surely they needed to say goodbye on a much larger scale.

Post-Atlanta, Hester (along with Joe Camilleri) had purchased the Elwood Beach House Café, and it had become a draw for Crowded House fans. In November 1996 the band gathered there for a press conference. It was revealed that after much backroom negotiating, particularly by their Australian manager, Grant Thomas, Crowded House would sign off in grand style with a free show on the forecourt of the Sydney Opera House, where the Royal Botanic Garden would provide a stunning backdrop. The only other time Neil had played at the Opera House—*near* the Opera House, to be precise—was the November 1979 Concert of the Decade, sponsored by 2SM, which was staged on the steps. Split Enz tore through 'I See Red' and 'Give It a Whirl' on a day that featured everyone from Skyhooks to Stevie Wright to the Captain Matchbox Whoopee Band. But this would be bigger. Far bigger.

The concert, known officially as 'Farewell to the World', was set down for Saturday, 23 November, with local acts Custard, You Am I and Powderfinger helping warm up what was anticipated to be a sizeable audience. All proceeds would go to the Sydney Children's Hospital and the Australian Cord Blood Foundation. And Hester agreed to rejoin the band for one final hurrah. This would be a far more fitting finale than a dispirited set at the Horseshoe Tavern.

In an effort to dust off the cobwebs, Neil and the band played two warm-up gigs at the Corner Hotel in the Melbourne suburb of Richmond, on 20 and 21 November. The audience was made up primarily of insiders, Crowded House fan club members and a few well-informed punters. The mood was upbeat; on the first night, in between 'Don't Dream It's Over' and 'There Goes God', Neil squeezed in a few bars of Patrick Hernandez's disco hit 'Born To Be Alive'.

On the second night, during a lengthy encore, Hester forgot the lyrics to his own 'Italian Plastic'. 'You wrote the bloody thing,' said a smiling Neil as he gave Hester his cues.

All four band members sang a verse, before Hester took over, conducting the audience like the master of ceremonies he was born to be. Then they tore into 'I'm Still Here', a madcap jam that had been recorded while everyone was high during the *Woodface* sessions. Neil played drums as Hester rapped: 'We're going up to Sydney town/ We're gonna make a lot of noise/ And then we're gonna go.'

Neil arrived in Sydney on the Friday and checked into the Sebel Townhouse, a favourite haunt of visiting musicians. He dropped in to see Hester and they shared a joint in Hester's room. It didn't help relax Neil, who was slowly coming to grips with the enormity of the upcoming event. 'I had one puff,' Neil recalled, 'and it absolutely destroyed me.' He had to walk around Elizabeth Bay for an hour or so to clear his head. This would be one gig best played straight.

Later that afternoon, the band played a short afternoon set for patients and their families at the Sydney Children's Hospital in Randwick, a reminder to everyone involved that the event was not only a farewell to the band but a fundraiser.

On what was meant to be show day, Saturday, a rainstorm forced the organisers to delay the concert by 24 hours. But there was one problem: several thousand fans had already reached the site. Neil made it known that the fans—especially those who couldn't make it back the next day—were welcome to stay for the soundcheck, which would still go ahead. A crowd of several thousand looked on as Neil and the band played for about an hour. It could well have been both the longest and the best-attended soundcheck in local music history.

Afterwards, when Neil spoke with some fans who hadn't planned for an extended stay—many had travelled interstate and now wouldn't be home until Monday—he offered to call their bosses and explain why they couldn't make it back to work on time. He figured it was the least he could do.

Fortunately, the weather was fine on the Sunday and by late afternoon the Opera House forecourt was awash with fans—'a human sea', in the words of *The Sydney Morning Herald*'s Jon Casimir. The crowd built and built and just kept on growing; an official estimate put it at around 150,000, way bigger than the band or promoter Michael Chugg could have ever imagined.

Backstage, Tim Finn hugged his father Dick, while Sharon, Liam and Elroy were nearby, as they so often were for Neil. Noel Crombie, who'd helped the band design their stage set for the night, was also in the house. NSW premier Bob Carr dropped by for a photo op.

Then it was showtime, early evening, as a full moon lit up the harbour city. 'The moment I walked on stage,' Neil said afterwards, 'I said, "This has got to be one of our best shows."' He bounded into the spotlight wearing a short-sleeved shirt that he'd picked up that morning in a shop on Oxford Street, which, most appropriately, featured a New Zealand kiwi on the front. It was possibly the first time Neil had bought his own stage outfit—that was always Seymour's domain, or Noel Crombie's during his days with Split Enz. As for Seymour, he looked out over the huge crowd and channelled British actor Sir Alec Guinness, quietly telling himself to know his lines 'and don't bump into the furniture'.

Neil couldn't stop grinning as they launched into 'Mean to Me'—there were just so many people looking on. But that came with its complications—as the set progressed, things got very lively on the forecourt, and bodies and a few inanimate objects (some inflatable) flew in all directions. The more daring punters crowd-surfed on boogie boards. 'There are some spectacular acrobatics going on out there,' Neil said warily between songs. 'Just be careful.' During an urgent 'Locked Out', members of the crowd down the front soared into the air as if they were bouncing on a trampoline. A particularly adventurous onlooker then scaled one of the Opera House's sails. 'Please be careful up there,' Neil implored. The band was relieved to learn that no one was seriously hurt during the show, although the St John Ambulance team did a lively trade throughout the night.

As he played, Neil, by his own admission, tried to stay both in the moment and outside it, too, reminding himself to take 'mental snapshots' of the event unfolding before him. 'It was an extraordinary sensory experience having that many people,' he said. It was also a huge adrenaline rush—the band needed to remind themselves not to play too fast or too hard, even though their bodies were telling them something else altogether.

Still, Hester's bony backside hardly touched the chair during a frenetic 'When You Come', an early peak of their 25-song set, while Neil bounded across the stage as though he had springs in his shoes, thrashing away at his acoustic guitar. And thousands of hands reached skywards during 'Four Seasons in One Day' and again during 'Better Be Home Soon', Neil conducting the audience like a maestro. 'That was great; we almost lifted the Opera House six inches then,' Neil said as the crowd roared their approval. 'We'll have it by the end of the night.'

After a stirring 'Distant Sun', Neil shielded his eyes and looked out over the mass of humanity, paying his respects to the 'people right on the back steps up there—how you doing?' And then he glanced towards the many boats that had gathered on the harbour. 'Anybody fallen over yet?' he asked.

Just at that moment, a tired and emotional punter somehow made his way on stage, embracing a stunned Neil in a fierce man-hug before being escorted away by security. As Neil began the next song, 'Into Temptation', a chant broke out in the mosh pit at the front of the stage: 'Water! Water!' Neil quickly changed his lyrics to get their message across. 'You opened up your door/I think they need some water.' Hester and Seymour obliged by throwing out bottles of Evian. Problem solved.

A run-through of 'Sister Madly' followed, with Hester's replacement, Peter Jones, taking over the drum kit while Hester played up front with Neil and Seymour. Neil then announced, 'It's time we had a little bit of brotherly presence on stage now,' and Tim—who seemed to be dressed for a cruise, in cream pants and a T-shirt, teaming sandals with socks—strode on stage. The brothers sang 'Weather With You' and as they did, Neil and Tim locked eyes. It was a rare public moment of intimacy. During the instrumental break, Neil swayed and danced around his brother, who grinned broadly. It was yet another massive moment.

'It's a bit emotional for us tonight,' Neil, the master of Kiwi understatement, told the gathering. 'But it feels more like a celebration than a funeral, doesn't it?' The audience response made it clear that Neil was right. Plenty of tears would be shed afterwards, of course—some during the show, too, as the TV cameras zoomed in on many fans who were choked up, bawling their eyes out as they tried to come to terms with the end of Crowded House.

The band played two lengthy encores. The big closer was, naturally, 'Don't Dream It's Over', their signature song. Emotions were heavy; Seymour admitted that he started to choke on the harmonies. He forced himself to think of something else—anything, really—to get him through without bursting into tears. 'Thanks' was about all Neil could manage, as the closing notes of 'Don't Dream' wafted over the huge gathering and nearby Sydney Harbour. 'It's been a blast.' Fireworks then lit up the sky.

But the night wasn't quite over. The four band members, still flying high from the show, reached their small trailer backstage and were shocked to be greeted by a complete stranger, who'd somehow evaded security.

'Who are you?' Neil asked him.

'I just climbed over the back fence, mate.'

Neil, Hester, Seymour and Hart looked at each other, shrugged, gave the man a beer and asked him to join them. It was a bizarre coda to what had been an otherworldly experience. As far as Neil was concerned, 'It summed up the whole day, really.'

Farewell to the World wasn't just a fabulous last hurrah for Crowded House. The concert raised a staggering $387,825 for charity.

13

'No one knew what the fuck was going on'

A few months after Crowded House's emotional swan song, a reporter asked Neil, 'What's your primary aspiration?' It was a big question to ask of someone who'd been through so much over the past three decades. Neil considered his answer for a moment before responding. 'Raising good children with my wife—and to make the transition to solo artist with a reasonable amount of grace and good humour.'

That transition wasn't always easy. Local artists Jimmy Barnes and James Reyne may have been in the midst of solid solo careers, but neither scaled quite the same heights as they had when they'd fronted Cold Chisel and Australian Crawl, respectively. And Neil had been in groups since he was in his teens; this was all very new. Neil laughed at how being in a band was 'like being married but without the sex. I've done it for twenty years and I think I'm beyond that now.'

Spare time was a new thing for Neil, and he spent much of his noodling away in his home studio or watching Liam play soccer. He'd also try to get to the beach every day; boogie boarding had become something of a new sensation. He started to focus more on painting, too, inspired by an artist friend from Brisbane, Robert Moore (who also played bass). Not long after the Opera House show, Neil and Moore shared ten days on the wild west coast of Auckland; they spent much of their time working on canvases in the middle of an empty field. Over this time Neil produced about half a dozen pieces of art. 'It was a delicious feeling,' Neil said of their getaway. After the trip, Moore would swing by Neil's home and listen to new songs he was writing. His job, as Neil saw it, was quality control. 'Friends would tell me if something sucked.'

As for Neil's former bandmates, they'd moved in very different directions. Nick Seymour started a new life in Dublin, where he established Exchequer Studios with collaborator Brian Crosby. Part-time barista Paul Hester, meanwhile, had formed his own new group, the Largest Living Things, alongside relocated American Kevin Garant. Hester was responsible for everything from setting up their gigs to rehearsals—even making sure his bandmates were fed.

'I'm doing all this stuff like a nanny,' Hester sighed. And finally he understood what it felt like to have tardy bandmates. 'Now I've got a band, I'm there half an hour before anyone else . . . I keep thinking about Neil having to chase Nick and I down all the time.'

He also began to grasp the pressure that came with writing songs. Hester had seen the emotional impact this had on Neil during the days of Crowded House, but never imagined it would one day bother him. According to Hester, 'I always thought Neil focused too much on the music. Now

I realise what he was going through. I really want to ring him up and say, "Neil, now I know how you felt, I'm so sorry for everything I did."' That chance would come soon enough.

★

Neil, typically, hadn't stayed idle for too long; he was already at work on his first solo record. He spent January 1997 in New York, working at Philip Glass's Looking Glass Studios on songs that he'd started at his home studio. He stayed with his friends, the Lizottes, Mark (aka Diesel) and his wife Jep. (Neil returned the favour by co-writing 'Burning Water' in 1999, a standout from Lizotte's *Soul Lost Companion* album.) Neil would walk to the studio each day, enjoying the New York lifestyle, 'getting a burst of energy from the Northern Hemisphere'.

Neil had no regrets about closing down Crowded House. 'Making the break was very liberating,' he said. 'When I started making the [solo] album, I was basically left to my own devices.' He had no deadline, there was no record company looking over his shoulder, and he could work with whoever he liked. Over the course of the year, Neil would make music with Jim Moginie from Midnight Oil; American bassist Sebastian Steinberg, from the band Soul Coughing; drummer Pete Thomas, best known for his work with Elvis Costello; and Afrobeat great Tony Allen, a drummer who'd worked with the legendary Fela Kuti. Neil's long-time collaborator Mitchell Froom also helped out. 'I'm enjoying the freedom,' Neil told New Zealand reporter Paul Holmes.

As for big brother Tim, he'd finally found his soulmate, a stunning, dark-haired woman named Marie Azcona whose family were originally from the Philippines. Nineteen years younger than Tim, she'd been an MTV VJ in Australia and, later on, would host New Zealand program *Music Week*. They bonded over music. When she mentioned to Tim that her favourite song was Small Faces' 'Tin Soldier', he memorised the lyrics and spent much of their first date singing it to her. Tim wrote a song called 'Forever Thursday' that recounted that date. He nicknamed her 'Absolutely Sweet Marie', a neat lift from a Bob Dylan song.

They were married in Sydney on 29 September 1997; by that time Marie was pregnant with their first child. The baby was due in February.

With his solo debut slowly nearing completion, in January 1998 Neil travelled to Vietnam, as part of his work with the Fred Hollows Foundation. He performed for village kids and on Australia Day played a special show in Ho Chi Minh City. His touring band included his fourteen-year-old son Liam (who already had his own group in New Zealand). Neil may have been biased, but he was struck by Liam's musical ability. 'Liam is very talented,' he said. 'There's potential for early retirement for me.' Neil realised that his son was 'very set' on becoming a musician. All the time that Liam had spent backstage and in tour buses clearly hadn't been wasted.

★

Paul Hester was a self-confessed TV junkie, so it came as no surprise that he was finally granted his own show on the ABC, which was called *Hessie's Shed*. It was a laidback mix of humour and music, and Hester was a natural host. The show was filmed at the Gershwin Room at Melbourne venue The Esplanade. The Largest Living Things were the house band, while Hester's buddy Brian Nankervis also helped out. Over time, musical guests included Renée Geyer, Vince Jones, Reg Mombassa, Colin Hay and Deborah Conway, Hester's former girlfriend/bandmate. The pick of local comics also appeared on each program. The set design was pure Aussie larrikin—it mirrored the inside of a shed, with couches, a bar, plenty of room for the players and a bust of TV icon Bert Newton. A painting by Neil's mate Robert Moore hung on the wall. It was the perfect man cave well before the term was even invented.

In April 1998, musicians and crew set up in the Espy for what would be the ideal first episode—a (sort of) Crowded House reunion. Paul Kelly would also perform, while peerless Kiwi wit John Clarke provided the laughs. When asked about this brief re-formation, Neil was at his pragmatic best. 'It'd be crazy if we didn't feel comfortable about playing together every now and again when the situation is right,' he said.

The night began with some shed chat between Neil, Hester and Kelly—Neil remembered chopping wood in the family shed when he was a kid—followed by a few songs by Kelly and then some music by Hester and The Largest Living Things. Neil then joined Hester and his band on stage, handing over the $10 he'd bet Hester some years before. As Hester recounted, Neil had told him, 'If you ever get your own show, Hess, there's a tenner in it from me.' It was time to pay up.

This segued neatly into a discussion about the many TV studios that Neil, Hester and Seymour had visited around the world during their time in Crowded House. They shared a laugh recalling the German studio where they performed 'Don't Dream It's Over', coming on after a magician who hypnotised chickens. Neil had observed how these places were almost uniformly cold and dull, and how it seemed that every effort went into making things look, rather than sound, right. This bothered Neil. 'No one really cared if the performance was any good,' he said. He revealed that he, Seymour and Hester had a shared dream about playing this 'mythical TV show' where the musicians came first. It seemed that Neil was about to nominate *Hessie's Shed* as that very show, but then came the punchline.

'I got here this afternoon for soundcheck,' said Neil, 'and no one knew what the fuck was going on.' So much for their dream, although, when the laughter died down, Neil did add, 'He's done it. He's done exactly what we were talking about.'

Neil also took the time to remark on the set, recognising a sombrero he'd once owned, which was hanging on the wall. 'It's very cosy in here, I must say,' he remarked. 'It doesn't feel like a gig, really.'

The first song Neil played was 'She Will Have Her Way', a sneak preview of his new music, which was warmly received. (Neil described it as 'a homage to all women and girls'.) Later in the show, Hester had an announcement to make: 'Well, there's only one thing I can do at this point and I suppose that's introduce Nick Seymour, ladies and gentlemen.' The crowd erupted as Seymour, all in black, his hair bleached blond, strapped on his bass. Before they started playing, Hester offered 'a general apology for leaving you guys in Atlanta . . . just to set that straight'. In response, Neil and

Seymour feigned their own walkout, squeezing a laugh out of what had been a fraught situation.

Before they played, Hester took a moment to read out some audience questions and the first was a doozy. It read: 'What the fuck went wrong?'

'It can't have gone *that* wrong,' Neil replied, 'because here we are.'

He couldn't have scripted a more perfect response; the crowd lapped it up. They went on to share some curious road stories, among them the night on stage in Los Angeles when Hester decided to find out what sound was generated by whacking his penis against a microphone (it was 'an experiment in sound', he insisted). They also revisited the push-and-shove that went on between Neil and Hester after the dodgy show in Milan during Hester's final tour with the band. 'Our worst moment of violence,' confessed Neil, who feigned disappointment at their shared wimpishness. More laughs ensued.

Issues that the three men once might have found hard to talk about were now public property, little more than slightly ridiculous snapshots of their time spent together. They were friends, no longer bandmates, and it would be churlish if they weren't able to laugh at their moments of prima donna rock star behaviour.

Then it was time to play 'Sister Madly', Seymour vamping on Deep Purple's 'Black Night' during his bass solo, and the three former bandmates harmonising as though they'd just rewound time. There were hugs all round at the end of the song, before Paul Kelly joined them for the finale, 'Leaps and Bounds'.

'That was a really effortless evening,' Neil said of *Hessie's Shed*. 'It was like a therapy session.'

A few weeks later, on the brink of turning 40, Neil was back on the ABC, speaking with 'Rampaging' Roy Slaven and HG Nelson on their show *Club Buggery*. How did he feel about reaching that particular milestone? Neil revealed that he'd arranged a tour, so he didn't have time to think about his upcoming birthday. 'I'm trying to let it slip by without any fanfare at all.'

★

Soon after arriving in London in 1977, Neil had found himself in Abbey Road Studios. He met Beatles producer George Martin during that Split Enz session, which was a pretty heady start to his new life. Now, on the night of his 40th birthday, 27 May 1998, Neil was back at Abbey Road. He was to play a showcase set of mostly new songs but with the occasional classic, such as 'Private Universe' and 'Fall at Your Feet', added for good measure. He'd come a long way since '77.

He may have downplayed his plans when talking with Roy and HG, but Neil did celebrate his birthday with some gusto. The day after his showcase he met with a reporter from *The Irish Times* and told him, 'I went out last night and got trashed.' But while his head may have ached, he was in an upbeat mood. 'I still have a huge affection for music and what I do,' said Neil. 'I have a fantastic family, I've made some money out of what I do, so I'm comfortably off.' He also said that he was a calmer man nowadays. 'A modicum of wisdom has been achieved in all those years.'

Abbey Road was the second public preview of *Try Whistling This*, which was released on 15 June. Neil had also hosted a special gig in Sydney, which started with an invited-guests-only ferry ride around the harbour followed by a showcase at the Slip Inn. These were the first two of some 90 shows that Neil would play over the next six months. Neil had signed a new deal with Work Group, which was part of Sony Records, and happened to also be the recording home of 'Jenny from the Block'. 'I'm pretty impressed by Jennifer Lopez,' Neil said a bit sheepishly when asked about his new labelmate. The co-president of Work Group, Jeff Ayeroff, was a big fan of Neil's, comparing him with another former bandleader who'd gone on to a stellar solo career. 'I liken this record,' he said of *Try Whistling This*, 'to when Peter Gabriel left Genesis.'

Try Whistling This was, in its own way, a family affair. The cover featured a painting by Elroy Finn, which went on to win the New Zealand Music Award for album cover art, quite the accolade for a nine-year-old. Neil referred to Sharon as a 'mentor' for the project; she also sang on a song that didn't make the final thirteen tracks. Liam played drums on the tracks 'Souvenir' and 'Loose Tongue' and guitar on 'She Will Have Her Way' (the video for this song was filmed on the set once used for *Little House on the Prairie*). When Neil appeared yet again on TV's *Later... with Jools Holland*, Liam was part of his band, looking sharp in a black leather jacket, his long hair falling into his eyes. 'He's one of the youngest people we've had in the studio,' noted a suitably impressed host. Liam seemed completely unfazed by the 300-strong studio audience, the ever-present cameras, or the million-plus viewing audience as he played guitar on 'She Will Have Her Way' and then beat the hell out of the drums during a thunderstruck 'Loose Tongue'.

The always fickle British music press maintained a grudging respect for Neil's work—he'd once noticed that 'when we started getting good reviews people would always preface it by saying, "I know I'm not supposed to like Crowded House but . . ."' Yet they had no such qualms with his new album. *Q* magazine stated that Neil 'appears to have struck gold in his attempt to remould his undisputed talent for classic melody', which was a roundabout way of saying it was a record worth buying. It was a hit in the UK, reaching number 5, and topping both the Australian and New Zealand charts, although it didn't sell in Crowded House numbers, going platinum only in Oz.

The album title was a private joke of Neil's, 'a wry comment on . . . my stock and trade': that is, melody and harmony. As he chipped away in the studio, sometimes straying far from his usual recording methods—he often worked alone, using computers a lot more than in the past—there were moments when he thought to himself, *This would be impossible to whistle.* But Neil made it clear that this was no *Metal Machine Music,* Lou Reed's unlistenable, four-sides-long 1975 up-yours to his record company. 'It's not *that* radical.'

A key inspiration for Neil at the time of *Try Whistling This* was Beck's *Mutations,* a genre-jumping release from one of the 1990s' more interesting musicians. 'I wasn't pretending to make a record like that,' Neil clarified, 'but I did like the fact that he was using computers and loops [yet] somehow it sounded like a garage band—there's a real skill to that'.

*

Not too long after the birth of his first child on 24 February 1998, a boy named Harper, Tim brought his family back to New Zealand. His decision to come home was sparked by an accident that left Harper with burns so serious that he required two weeks of hospitalisation. It happened while they were visiting New Zealand, and over that fortnight, as Tim would relate, they were 'deluged with love' from friends and family, a reminder of how strong their ties were to the country. But there was another reason: Mary Finn had been diagnosed with cancer. Tim and his family bought a home close to Neil in Parnell, and the brothers began hanging out and making music together, when Neil wasn't on the road promoting *Try Whistling This*.

On 19 December, Neil and Tim were guests of honour at the opening of the *True Colours* exhibition at the Te Awamutu Museum. It was an impressive collection of Split Enz artefacts, including handwritten lyrics and a selection of Noel Crombie's costumes. Dick Finn's home movies showing Neil and Tim as carefree boys played on a loop.

Later that day, at the Waipa District Council chambers, the brothers stepped forward to say a few words. Tim thanked his parents for sharing their love of music, while Neil thanked Connie Nicholson, his childhood piano teacher—he had just come from attending her 90th birthday—and Felicity Saxby, from the All'n'Some folk club. He noted how his former musical mentor and her family 'were always very kind to me'.

Neil and Tim played a heartfelt 'Weather With You' on acoustic guitars, a song that, although written in Melbourne, could easily have been about their hometown. Neil then spoke about Te Awamutu. 'I don't get back that much,' he said, 'but I still feel quite connected to the place.' And he meant every word.

14

'A lot of things I've been worrying about weren't important at all'

Neil was invited to appear at The Concert for Linda, an event organised by Chrissie Hynde and staged at London's Royal Albert Hall on 10 April 1999. Hynde's close friend Linda McCartney had died from cancer, at the age of 56, almost exactly a year earlier. It was a highly emotional evening for the 5000-strong audience, a fundraiser for various causes, with Paul McCartney making a special appearance; he had rarely performed since his wife's death. Neil, too, was becoming something of a recluse after all the heavy touring for *Try Whistling This*—this was one of just ten performances he'd undertake over the next twenty months.

It said a lot about Neil's standing in the world of music that he was invited to appear at the Royal Albert Hall; there was even a whisper that Paul McCartney had called Neil 'the best songwriter in the world'. (When asked about this, McCartney admitted, 'I love his songs.') Neil appeared alongside Sinead O'Connor, The Pretenders, Elvis Costello, Heather Small from M People, Tom Jones, George Michael, Marianne Faithfull and Ladysmith Black Mambazo. The host was cross-dressing comic Eddie Izzard.

Neil and O'Connor, both in red—'I had no idea when I chose this shirt,' Neil made clear—performed the *Woodface*-era 'She Goes On'. It was an apt choice, a powerful ballad that Neil had written for a friend's mother who had died. As he played, Neil, every bit the professional, dealt with a broken guitar strap with an absolute minimum of fuss. The audience barely noticed his mishap.

'I think Linda and Paul were an inspirational love story for those of us who have families and try and navigate the distances and battles of the music industry,' Neil said between songs, speaking very much from experience. He dedicated 'Don't Dream It's Over'—which went down a storm—to his own family, 'the Finns, generally' on the other side of the world. It was always family first for Neil.

Backstage after the show, he was introduced to Johnny Marr, the former guitarist for The Smiths and a man with an even finer thatch of hair than Neil's (which was saying something). Marr had just delivered a devastating version of The Smiths' 'Meat is Murder', a nod to Linda McCartney's vegetarianism, and one of the musical highlights of the evening. Coincidentally, both Neil and Marr had attended Sacred Heart schools as kids, but on opposite sides of the planet: Neil in Auckland, Marr in Manchester. They'd also both been playing in bands since their teens; Marr formed his first group when he was thirteen. They clicked and agreed to stay in touch. It would prove to be a rewarding friendship for both men.

*

Death, tragically, dominated this phase of Neil's life, while he chipped away at a new solo project. As his mother's health gradually declined, he ventured outside New Zealand for just a few events—the June 1999 Tibetan Freedom Concert in Sydney, April 2000's East Coast Blues & Roots Festival in Byron Bay, plus a handful of dates at LA club Largo, which had become a favourite spot of Neil's (and of many other acclaimed musos). When Mary died in October 2000, aged 78, Neil stopped work on his next album.

He'd lost a key figure in his life, the woman who had inspired him as a boy to sing and enjoy music—which, of course, became Neil's obsession, his life's work. The impact was devastating, overwhelming. At that moment, the notion of completing a new record for imminent release had no appeal for him. 'It was a difficult year,' Neil said. 'I didn't feel like touring or doing anything.'

In front of 350 mourners at St Peter's Church in Cambridge, just outside Hamilton, Neil and Tim sang 'Irish Heartbeat', one of Mary's favourite songs, as Dick Finn, her husband of 51 years, wiped the tears from his eyes. 'She was an inspiration,' Tim said of his mother. 'She always was.'

In the wake of Mary's death, Neil came to realise that some things he once might have obsessed over weren't worth the bother—and that he should stop trying to, as he put it, 'mould the world to fit how I see it'. 'I've learned not to worry about stupid things and expend energy on pointless arguments—and to accept people a lot more for what they are and not attempt to change them,' he told Australian music writer Barry Divola.

Neil also decided that some house cleaning was in order. He parted ways with Grant Thomas, his manager since the days of Crowded House—who duly left the music biz altogether—as well as his American record label, Work Group. While his next solo project was on hold, he did, however, involve himself in one-offs, such as a collaboration with Australian cartoonist Michael Leunig, entitled 'Parables, Lullabies and Secrets', in which Neil performed with the Australian Chamber Orchestra at a concert in Melbourne. He also composed music for the New Zealand film *Rain*. And, brought together by grief, Neil began talking with Tim about possibly making another Finn Brothers record.

When the family got together for their first Christmas without Mary, Neil made a new year's resolution. He was wary of becoming 'good old Neil', the Kiwi legend; that was too comfortable, too easy. He wanted to shake things up. As he revealed, he was in the mood for 'collaboration and lots of it'. Neil decided that 2001 would be his 'year of living differently'.

★

In the 1990s and early 2000s, music TV shows were all the rage (pun intended) on Australian TV. The ABC alone had produced *Hessie's Shed*, *Recovery*, *The 10:30 Slot* and *Studio 22*, along with the ubiquitous *Rage*. SBS produced *Nomad* and *Alchemy*. MTV Australia first screened on Channel 9 and then shifted to Optus Television in 1996. Yet another new live music program, MTV's *Cold Live at the Chapel*, featured Neil as a special guest on 21 January 2001, just days after he and Tim were presented with honorary doctorates from the University of Waikato's Academy of Performing Arts. The show was filmed at a renovated chapel in the heart of Melbourne. It was probably deconsecrated, too, given that the key sponsor of the program was the beer company Carlton. Neil was there ostensibly to promote the solo album he had finally completed, called *One Nil*. But he had some surprises in store.

Neil took the stage in a crisp collared shirt, his hair swept back from his eyes. He bowed to the audience before starting with a new song, 'Turn and Run', which was vintage Neil Finn, heartfelt and melodic with a strong whiff of melancholy. This was followed by 'Rest of the Day Off', which, as Neil explained, was all about 'slacking off, something I've learned to do in recent years. I'm learning to be lazy.' It was quite an admission from a man with a work ethic to rival anyone in the music business.

Neil's first guests for the night were Jim Moginie, playing some spooky guitar, and Richard Tognetti, from the Australian Chamber Orchestra, on gypsy violin. Together with Neil they played 'Wherever You Are', a highlight of *One Nil*. That was followed by 'Anytime', a song about mortality that, as Neil explained, was inspired by a near-fatality when his dog, Lester, chased a cat into traffic. 'Dogs become more and more important as time goes on,' Neil added, dedicating the song to Lester. But there was little doubt that his mother's death was also on his mind.

Soon after, Neil answered questions from the audience— or in the case of a bogan named James, heard a revelation about 'Wherever You Are'. 'Me and my girlie'—his girlfriend Jo, apparently—'had one of our first big pashes to it,' James admitted. 'It's good to pash to.'

Neil didn't quite know how to respond, but he did hope, for James's sake, that he and his partner had 'moved onto the next stage possibly by now'. The crowd loved it.

In between numbers, Neil talked about his new website, neilfinn.net, which he had recently launched with an 'ancient' and obscure Crowded House video that featured some band nudity. 'If that's not motivation to check out my site,' he chuckled, 'then I don't know what is.' Neil was an early adopter; not all musicians had embraced the mysterious beast called the internet, especially in the wake of Metallica's much-publicised lawsuit with Shawn Fanning and Napster. But Neil could see its potential. 'There are no gatekeepers,' he noted, 'and you can connect directly with an audience.'

While his new material was warmly received, the crowd at the Chapel really burst into life when Neil introduced his next guests. 'Please welcome Paul Hester, Nicholas Seymour and, filling out the crowded house for tonight, Mr Jim Moginie.'

'How we looking?' Neil asked as the others plugged in.

'You're always looking good from back here, Neil,' deadpanned Hester, and they eased into a beautiful 'Distant Sun'. It was hard to believe they hadn't shared a stage for almost three years since *Hessie's Shed*. And they seemed genuinely thrilled to be playing together again, Seymour bouncing around the stage like a teenager, Neil smiling broadly.

This was followed by 'Fall at Your Feet', Neil closing his eyes tightly as he sang, lost in the music. Neil then led the audience—and the band—in a sweetly sloppy run-through of Mary Hopkin's 'Those Were the Days', as Hester joined Neil and Seymour down front to play his stripped-down drum kit while Moginie retired to the wings. 'Four Seasons in One Day' followed, and Seymour's ad-libbed harmonies were rewarded with a quick sideways smile from Neil—they were still finding new twists in songs that they'd played thousands of times.

Soon enough, though, it was all over. 'Thanks a lot, this has been a bit of a special evening—lots of new things, lots of old things,' Neil said in closing. 'They seem bloody new to me and Nick, let me tell you, son,' chirped Hester from behind his kit. 'I didn't know where we were. Just as well you're here, Neil.'

Neil and friends closed proceedings with a revved-up 'Mean to Me', the group almost lifting the roof clear off the Chapel—by now, the crowd were up on their feet and cheering. 'Have a good year,' Neil said, before disappearing into the wings, applause still ringing in his ears.

Though Neil thoroughly enjoyed himself, there was a caveat. 'It felt good, easy and comfortable,' he said afterwards. 'It didn't feel all that nostalgic. But it's not an indicator of anything other than that we had a good time.' Neil was concerned that it might start rumours about the chance of a Crowded House reunion, 'because as far as I'm concerned, there's not'.

Rather, Neil's focus was on *One Nil*, the album that he'd put on ice while dealing with his mother's death. The time was now right to share it with the world.

★

The spirit of collaboration was a big part of *One Nil*, which was released in early March 2001 (apart from the US, where it was released in 2002 as *One All*). The guest list was long and impressive. Lisa Coleman, a big part of Prince's band The Revolution, co-wrote 'Hole in the Ice' with Neil. Jim Moginie also contributed, as did Mitchell Froom and Tchad Blake and a pair of Finns, Sharon and Liam. Sheryl Crow, whose drummer Neil had 'borrowed' in the wake of Hester's sudden departure in Atlanta back in 1994, also helped out. And American Lisa Germano, best known for her work with John Mellencamp, brought her multi-instrumentalist skills to the record. Many of these people would continue working with Neil beyond *One Nil*, a record whose title, Neil revealed, celebrated the final score in the soccer final that Elroy's team had recently won—and he scored the winning goal.

But the collaborator who had the most impact on his new album was 37-year-old Los Angeleno Wendy Melvoin, another key member of The Revolution. She had a remarkable musical bloodline: her father, Mike, was one of the legendary LA studio musicians known as The Wrecking Crew, playing piano. Her brother Jonathan was the touring keyboardist with Smashing Pumpkins, and her twin sister Susannah was a singer and composer. Melvoin had been the romantic partner of Lisa Coleman, and the pair performed together as Wendy & Lisa.

Neil met Melvoin at Tchad Blake's home in Los Angeles, and they co-wrote their first song, 'Secret God', within hours. 'It felt good and natural,' said Neil. It was as simple as that. Neil invited Melvoin to New Zealand and together they co-wrote four of the album's dozen tracks. She also played everything from fuzz guitar to 'low bass' and drums on the record. When Neil spoke with the press, he noted that there was 'a good groove running through [*One Nil*], courtesy of Wendy Melvoin'.

'She's an amazing musician,' Neil said, noting that Melvoin hit the drums 'harder than any man I've ever seen'.

One Nil did some miles during its creation, from New Zealand to the US and back again. When Neil was completing the album in Auckland's Revolver Studios, he conjured up what he described as a 'living room/circus/opium den' vibe, installing a parachute canopy and comfy sofas, with candles flickering nearby. Catering was courtesy of the nearby Sanitarium Foods factory, the air thick with the smell of breakfast cereals. When asked to compare the finished record with *Try Whistling This*, Neil replied: 'It feels a bit more romantic in a way . . . a little less angst-ridden. I was a bit of a stress merchant there for a few years. I'm a bit more relaxed now and I wanted the lyrics to reflect that.'

Neil also adopted a more relaxed method of introducing the record to the broader public. During the track 'Rest of the Day Off'—a song so mellow it was hard to believe it came from Neil—he namechecked Piha Beach, which was 40 minutes from Auckland and famous for its black volcanic sand. He and Sharon kept a holiday home there. And it was at Piha that Neil previewed *One Nil* to an audience of 100 locals at the Returned Services Association Club, just prior to its official release. The walls of the hall were adorned with photos of past club presidents, many of them sporting war medals. 'I've always wanted to do a gig at Piha,' said Neil, taking it all in. Members of the ladies' auxiliary passed around plates of sandwiches and finger food, as Neil (helped out by Liam on drums) set up.

Before Neil played 'Rest of the Day Off', he asked if there was a piano player in the audience. Up stepped a 60-ish local named Roger, in shorts and a white T-shirt. Neil talked him through what was required, pointing to the appropriate keys, advising Roger, 'If you hit any of those notes at any time it should be okay.' When Roger found that a bit of a struggle, Neil tore off some gaffer tape and used them to mark the three keys Roger needed to play. That did the trick.

It was the most informal launch of Neil's career.

*

In keeping with his 'collaboration and lots of it' mindset, an idea had come to Neil after he played a one-off show at London's Palace Theatre on 4 February. During the concert, three members of the audience joined him on stage; he was struck by how well they played and how they knew his music pretty much inside out. It dawned on Neil that many of the songs he'd recorded with Split Enz and Crowded House 'have reached a point where they're like folk music'. Everybody seemed to know them. This is how Neil came up with the idea for the Band of Strangers, a tour unlike any other he'd been part of before.

Upon returning home, Neil put in place a plan to hit the road less toured—at least by an act of his stature. His tour would start at the University of Canterbury at Christchurch on 20 February, then he'd play the Dunedin Town Hall and the Taihape Musicians Club before visiting Palmerston North, Christchurch, Wellington and Hastings, and winding up at the 1250-capacity Founders Theatre in Hamilton on 6 March.

The set-up was simple: Neil would essentially be the night's MC, playing a short solo set of new material and then leading a group of local musicians, selected in advance, to play some Neil Finn classics. (More than 80 audition tapes were sent in for the Wellington show alone, and another 60 for the gig in Christchurch.) It was a freeform, anything-goes concept that, while great in theory, had the potential to go awfully wrong. It was also Orientation Week on the university campuses he was visiting, typically a boozy, raucous time, which was bound to add to the chaos.

Yet when Neil spoke on the morning of the first show, he insisted that he was up for the challenge. 'Since I've become solo, I've decided to embrace all the diversity of what goes on out there, so this is just an opportunity to set the cat amongst the pigeons and stand back and watch what happens.'

On the afternoon of this and every gig, Neil would meet with the players who'd been selected and get a feel for what they could do. This would typically consume most of his day, right up to the time of soundcheck. Then he'd grab a nap, and if the run-through hadn't been too great, he'd sometimes say a quick prayer to the music gods about the upcoming show. But, as Neil admitted, that nap always seemed to ease any concerns he might have had. 'I came back every time feeling confident it would be okay.'

As expected, the crowds for each of the shows were large, rowdy and noticeably younger than his normal fan base. 'I loved looking out on these people, half of whom probably weren't born when I wrote those songs,' said Neil. 'They were singing along and digging it. More proof that there's no such thing as a generation gap.'

Playing to a crowd of 3000 at the Dunedin Town Hall, Neil watched on wide-eyed as a punter, in front of the stage, slugged beer from a yard glass, which he'd somehow smuggled into the room. Then a drunken stage invader almost derailed 'Don't Dream It's Over'. But any concerns he had about crowd behaviour were offset by some great discoveries among the players who joined him on stage. He met a fourteen-year-old piano virtuoso in Cambridge, who was classically trained. Neil feared that the teen would be 'swamped' by a band, so he let him perform some Mozart by himself, which bled seamlessly enough into 'I Got You'. In Palmerston North, Neil shared the stage with three home-schooled brothers, Peter, Jon and Dann Hume, whose group was named Evermore. They'd go on to commercial success in Australia and at home.

Midway through the tour, a buoyant Neil spoke with *TV3 News*. 'It's pretty easy to get into a comfort zone when you're a musician,' he explained, 'but I actually like the moments when it's teetering on the edge of collapse.' Covering the Wellington show for *The Evening Post*, reporter Steve Rendle stated, 'This wasn't amateur night . . . it was a rock concert transformed into a party.'

Although Evermore was an exception, for most of the Band of Strangers players, these gigs were the biggest events of their musical lives. 'It was a dream come true,' said Robine Prigg, who got to sing 'Better Be Home Soon' with Neil at the Wellington gig. 'It's just so strange to go up and bow in front of so many people when you're used to playing in front of . . . not very many,' said 24-year-old drummer Ben Chapman, who also played at the Wellington concert. After each show, Neil would drink a toast to his guests, sign their lanyards and pose for photos, very much the happy elder. And Neil was comfortable with the fact most shows were pretty ragged; that was in keeping with the spirit of the event. 'That was as it should be,' he insisted. The concept was a stayer, too—Neil recycled it when he took *One Nil* to the UK in August 2001.

Yet the Band of Strangers tour was just the beginning. Neil had an even bigger collaboration in mind, the kind of A-list event that had never been witnessed before in New Zealand.

15

'I would hope that a genuine musical exchange takes place'

The spark for what became 7 Worlds Collide came about from a conversation Neil had with Radiohead guitarist Ed O'Brien. They compared notes about all the people they'd met over the years, especially the like-minded ones, in places frequented by touring musicians: backstage, hotel lobbies, catering rooms, airport check-in lines and so on. 'If you hit it off with somebody,' Neil explained, 'and there's a mutual appreciation of music, quite often you think, "It'd be nice to do something someday."' Neil craved something more substantial than 'just having a chat and a beer' in passing with these acquaintances. He also wanted the chance, as he admitted with a grin, to form 'a great band and then break up. With no baggage or management disputes'.

When he spoke with O'Brien, Neil mentioned that while he did live 'at the bottom end of the world', he wondered what would happen if he made a few calls to friends and suggest they play some shows in New Zealand, for a good cause. It would be as much a holiday for the visiting players as a series of concerts. Neil made some calls and a plan was devised to play some shows in early April 2001.

Neil prepared an official invitation for his guests, which said this of the proposed event: 'Given a bit of preparation time and careful planning, it should go far beyond the sometimes token nature of one-off all-star shows. I would hope that a genuine musical exchange takes place and that everyone involved feels inspired and stimulated at the end of it.'

O'Brien was up for the gig, as was his Radiohead bandmate, drummer Phil Selway. Pearl Jam's Eddie Vedder was another early invitee. 'Okay, that sounds great,' said Vedder, who'd taken to sometimes calling Neil in the middle of the night while listening to rare Split Enz and Crowded House tapes. Another invitee was Johnny Marr, who Neil had befriended at the Concert for Linda, although his schedule would only allow one day of rehearsal prior to opening night. Still, Marr was in—and when he arrived, he went straight from the airport to rehearsals and stayed for five hours. ('That's someone who loves music,' noted Neil.) Ponytailed Sebastian Steinberg, who'd worked with Neil on *Try Whistling This* and was a dab hand with both electric and upright bass, among a number of other stringed instruments, also agreed to participate, as did musical all-rounder Lisa Germano. Neil would bring the family, too, inviting Liam and his band Betchadupa, as well as big brother Tim.

In short, Neil had somehow managed to wrangle key players from The Smiths, Radiohead and Pearl Jam with a few calls, which said plenty about his standing among his peers. A run of five concerts, beginning 2 April, was booked at the St James Theatre in Auckland, a stately venue that had hosted everyone from Joni Mitchell to James Brown and Megadeth—and even a visiting royal couple, Prince Charles and Princess Diana, in 1983. A live DVD would be collated from the shows, with the proceeds going to the charity Oxfam.

In the week prior to opening night, Neil and the entire ensemble retired to Karekare for musical bootcamp, an intensive four days of rehearsal, playing for ten hours every day, jamming 40 possible songs. 'We worked like dogs,' Neil reported. Yet even before they'd played their first show, Neil was buoyant. 'I can honestly say it's the best thing I've ever done,' he told writer Barry Divola, who was watching the magic unfold at Karekare.

During the rehearsals, Neil talked Johnny Marr into a run-through of The Smiths' 'How Soon Is Now?', a track Neil had listened to frequently while making the first Crowded House record. Marr, however, hadn't played the song since The Smiths' final show in 1987. 'I never thought I'd do it again,' Marr admitted. 'Too much baggage. But it's Neil. He's so cool and such a nice guy that you just say "Yeah, let's try it."' (Marr played the song once during the five shows, ad-libbing the second verse, singing: 'So you go out and you bust some moves/And you go home and there are 40 people in your house/And they're putting drugs in your pockets.' It was close enough.)

During their time at Karekare, Neil confessed to Marr that he'd dreamed about bringing him into Crowded House after Tim's sacking. 'So why didn't you call me?' Marr shot back. Neil said at the time he still saw himself as a bit of a rube, 'a small-town boy going to the big city'; there was just no way he could possibly pick up the phone and ask someone as renowned as Johnny Marr to join his band.

The easy familiarity that now existed between the pair was evident during the opening show at St James. 'Always been one of my favourite nights, Thursday night,' Neil said between songs.

'You say every night is your favourite night,' Marr said with a grin.

'Just play a fucking Smiths song,' Neil shot back.

'And it was going so well up to now,' Marr replied, as they launched into 'There Is a Light That Never Goes Out', Neil delivering Morrissey's gloomy lyric as if it was the most natural thing on earth.

When patrons entered St James before each show, they were handed sheets of A4 paper that came with the printed instruction: MAKE ME FLY. Accordingly, paper planes littered the theatre and many reached the stage, some carrying song requests, others unrepeatable comments and suggestions. On opening night, Neil examined a stray that had crash-landed nearby. 'You've got one flap up and one flap down,' he noted, ruefully shaking his head. 'That'll end in disaster.' After a few small adjustments, Neil proclaimed: 'Let's will it into flight.' And he did, sending it floating off into the darkness. This typified the mood during 7 Worlds Collide's five-night stand: there was magic in the air. And the 2400-strong audience got involved with the music, too, taking over from Neil each night during 'Fall at Your Feet', singing the song back at its creator with the gusto of a much larger crowd. It was one of many singalongs.

Reinvention was a big feature of the shows. Germano's sweeping violin and soulful backing vocals underscored

'Private Universe', which reached a stirring crescendo. As for 'Four Seasons in One Day', it now resembled a hymn, with Marr blowing a mournful harmonica while Tim sang and played piano. The voices of Neil, Marr, O'Brien and Germano, meanwhile, gelled beautifully during 'Anytime', transforming a song about mortality into something far more life-affirming. Up the back, drummer Phil Selway kept a steady beat throughout with all the understated class of Rolling Stone great Charlie Watts. (Selway also dressed in a cool style similar to Watts, favouring smart suits.) While Selway typically maintained a poker face, when Neil played 'She Will Have Her Way' on opening night, he and his bandmate O'Brien grinned as though they'd just won the pools, mouthing the lyrics. Germano, meanwhile, stood at her keyboard, swaying in time to the music, eyes closed. In fact, there were just as many smiles on stage as there were in the audience—there was no doubt that Neil's hope of a 'genuine musical exchange' had been achieved.

Then there were the real surprises. Crowd favourites most nights were Liam's band Betchadupa—all teenagers—who rocked the bejesus out of 'I See Red', with Vedder on vocals, along with Tim, who would literally run on mid-song to join him. They did likewise with 'I Got You', playing, noted Barry Divola, who was covering the event for Australian *Rolling Stone*, 'at such volume and with such veracity that you're pinned back into your seat and unable to move'. Ed O'Brien stated for the record that Betchadupa was, to quote an old Enz track, a hard act to follow. 'They're definitely the high point of the night as far as crowd reaction is concerned,' he said. 'It's really difficult going on after them.' Divola wasn't alone when he described Betchadupa as the 'best Split Enz tribute band on the face of the earth'.

Vedder was also in fine form, typically pogo-ing his way through Split Enz's 'Take a Walk', swapping verses with Neil. He also took lead vocals on the gorgeous 1978 Enz track 'Stuff and Nonsense', with Tim playing piano. As for Tim, he threw himself around the St James stage so vigorously that he required a thorough rub-down after each show. 'He hasn't moved like that for twenty years,' Neil observed slyly.

7 Worlds Collide was a huge success, probably the highlight of Neil's year of living adventurously. At the end of the first show, after introducing each of the players, Neil punched the air and proclaimed: 'What an incredible night.' And his overall assessment of the five shows? 'It was like the planets were lining up.' Ed O'Brien admitted that at the close of the final show, as Neil played the last note of 'Don't Dream It's Over', the entire ensemble was overcome with emotion. 'We all sat on the edge of the stage and we thought, *Oh no, it's over.*'

The ensuing *7 Worlds Collide* DVD, released in November 2001, was a success, reaching number 9 on ARIA's DVD chart in Australia and proving to be a nice little earner for Oxfam, Neil's charity of choice.

★

Anniversaries and accolades marked the next phase of Neil's life. He and Sharon celebrated twenty years of marriage in February 2002, dancing cheek to cheek to Neil Young's 'Harvest Moon', a song that Neil believed to be 'one of the most romantic ever'. They didn't celebrate alone, as Neil revealed: 'Couples were cavorting and carousing left right and centre.' The invited guests included Neil's former bandmates from Split Enz, and over the course of the night they got up and played a few songs together. 'There was a lot of rough edges,' Neil said afterwards, 'but it was still fun.'

On 4 April 2003, Neil appeared at the inaugural Pride of Te Awamutu Awards, where he and Tim were honoured with the first spot on the town's Walk of Fame. A plaque with their names was then set in concrete on a nearby street. Tim was unable to attend as his wife Marie had just given birth to their second child, a girl named Elliot Maisy, but he did send a thank-you text. (Tim wrote a new song, 'Luckiest Man Alive', to celebrate Elliot's birth.)

Neil, wearing a smart ensemble of buttoned-up shirt and sports jacket, addressed the gathering with heartfelt gratitude. 'It's a fine thing to be acknowledged by your hometown. When you're born in Te Awamutu, you're always from Te Awamutu. You never lose that.' Neil then sang Van Morrison's 'Irish Heartbeat' a cappella, his voice ringing out through the auditorium. 'It's a song we sing at all the family gatherings we have,' Neil told the townsfolk and dignitaries, who gave him a big ovation. It was also the song that he and Tim had sung at their mother's funeral.

Soon after, in May, Neil and Tim's alma mater, Sacred Heart College, celebrated its 100th anniversary. It was only right and proper that two of their most famous sons joined in the occasion, playing a surprise 30-minute set before a crowd of 1200 at the Ellerslie Racecourse, just after taking in a rugby match between Sacred Heart and King's College. 'Finn brothers bring house down,' reported *The New Zealand Herald*.

The Finns had become involved in other enterprises beyond music. Neil and Sharon opened a small bar-slash-venue in Auckland that they christened Bar Tabac, a nod to the cigar bar that was formerly on the site. (*Tabac* is the French word for tobacco.) Neil would often stop in for a glass of red wine, if the mood struck, or a Steinlager. When Dick Finn turned 80, the family celebrated there, Neil and Tim stepping forward to sing a few songs. Sharon, meanwhile, had turned her talent for design into a business named, appropriately, Sharondelier, situated in a 1928 art deco building in Auckland's Newton Road; in a few years, Neil would set up a new music studio next door. And Neil wasn't the only Finn spreading his wings—Liam, their eldest, had followed in the footsteps of Split Enz and relocated to Melbourne with Betchadupa. The band had signed a deal with Liberation Records, which was part of Michael Gudinski's Mushroom empire, and had begun recording a new album.

Neil, too, was headed overseas, along with Tim, to record some new songs with American producer Tony Visconti, who'd made his name working with Marc Bolan and David Bowie—*Hunky Dory* had been huge for Neil when he was a teenager. 'The songs are great, the brothers sing in perfect harmony,' Visconti wrote on his website after Neil and Tim previewed some material via webcast from New Zealand. 'Did I say,' Visconti noted in his next post, 'that the Finns wrote the most amazing songs I've heard in years?'

In July 2003, the Finn brothers, along with moonlighting Midnight Oil bassist Bones Hillman (who'd played with Phil Judd in The Swingers) and drummer Ross Burge, set up with Visconti in Allaire Studios, where he had recently produced

David Bowie's *Heathen*. The studio was more like a retreat, with sweeping views of the Catskills and Woodstock. 'Should be a treat,' Tim declared in an online post. But unlike 1995's *Finn*, this album, which they would title *Everyone Is Here*, had a complicated evolution.

*

Over the course of four weeks with Visconti, the Finns recorded sixteen tracks—and for that entire stretch, Tim never wore a pair of shoes, much to Visconti's surprise. 'Coming along great,' a barefoot Tim noted in an online post. The troupe pretty much lived together for the month, eating in the communal dining room, swimming in the studio's pool and, as Visconti reported, 'enjoying the lofty environment of recording on a mountain top'.

Among the new songs recorded was 'Disembodied Voices', a big-hearted flashback to the brothers' childhood, the lyric recalling the nights Neil and Tim spent lying awake in the dark, talking together quietly, 'keeping all our hopes alive'. Neil at first considered the song too personal to include—'I thought it wouldn't be interesting to anyone else'—but was persuaded otherwise. 'Luckiest Man Alive', the song Tim had written to celebrate his daughter's birth, also made the cut, as did 'Nothing Wrong With You', which featured a lyric Tim had written after his wife received a racist slur. It was a storming pop/rock track, a standout among a batch of memorable new material, much of which, Neil admitted, was inspired by the death of their mother—he described it as the project's 'subtext'.

'On this record, we were unafraid to talk about things

close to us,' said Neil. 'Family, our relationship, things that we care about.'

In October the production moved to London for mixing, again with Visconti. The Finns had signed a deal with Parlophone for this new album, and the label's MD, Tony Wadsworth, dropped by the studio for a listening session. 'It's *Woodface* ten years on,' he declared—a big statement given how successful that record had been in the UK. Another visitor was Miles Golding, an original member of Split Enz now living in England, who added some violin to the record.

One night, when they weren't needed in the studio, Neil and Tim unwound at the home of New Zealand–born actor Sam Neill. Joined by Andy White, Tim's ALT bandmate, they gathered around the piano and belted out 'Penelope Tree', a song from the ALT album of a few years back. Many drinks were consumed; spirits were high.

Tim soon posted another very upbeat message, describing the tracks as 'live and heated, not too tarted-up but crisp and delicioso all the same'. Producer Visconti also provided an update, announcing that they had reached a crucial stage: 'Neil and Tim have to make the difficult decision to choose the 12 best songs' from the sixteen they had recorded. As far as Visconti was concerned, 'I'd have them all.' He also posted that the record was due out early in 2004. All seemed to be in order.

But then the Finns' feelings towards the record changed. 'The egos got involved,' said Tim, although he would later refer to their problems as 'good conflict'. Neil had made it very clear that he had to feel absolutely comfortable and satisfied with the songs, otherwise they wouldn't see the light of day. Just as he had done during the complicated early stages of what became *Woodface*, Neil decided to put the release on hold—for several months, as it turned out.

'It's mysterious what makes things right or not right in music,' Neil said of his reaction. 'I can't be more specific than that. It wasn't Tony's fault. It just didn't seem to have the vitality we wanted it to have.' Visconti remained silent about *Everyone Is Here*, but his manager, Joe D'Ambrosio, offered this: 'I have a copy of Tony's record . . . I fucking love it to death.'

Once reconciled, the brothers took just one track—a song called 'Gentle Hum'—to Cello Studios in Los Angeles in February 2004, where they played it to Jon Brion, a regular performer at Largo, Neil's favourite LA club, and Mitchell Froom, Neil's frequent collaborator. 'Los Angeles was a desperate last resort after trying every other city in the world,' Neil would later joke (half-joke, maybe). With their input, the track came alive. 'We were so pleased,' said Neil, 'that we thought if we tried another song, it would be better as well.' By the time they had finished working together, only fragments of the Visconti sessions—for the tracks 'Nothing Wrong With You', 'Disembodied Voices' and 'Edible Flowers'—remained. Everything else was re-recorded with Brion and Froom and such in-demand players as Sebastian Steinberg and drummer Matt Chamberlain.

As the album was being prepared for an August 2004 release, long after the initial due date, back home, Neil and Tim gathered for the cover shoot. The image that was used was perfect for a record that was dedicated to their mother and inspired by family: the brothers were photographed standing on the banks of the Waikato River, not far from

Te Awamutu. In an outtake from the shoot, Dick Finn's hands could be seen resting on his sons' shoulders.

The album, by now, had done some serious miles; over the past year, Neil and Tim had bounced between New Zealand, the US and the UK. In the final wash-up, they used five different studios to complete *Everyone Is Here*, with individual production credits to Visconti, Brion and Froom, as well as Neil and Tim. 'We explored a lot of territory with this record,' Neil noted, with considerable understatement.

Its creation may have been haphazard, but that had no noticeable impact on the response to the album. Critics loved *Everyone Is Here*—and with due cause, because the songs were great, among the best they'd ever written. 'All things considered,' noted *The Guardian*'s Adam Sweeting in his review of the album, 'a bit of a classic.' 'The Finns' latest is glossy, emotional and sure to satisfy longtime listeners,' wrote Pitchfork's Marc Hogan; he thought it combined 'the skillfully crafted pop effervescence of *Woodface* and the moodiness of *Finn*'. The PopMatters critique was just as praiseworthy. 'These dozen songs are a cause for celebration for fans of Crowded House, Split Enz, and music in general—*Everyone Is Here* delivers the kind of Finn Brothers album that people have long been awaiting.'

The album was a commercial success, too, reaching number 1 in New Zealand, 2 in Australia and 8 in the UK.

★

Neil and Tim toured the record long and hard, starting out in Vancouver, Canada, on 9 July and then playing more than 60 shows during 2004, covering Australia, New Zealand, the UK and the US. 'We really took the considered and long and dedicated approach to making the album,' Neil said, when guesting on *Morning Becomes Eclectic*, a show on US radio station KCRW, 'so we want to tour the hell out of it.' And, as Neil noted, he'd accumulated some handy Frequent Flyer points. 'Masses,' he pointed out.

The tour's lengthy road eventually led them to the Arts Centre in Melbourne in November, to film a set for *The MAX Sessions*, a music show on cable TV channel MAX that was also Paul Hester's latest hosting gig. The Finns got straight to business, beginning with 'Won't Give In' and following it with the album's uplifting title track. 'Everyone I love is here,' sang Neil and Tim, their voices as sweet and supple as ever. As the song built to a rousing climax, Tim stepped away from the piano and shimmied around the stage—he may have now been 52, but the natural-born frontman still had energy to burn. Next up was 'Nothing Wrong With You', another storming pop song, Tim now sharing centrestage with Neil as they both sang their hearts out. The lights were dimmed for 'Edible Flowers', a sombre piano ballad of Tim's that roared into life when Neil chimed in. If you closed your eyes, you could have sworn that the Finns were kids again, on vacation in Mount Maunganui, harmonising with the Durning brothers.

It was inevitable that Hester—who revealed to Neil on camera that he still had one of his guitars that he'd 'borrowed' seven years back—would join in at some point. After they played 'Disembodied Voices', Neil gestured to him: 'Jump on those skins, Hess.'

'We've got to get that vibe going,' added Tim.

'I remember now,' chuckled Hester, as he eased the group into the melodic groove of 'Weather With You'. Midway through the song, Neil, strumming an impressive cherry-red twelve-string guitar, took a few steps towards Hester, a smile lighting up his face. It was good to be back, at least for a song or two. After 'Six Months in a Leaky Boat', which rocked like a hurricane, their set ended with 'Part of Me, Part of You', which the brothers dedicated to their father Dick. 'Eighty-two and going strong,' noted Tim, every bit the proud son.

During a brief Q&A segment with the audience, Neil spoke about 'having a sense of community with the people you're playing with. It's a true and bloody wonderful thing to be part of.' Paul Hester remained a big part of that community. It had now been some twenty years since he, Neil and Tim had first joined forces in Split Enz, when Hester, for a time, breathed life back into a band that was unravelling. 'It was great seeing Paul behind the drums again,' noted one audience member after the session. 'It was fantastic.'

A few days later, Hester again joined Neil and Tim—and Nick Seymour—at the Palais in Melbourne. Together they played 'There Goes God' and then 'I Got You', with Neil's boys Liam and Elroy helping out. Neil, Tim and Hester closed what had been a huge night with a rousing 'Four Seasons in One Day'.

Tragically, it was the last time they would ever share a stage.

16

'I am deeply saddened by the loss of a close friend'

On Saturday, 26 March 2005, Neil and Tim were about to begin a three-night run at London's Royal Albert Hall when they received some terrible news: Paul Hester was dead. He'd taken his dogs for a walk on Friday night and hadn't returned. The body of the 46-year-old had been found hanging from a tree in a park in suburban Melbourne. Ambulance officers reached the scene at 2 p.m. on Saturday but couldn't revive Hester, who was pronounced dead soon after.

Hester left behind his two daughters, ten-year-old Olive and Sunday, who was eight, and although he'd split from his partner Mardi Sommerfeld, they still lived close to each other. Everyone who knew Hester was deep in shock; many knew that he suffered from dark moods, and had been in therapy, but nobody suspected that something this awful might happen. His former partner Deborah Conway, who'd seen Hester only two weeks earlier, was so rocked by the news that she speculated whether foul play had occurred.

'I suspect he may not have entirely meant to kill himself,' she said. Hester had never spoken to her about suicide.

A message posted on the Frenz of the Enz website tried its best to express the depth of that shock. 'He loved life too much,' it read, 'and it really seems like a bad dream . . . At the moment we are trying to look after Paul's family.'

A simple tribute—a single protea flower with homemade drumsticks—marked the spot where Hester took his life.

Peter Green had been working closely with Neil in a sort of 'front office' role since the days of Split Enz; he was a trusted insider. He flew to London to meet with Neil. 'Should we come back?' Neil asked him.

'No,' Green replied. 'Stay and play.' He firmly believed that's what Hester would have wanted.

Neil quickly prepared a statement: 'I am deeply saddened by the loss of a close friend . . . The Finn Brothers shows . . . will go ahead as we don't know what to do at this time other than to be with those closest to us and Paul and play music to remember him by.' Nick Seymour flew in from Ireland to join Neil and Tim. The opening Royal Albert Hall show would now be a musical wake for their dear friend.

Back in Oz, reporters did their best to capture the spirit of Paul Hester in print. 'Never missed the beat or a laugh' was the headline of one obituary. Hester was the 'cheeky larrikin' who 'stole the show', in the words of his friend John Clifforth, who first met Hester in 1978 and played with him in the band Deckchairs Overboard. Clifforth disclosed that when Hester was still a schoolkid, he had written in his diary that he intended to be 'a famous drummer and not get into trouble with the police'. Hester had achieved much more than that. 'Paul was openly ambitious and with Neil Finn he found the perfect Beatles-influenced partner to realise his dreams.' In conclusion, Clifforth wrote this: 'Dark moods would temporarily swamp him and shame him into isolation. [But] Paul was my dearest and funniest friend.'

When the curtain rose at the Albert Hall on 28 March, the audience was greeted by the sight of three microphones arranged at the front of the stage, along with a single snare drum. It was the set-up that Crowded House used whenever Hester joined Seymour and Neil in the spotlight, a poignant gesture that wasn't lost on the crowd. Most shows on the Everyone is Here tour began with Dick Finn's home movies of the Finns as kids flickering on a screen, but not that night. Instead, a light swooped around the hall, settling on a pantomime horse, stage left, that stumbled onto stage and collapsed in a heap. Neil and Tim emerged from the costume, and with a quick, 'Hey, Nick' were joined on stage by Seymour.

A sadly beautiful 'Don't Dream It's Over' was their first song for the night. The audience clapped until their hands hurt. Neil then spoke for the first time, doing his best to avoid sentimentality, despite the almost unbearably heavy emotions he was experiencing. 'We're just feeling a lot of stuff,' he said. 'We're glad you're here tonight because we know you're feeling it too.' Together, Neil, Tim and Seymour then played 'Fall at Your Feet', 'Four Seasons in One Day' and Hester's own 'Italian Plastic'. Neil later admitted that he struggled to get through these Crowded House songs. 'It was a very hard and difficult thing,' he said. But, as he also recalled, 'We were very blessed to be together, and in a room full of people . . . who all were united in sadness.' Neil said it was a 'very profound experience'.

It was only when they were deep into their twenty-song set that Neil spoke directly about his friend. 'Paul Hester is gone and we're pretty fucked up about it, but all we can do is play music and remember him.' A remarkable night of sadness and joy ended with 'Throw Your Arms Around Me' and then a sad, solemn 'Gentle Hum'.

'It was an incredibly emotional night, as you could imagine,' Neil said soon after. But something positive also came out of the evening—Neil reconnected strongly with Nick Seymour, who he'd rarely seen since the end of Crowded House. Seymour had stated publicly that he was angry about Neil's decision to break up the band in 1996; in May 1997, upon the release of Radiohead's era-defining *OK Computer*, Seymour left Neil a phone message. 'That was the record we were supposed to make.'

But all that was now in the past. 'We were embracing that wake-type need to be together,' said Seymour.

After the Albert Hall dates, Neil and Tim returned briefly to Melbourne for Hester's memorial service. Seymour travelled with them. Mark Hart was also at the service, and he joined Neil and Seymour to play a few songs. 'It was incredibly powerful,' said Neil. 'The music was really good.'

★

In 2005, The Finn Brothers played 50 more shows, returning to Australia in July and settling in for four nights at the Sydney Opera House, where Crowded House had said farewell nine years earlier. This time, though, they played in the smaller (but no less stately) Concert Hall.

While in Oz, another accolade was given to Neil and Tim when Split Enz was inducted into the ARIA Hall of Fame on 14 July. The *True Colours*–era version of the band made the most of the night, too. Wearing matching tattered black suits that looked as though they'd been put through a shredder—a classic Noel Crombie design touch—they stumbled onto the stage as if they'd just come straight from a backstage brawl, pushing and shoving each other, all the while making it clear that it was a put-on. The group performed 'Poor Boy' and 'History Never Repeats', sounding pretty damned good for an outfit that hadn't played in Australia for 25 years. The industry-heavy crowd jiggled in their seats like teenagers. (The event inspired the band to re-form for a series of nine large-scale Australian shows in June 2006, supported by Evermore, who'd appeared on Neil's Band of Strangers tour. Split Enz also played some New Zealand concerts in 2008.)

In October, during a rare break from touring with Tim, Neil appeared at the ARIAs, which were staged at the SuperDome at Sydney's Olympic Park. 'You can sing one for Paul with me if you want,' Neil said from the stage as he began 'Better Be Home Soon', and the crowd did just that, as they left their seats and moved towards the front. Try as he might, Neil struggled to hold it together, his voice faltering at times, as a video montage of Hester played on the big screen behind him. For the final refrain of the chorus, Neil stepped away from the mic, letting the crowd, many of whom were crying, sing the words.

'Love you Paul,' Neil said, then he left the stage.

Missy Higgins may have been the big winner on the night, with five gongs, but Neil had left the deepest and most lasting impression on those inside the SuperDome—and the millions watching the TV broadcast. Jimmy Barnes, who was in the backstage dressing room next to Neil, popped in afterwards to congratulate him on such a gutsy, vulnerable gesture. But he could see Neil wasn't in the mood for company. He was in tears. 'It was an incredible performance under such tough circumstances,' said Barnes.

Neil's one-song performance has since been rated the most memorable of the awards' 30-plus years, and justifiably so.

*

Neil had always left himself open to creative accidents and shifts in purpose. 'Don't Dream It's Over' was a great song, but it truly came to life when Mitchell Froom added his soulful organ solo. If it wasn't for his frustrations with the record company, Neil may have never created the great songs with Tim that became such a huge part of *Woodface*. There had been dozens of such instances in his career. And something similar was about to happen again to Neil when, in early 2006, he began a new album project—a project that would consume much of his creative energy well into the following year.

Neil set out on what he intended to be solo record number three in his new Roundhead Studios, which he was building next door to his wife's business, Sharondelier. Neil had a lot of great gear at his disposal, including a Steinway grand piano; a 1960s Chamberlin Music Master 600, a forerunner of the Mellotron, which Neil had acquired in LA a few years before; and an Optigan, a 1970s-era electronic keyboard that could produce a seemingly endless array of effects. 'It sounds very low-fi but is very atmospheric,' said Neil. 'Not only is it great fun at parties but I've written songs on it.' These included 'Chocolate Cake', 'Not the Girl You Think You Are' and 'Instinct'. 'Best $300 ever spent,' he added.

But the big attraction of Roundhead, at least for an equipment nerd like Neil, was the Neve 8088 console that was installed in the main room, Studio A. (There was a second studio called the Brick Room.) The console had until recently been installed at Bearsville Studios in Woodstock and was used to record such era-defining LPs as REM's *Automatic for the People* and Jeff Buckley's *Grace*. But its even bigger claim to fame was that it had been originally built for The Who. A close inspection of the console revealed remnants of a cigarette butt—on Track 28, to be precise—which was said to have been smoked, and stubbed out, by Keith Moon. The console could be glimpsed briefly in the film clip for The Who's 'Who Are You'.

In the wake of his reconnection with Seymour, Neil invited him to play bass on his new songs. 'At that point,' said Neil, 'we were just a couple of old mates getting together and making some music.' American Joey Waronker was brought in to play drums. Over time, Neil hired Londoner Ethan Johns, who'd been recommended to him, to help out. Johns' father, Glyn, was rock royalty, having worked with The Beatles, The Rolling Stones, The Who and Led Zeppelin, but over recent years his son had emerged from his lengthy shadow. A multi-instrumentalist and producer, whose salt-and-pepper beard belied his age of 37, he'd most recently worked with American rockers Kings of Leon on their upcoming album *Because of the Times*. He'd also worked with Counting Crows, Ryan Adams and Rufus Wainwright. The producer was hugely impressed by the songs Neil presented to him—Johns felt that he was using his music in a 'cathartic way' to try to come to terms with what had happened with Hester.

And Neil did have strong new material to work with: some songs written in the wake of Hester's death, others drawing on different experiences and inspirations. Neil had read the Ian McEwan novel *Saturday*, and a scene in the book inspired the line 'people are like suns', which he used as the title for a solemn ballad that would close the new album. As for 'Silent House'—which would become the emotional centrepiece of the record—Neil co-wrote it with the three Dixie Chicks, Martie Maguire, Emily Strayer and Natalie Maines, who recorded it on their 2006 LP *Taking the Long Way*. Interestingly, Neil was drawn to working with the trio for reasons beyond music. 'I knew they were great singers . . . I didn't really know more than one or two songs of theirs, but I loved their political stance,' he said. (Maines had publicly criticised George W. Bush, which led to the group being black-banned by many US radio stations; they eventually changed their name to The Chicks.) 'It's something I very rarely do,' admitted Neil, who was very selective about writing with others, 'but it's good for you.'

Maines wrote the lyric about experiences with her grandmother, who was suffering from Alzheimer's, but it wouldn't be a stretch to suggest that Neil was thinking about Hester when he recorded the song. 'It's true/I'm missing you,' a heavy-hearted Neil sang. 'And I stand alone/Inside your room.' It was a haunting, powerful song, featuring at times angry, at other times heartbreakingly sad guitar from Neil, some of his best playing ever captured on record.

Neil confirmed that Hester was 'a strong presence' on the record. 'There is definitely an underpinning of sadness and reflection. It was a profound event in our lives—and we miss the little bugger.' The title that Neil chose for the album, *Time on Earth*, felt very much like a reflection on mortality and existence. The finished record would be dedicated to Hester.

At the end of the sessions with Ethan Johns, Neil shifted operations to Real World in Bath, the studios established by Peter Gabriel in the late 1980s as a state-of-the-art facility to be used by artists from around the world (the work of many would be released on Gabriel's label, Real World Records). While staying at a nearby village called Freshford in Somerset, Neil wrote a song about a road trip that had just gone awry, with Sharon at the wheel and Neil trying to guide her home via GPS. 'God knows where the satellite's taking us,' Neil sang in the demo, his voice switching between fear and frustration. It was titled 'Don't Stop Now'. Neil also wrote an oddity named 'Transit Lounge', in which he captured the weird sensation of being stuck in yet another airport terminal—and he'd seen plenty of those—where, regardless of the locale, everything tended to look and feel the same. Bordering on acid jazz, it sounded unlike anything Neil had ever written before. British singer Beth Rowley contributed dreamy, mysterious vocals to the track.

At this point it was still very much a Neil Finn solo record, although that would soon change. Then, 'with some degree of afterthought', he travelled to London's RAK Studios to record some new songs—including 'Don't Stop Now' and 'Transit Lounge'—with producer Steve Lillywhite, who'd been on the shortlist for *Together Alone*. Lillywhite was a very different type of producer to Johns: he rarely left the desk, while Johns got more involved on the studio floor. Lillywhite would tell the players, 'I'm not a musician. You work that out.' Neil wanted Lillywhite to add some energy to the record, which he delivered with the four songs he produced—'Don't Stop Now' in particular. It had the most momentum of any song on the finished record and would be picked as the lead single.

Neil invited his friend Johnny Marr to play guitar on 'Don't Stop Now', and they also recorded 'Even a Child', a song they'd written together on the beach when Marr had visited the Finns in Auckland. Neil and Marr had made a pact—if either of them was nearby when the other was playing a show, they were welcome to come along and join in. That pact now extended to the studio.

As the recording continued into the early months of 2007, players lined up to contribute, including Eddie Rayner, Mark Hart and a trio of Finns—Liam, Sharon and Elroy. Neil also brought in versatile California-born drummer Matt Sherrod, who'd worked with Beck and Macy Gray. Despite the array of musicians, the desire to again be part of a full-time group—something missing from his life for more than a decade—had taken hold of Neil as the recording progressed, and he had decided that not only would this be marketed as a Crowded House album, but it was time to get his old band back together. And in Hart, Sherrod and Seymour, Neil saw the nucleus of the new Crowded House. Hester's death, in its own way, also played a part in igniting Neil's desire to relaunch the band. For one thing, it had got him back into the studio with Nick Seymour. 'We wanted to . . . remind ourselves of the goodness of what had gone on,' said Neil. 'And make some new stuff.'

★

Word of Crowded House's rebirth leaked out in a clumsy fashion. Seymour intended to text a friend about the re-formation but mistakenly sent it to Melbourne journalist Nui Te Koha, who broke the news in late 2006, well before Neil had intended. There was another unfortunate by-product of Seymour's wayward text. Matt Sherrod hadn't yet been officially hired, and Seymour mentioned in his message that they were on the hunt for a new drummer. Soon enough, Peter Green, who'd worked with Neil since the days of Split Enz, was swamped with tapes from hundreds of hopeful drummers, and just as many emails enquiring about the job.

The band had been back in the spotlight of late, due to a tenth anniversary CD/DVD edition of Farewell to the World (FTTW), which was released in November 2006 and reached number 1 on the DVD chart, selling more than 80,000 copies. FTTW was a handy reminder of the band's popularity, and the high emotions of their Opera House farewell. Hester's death made it all the more poignant. 'It's difficult to consider seriously the pop-rock scene of the late 1980s and the early 1990s without paying a measure of attention to Crowded House, one of the creative forces of the era,' noted reviewer Kirk deCordova. 'Though the show was intended to be the final hurrah for the band, it now serves as a prelude to the future.'

With the new album set to drop in July 2007, the Live on Earth Warm-Up tour began on 17 March when the new-look Crowded House assembled for a webcast at Real World Studios in Bath. Two days later they played a secret show at the Thekla in Bristol, just down the road from where they'd been rehearsing. But this was no ordinary gig: the Thekla was a former cargo ship that was docked on the River Avon.

The band played 21 songs in all, Neil mixing up what were now regarded as classics ('Distant Sun', 'Fall at Your Feet', 'Something So Strong') with a hefty serving of *Time on Earth* tracks. A run-through of Creedence's 'Born on the Bayou' continued the band's reputation for unexpected covers. 'It was raucous and fantastic,' reported Neil. And the first of 85 shows they'd play during 2007.

Crowded House's large-scale public return occurred on Sunday evening, 29 April, when they played the massive Coachella Festival in Indio, California—they'd warmed up with shows at Tempe, Arizona, and Pomona, California. A crowd of some 180,000 packed the polo ground where the festival was staged over the course of three days, there to see such big acts as Björk, Red Hot Chili Peppers and Arcade Fire. But as Neil and his fellow Crowded Housers discovered, taking the stage prior to another band that was staging a comeback—sonic destroyers Rage Against the Machine (RATM)—wasn't the optimum spot for his band. Not by any means.

It had been a sweltering day, and security regularly threw bottles of water into what was by mid-evening a heaving mosh pit. But those bottles were now weapons in the hands of impatient Rage Against the Machine fans. And it didn't take long for the crowd to make a statement; just the one song, in fact. As Neil tried to sing 'When You Come', he was hit in the head by the first of many bottles that flew the band's way during their set. Seymour was then struck by two projectiles in rapid succession—he suspected it was the same marksman, who had a particularly accurate arm.

Neil had encountered his share of unruly crowds over the years; playing gigs in Aussie beer barns without some kind of uproar was uncommon. But he'd not experienced mayhem on the scale of Coachella. During their third number, 'Don't Dream It's Over', he was nailed by another flying bottle. Neil stopped singing for a moment—Liam, who was in the touring band, briefly took over—but when he did recover, he had the perfect response. 'I'm walking again to the beat of the drum,' he sang to the crowd, 'And that bottle didn't hurt me/It didn't put me off.'

Soon after, Neil tried another approach, suggesting that all the Rage fans go to the bar and get themselves a beer. 'They'll be on soon,' he assured the black-shirted masses. This defused the situation, at least to some extent, but as one critic later noted, Crowded House were given a tepid response during their eleven-song set. 'You had to be there to appreciate just how thunderous [the] silence was.'

Speaking about the gig, Nick Seymour swore blind that they won over at least some of the mob. He told Aussie TV host Rove McManus that he spotted RATM fans 'waving during the ballads'—conceding, however, that it was possible that their middle fingers were raised at the time. 'It was good, it was synchronised,' insisted Neil, who, while acknowledging that getting bottled was 'a deeply confusing moment for me', thought they got off relatively lightly. 'I was expecting more, in some ways.'

It came as no great surprise, given the chaos, that press coverage of their high-profile return focused more on the madness than the music. 'Felt bad for the band,' ran a report at Stereogum. 'Their obvious enthusiasm on stage (this was their big reunion show, after all) was met with utter indifference from the dehydrated and impatient crowd.'

Fortunately, Rage Against the Machine fans didn't review Crowded House albums, and the response to *Time on Earth* was, in the main, very positive. 'This taut album possesses the immersive qualities and cumulative impact of a good novel,' wrote Bud Scoppa at *Uncut*—a comment Neil would have appreciated, given the influence of novelist McEwan. Crowded House were 'picking up where they left off', noted a review at Pitchfork, 'buoyed as usual by Neil Finn's brilliant and beautiful songwriting'. 'Thoughtful, warm and endlessly hummable even in its moodiest moments,' wrote Liam Gowing at The A.V. Club, '*Time on Earth* is a sweet epitaph.' Writing in *The Observer*, Stephanie Merritt drew comparisons to The Go-Betweens, even to Crosby, Stills & Nash. 'But this is still unmistakably a Crowded House album, even if that definition has subtly altered over the years.'

The album also connected commercially, reaching number 3 in the UK, number 2 in New Zealand and hitting the top spot in Australia, where it went platinum. *Time on Earth* also climbed to number 46 on the *Billboard* 200, their highest chart position in the US since *Temple of Low Men*. Coachella be damned—it had been a savvy decision by Neil to get the group back together.

'It's a glorious thing to feel like you're in a band,' he said when they reached Texas to play the in-demand *Austin City Limits* TV show, 'and there's no replacement for that, other than actually being in a band.'

17

'One of the most extraordinary musical experiences of my life'

Coachella proved to be a rare disappointment during the long haul spent promoting *Time on Earth*, which continued for much of 2007 and deep into 2008. Crowded House's headlining slot at the Live Earth concert at the Sydney Football Stadium on 7 July 2007 was a triumph, despite playing part of their show in the dark when the 'green' generator powering the lights gave up the ghost. 'I guess we're saving power,' Neil said from the stage, as they continued playing 'Something So Strong' without the aid of stage lights.

The voice of promoter Michael Chugg came over the PA as the group took the stage for an encore, searching for their instruments. 'Turn the house lights on, so the band can at least see you!' he roared. Neil, who'd taken to wearing a smart suit on stage (no tie), wasn't too concerned. 'You're all looking pretty beautiful from up here,' he assured the huge crowd, who he then serenaded with 'Better Be Home Soon'. Soon enough, 50,000 pairs of arms were waving in the night air.

Not all their gigs were on such a large scale. Two nights after Live Earth, they plugged in at the Corner Hotel in Melbourne for a fan club show, followed by another at Auckland's Kings Arms Tavern on 12 July. The next night Neil officially launched his Roundhead Studios with a short set, playing three songs, and then within days he and the band were back in the US, packing the Troubadour in West Hollywood, the famous room where Elton John's American odyssey had been launched back in 1970.

Paul Hester was never too far from Neil's thoughts. Before Neil and the band played 'Italian Plastic' during their *Austin City Limits* appearance, he dedicated the song to their late drummer: 'We love him. Bless you, Hessie.' Straight after 'Plastic', the band tore into 'Silent House'. 'It's true, I'm missing you,' Neil sang, his eyes closed. Live, the song was even more thrilling and dynamic than on record, Neil and Mark Hart both furiously cutting loose on their guitars, their heads bobbing madly, while drummer Sherrod pounded away behind them. The crowd lapped it up. 'It felt true and real and right,' Neil said after their rapturously received set.

Neil's lighter side emerged during an afternoon bracket at the Glastonbury Festival in late June 2008, which came on the back of a run of American dates during April and May. At shows such as these, Neil would look out from the stage and see a huge expanse separating them from the crowd, usually occupied by security and media, which hardly helped to build chemistry between band and audience. This was not Yamashiro's garden room, by any stretch.

At Glastonbury, Neil started calling out to the guards in front of the stage, whose shirts revealed they were from a company called Specialized Security, and tried to elicit a nod, a smile or even a wave. When he succeeded, the huge crowd erupted with cheers and roars of laughter. As the band finished 'Don't Dream It's Over', Neil tweaked his lyrics. 'We know who they are,' he sang, grinning broadly, 'Specialized Security . . . They build a wall between us/ Especially number 110.' Guard number 110 managed a smile and then got back to work.

★

In late July that year, Neil returned to the stage in a far more modest setting when a friend from Te Awamutu, Dean Taylor, invited him to play in his old school hall to raise money for a local disability services charity. Brother Tim was also invited. Billed as 'The Finn Brothers Play Graceland'—Gracelands Trust being the name of the charity, not the mansion in Memphis—they played to a crowd of 500 at the Te Awamutu College hall.

'We could be at home,' Tim said as he looked out at the crowd.

'We are,' Neil reminded him.

Neil and Tim shared many Te Awamutu memories as they played their set, which included songs from Crowded House and Split Enz as well as their own solo work, and, it being Māori Language Week, the siblings' own version of 'Hoki Mai', a Māori folk song that dated back to 1946. While seated at the piano, Neil recalled how, as a teenager, he once had the 'best gig in town', improvising 45 minutes of music for a swimwear fashion show. When he sang James Taylor's 'Fire and Rain', Neil remembered performing it on the same stage when he was a teenager. He added that he'd often sing it at parties, 'while the other boys got all the girls I liked'.

When the house lights finally came on, the audience stood and applauded loud and long. The Finns had helped raise $50,000.

★

Neil frequently cited 2001's 7 Worlds Collide collaboration as one of the best things he'd ever done—it was perhaps *the* greatest musical experience of his career, which was saying a hell of a lot. If a similar opportunity ever arose, he was up for the challenge. And when it did, in late 2008, it was purely by chance.

Neil's sons Liam and Elroy were big fans of the American band Wilco, who'd started life playing alt-country/Americana in the early 1990s but had since, via such critically revered and wildly experimental albums as *Yankee Hotel Foxtrot* and *A Ghost Is Born*, become arguably the most interesting band in the US, with a zealous following (including soon-to-be-president Barack Obama). *A Ghost Is Born* won the Grammy for Best Alternative Music Album in 2004. When Wilco played at the Bruce Mason Centre in Auckland in March 2008, Neil and Sharon went to the show, spurred on by their boys. Neil enjoyed what he witnessed and met with the band afterwards. It turned out that Wilco's frontman, Jeff Tweedy, had also been a fan of Neil's music since his high school days growing up in the Chicago suburbs.

Not long after, Neil sent Tweedy and the band what he described as a 'wishful email', inviting them to New Zealand for Christmas. Neil had recently been contacted by Oxfam, who floated the idea of him making a record for them. Their timing couldn't have been better. As far as Neil was concerned, it was synchronicity in action: why not make the record with Wilco? (And other assorted friends, as it transpired.)

'Let's make an album,' Neil suggested in his email to Wilco. 'And bring your families.' Tweedy spoke for all the band when he replied with a simple, 'Yes. We'll be there.'

Neil, as you can imagine, was pleasantly surprised. 'I guess it just tickled their fancy,' he figured.

Three weeks were set aside for the project, spanning Christmas and the new year. Over time, Neil reached out to many of the players who'd been involved with 7 Worlds Collide and had been itching to return: Sebastian Steinberg and Lisa Germano (now a couple) and Johnny Marr, as well as Radiohead's Ed O'Brien and Phil Selway, inviting them to what he described as a 'South Pacific sojourn'. They all quickly agreed.

Scottish singer/songwriter KT Tunstall, best known for her breezy 2005 hit song 'Suddenly I See', planned to be in the country at the time, driving a campervan with her husband on an extended holiday. When she contacted Sharon, keen on paying a visit to Sharondelier, she learned about Neil's summer project. Tunstall, too, was now in. Neil also invited local musicians, and old friends, Don McGlashan, from The Mutton Birds, and Bic Runga, while Liam, Elroy and Sharon would contribute, as would Aussie Glenn Richards, from the band Augie March.

A producer was needed, and Neil hired Jim Scott, who often worked at LA's Cello Studios, where Neil and Tim had re-recorded *Everyone is Here* in 2004. The silver-haired Scott had won a Grammy for his work on Tom Petty's album *Wildflowers* and had recorded extensively with Wilco; he also remixed the Finn brothers' song 'Suffer Never' in 1995. As well, he'd worked with Rage Against the Machine on their 2000 LP *The Battle of Los Angeles*, but Neil was unlikely to hold that against him, especially when Scott revealed what he knew about Neil: 'What everyone else knew—that Crowded House should have been the biggest band in the world.' Clearly, he was a fan.

The guest list kept growing, and would reach 40 people in all: musos, friends and family, including brother Tim. Neil decided that Piha was the ideal base—it was close enough to Auckland and Roundhead (where they would record) but would still feel very much like a holiday—and he organised fifteen rental properties for his visitors. But about two weeks prior to the start of the project, Neil began to panic. He asked himself whether this was just some ego trip.

He talked it through with Liam. 'Is it a bit of a wank?' Neil asked.

'If you could do this,' Liam replied, 'why wouldn't you?'

That made perfect sense to Neil. Liam had a handy knack of cutting through the crap.

Neil's role was, essentially, 'musical ringmaster', but he and Sharon were also hosts; they warmly greeted each party as they arrived at the airport just prior to Christmas 2008 and helped them settle into their digs. Jeff Tweedy, a keen 'tramper', not only loved Piha, which was a great place to explore on foot, but after one quick stroll through Roundhead he told Neil that when he returned home, he intended to toss all his equipment into Lake Michigan. 'It just doesn't stack up anymore,' Tweedy said, looking around him like a kid in a candy store.

Neil had asked all the invitees to 'bring a song if you have one', but some of the material they recorded was composed pretty much on the spot. Sebastian Steinberg wrote 'The Water' after a few hours at Piha Beach, mostly spent at a breathtaking spot known as The Gap. Johnny Marr wrote 'Run in the Dust' on New Year's Eve, also at Piha. Marr described the mood of the song as 'like 2 a.m. on some Mississippi back road'. Duly inspired, Tunstall and Bic Runga decided to pen a murder ballad, which they named 'Black Silk Ribbon'. The end result sounded like something Nick Cave would have been proud to claim as his own. Neil helped Tunstall with a song she'd partly written, 'Hazel Black', although he forewarned her that he'd already 'had a few' when she asked for his assistance. That didn't matter; the song came together seamlessly.

Sharon Finn, who shared vocals with Neil on the charming 'Little By Little', described the mood of the sessions as 'all inclusive', part work, part holiday. Accordingly, some of the players' children started to hang out in the studio (as did a variety of pets). Tweedy's ten-year-old son Spencer played drums on one track, while a group of sons and daughters got together to sing backing vocals on Lisa Germano's 'Reptile'. Liam Finn had a hand in writing three of the finished tracks, including the freaked-out pop of 'Bodhisattva Blues', a co-write with Ed O'Brien. Elroy, meanwhile, wrote and recorded 'The Cobbler'.

Dick Finn was another visitor to Roundhead—he was particularly approving of the bottle of Johnnie Walker Black he spied as he greeted Neil and the team. The notion that Dick might sing something for the record was floated but he politely refused, making it clear that, unlike his sons, he only sang in the shower. Roundhead was a very well-equipped studio, but not *that* well equipped.

As the songs started to come together during January 2009, Neil understood that the project was exactly the 'blessing' his studio needed. 'I wanted to fill it up with music,' he said. Neil also recognised that he had more than a single album on his hands. 'There was so much great music,' he realised, 'we had to make a double record.' The finished product, which was named *The Sun Came Out*, featured 24 tracks (although there was also a single-disc, thirteen-track version released).

'It was wonderful,' bassist John Stirratt told a writer from New Zealand's Stuff website. 'Neil was amazing; there are not many guys who can oversee a project like that.' The guys from Wilco were so taken by Roundhead that they also recorded a new LP in the studio, which they titled, simply, *Wilco (The Album)*. It reached number 4 on the *Billboard* 200 and received rave reviews.

Given that Neil had corralled such a great assortment of players, it would have been almost churlish not to stage a concert. They actually undertook a three-night stand, at the Powerstation in Auckland, from 5 January. And while the bill was star-studded, it was Liam Finn who stole the show (just as his band, Betchadupa, had done back in 2001). In the words of Russell Baillie, who covered the opening concert for *The New Zealand Herald*, Liam was 'the night's most valuable player'.

Not only had he grown into a versatile musician, but Liam was very comfortable on stage, as an exchange at the Powerstation with his father demonstrated. Neil had been pondering out loud what to call the group—Wilcohead, perhaps, maybe Radiosmiths or Crowded Head—when Liam interjected.

'Get over it, Dad,' he said with a smile.

'You're 25 now,' Neil replied. 'I guess you can say that to me.'

'You can hit me now,' Liam chimed in.

Neil thought better of this but did offer an alternative. 'Well, I could always stop feeding you.'

The gig itself, again in Baillie's words, 'was a show of two neatly unpredictable robust halves'. When the house lights went down, the ensemble took the stage and opened with a gorgeous 'Distant Sun', before playing both new and old songs from Runga, McGlashan, Tunstall, Johnny Marr and Liam. The second half of the show was devoted to the music of Wilco and Radiohead—Neil taking the lead for the latter's 'Bodysnatchers', Tweedy doing his best Thom Yorke on a fine 'Fake Plastic Trees', despite his pre-song warning: 'This is going to be like Paul Rodgers fronting Queen.' (On the third night, Tweedy took the surprise lead on the second verse of Split Enz's 'I Got You'.) Then Tweedy and his band played 'California Stars', the highlight of their Grammy-nominated 1998 LP *Mermaid Avenue*, which set the words of Woody Guthrie to music of their own making (with the help of Brit folkie Billy Bragg).

Following that, Neil and Marr joined forces for The Smiths' 'There Is a Light That Never Goes Out', which they'd also played during the 7 Worlds Collide shows, followed by a double whammy of the best of Neil Finn: 'Four Seasons in One Day' and 'She Will Have Her Way'. Then the troupe gathered for the most unlikely finale of all, a take on Thunderclap Newman's curiosity piece from 1969, 'Something in the Air'. The song's title rang true; there was definitely something magical happening at the Powerstation.

The show, as far as reviewer Baillie and the crowd squeezed into the venue were concerned, 'was anything but a predictable charity bash or a dull supergroup jam'. Neil had pulled off another minor miracle, a once-in-a-lifetime—okay, twice-in-a-lifetime—collaboration. It was the kind of genuine musical exchange he'd had with 7 Worlds Collide, where egos were checked at the door and strong bonds, both personal and creative, were forged and/or reinforced. A lot of tears were shed when the troupe reluctantly left New Zealand after three weeks, with the shows, and the album, done. The record was released at the end of August 2009, while the documentary of *The Sun Came Out* project would screen at film festivals in 2010.

Johnny Marr didn't hold back, describing the project as a 'love fest'. To Neil, it was a 'glorious summer holiday . . . one of the most extraordinary musical experiences of my life'. He'd also met one of his biggest personal challenges—he'd made a record in twenty days. With a lot of help from his friends.

*

A version of Crowded House played their only—unbilled at that—show for 2009 on 14 March at the Sound Relief concert, held at the MCG. It was a fundraiser for the Red

Cross Victorian Bushfire Appeal, leading on from the terrible Black Saturday fires that had claimed 173 lives. (A Sydney show was staged on the same day, headlined by Barry Gibb and Olivia Newton-John.) Neil and Tim had agreed to make an appearance at the MCG with Split Enz and were scheduled to take the stage just before 9 p.m. Liam Finn had his own spot on the bill, in the late afternoon, and the audience made a huge noise when Neil and Nick Seymour joined Liam and his band, running through 'Don't Dream It's Over', 'Weather With You' and 'Better Be Home Soon'.

It may have been a surprise spot—although it had been hinted at in press leading up to the event—but no one on the day received a warmer, or louder, response from the crowd. It felt like karaoke on the most massive scale imaginable. Neil was right; his biggest hits had become like folk songs, as proved by the 80,000 people singing along at the MCG. The twin concerts raised several million dollars for bushfire victims and proceeds from a DVD of the day's events—which sold a whopping 75,000 copies—went to the Red Cross.

It may have been the only show that Neil and Seymour performed during 2009, but momentum was building behind the scenes. Despite erroneous reports at the time of the Sound Relief concert suggesting that Crowded House were defunct, they were anything but. Neil was busy writing new material for the band, which now had a stable line-up of Neil, Seymour, Mark Hart and Matt Sherrod.

Between April and June 2009, inside Roundhead, Neil and the band chipped away at eleven fresh songs for a new LP, with a planned release date of March 2010. Neil again hired Jim Scott to produce, and the sessions continued in London and at Real World Studios. Neil brought in guests, including Sharon and Liam, Don McGlashan, Jon Brion and Lisa Germano. He named the album *Intriguer* (oddly, the title of the one track that didn't make the finished record).

Before its release, the band underwent more changes in management and recording home, signing to Universal-Mercury for pretty much everywhere on the planet except the US, where they struck up a deal with Fantasy Records (best known as the home of Creedence Clearwater Revival), part of the Concord music group. *Recurring Dream*, meanwhile, re-entered the Australian charts in late 2009, as it tracked its way to sales of more than 900,000 copies, making it one of the top 20 bestselling albums in Australian chart history, matching the sales of Fleetwood Mac's *Rumours* in Australia. And, in time, the paths of Neil and Fleetwood Mac would intersect.

18

'I don't like cards, so we decided to go and make a noise'

Neil and Sharon weren't old by any measure—he'd turned 50 in 2008—but they were on their way to becoming empty-nesters. Liam had long left home, having released his first solo record, the terrific and hard-to-define *I'll Be Lightning*, in 2007, after the demise of Betchadupa. Elroy was now twenty and about to set out on his own musical adventure. Sometimes at home, in the evening after a drink or two, Neil and Sharon would pick up instruments and jam. 'I don't like cards,' Neil explained, 'so we decided to go and make a noise.' Neil, like Tim, enjoyed jumping behind the kit and flailing away like Animal from *The Muppets*, as he'd once described Tim's drumming style. Sharon was gradually mastering the bass guitar.

On 20 November 2009 Neil and Sharon performed as a duo in public for the first time, at a benefit staged at the

Kings Arms Tavern for Chris Knox, 'a local luminary of the New Zealand scene', in Neil's words, who'd suffered a stroke. (Neil had appeared on a benefit album, released earlier in the year, singing Knox's 'Not Given Lightly' with Liam and Eddie Vedder.) They played a song they'd written together, called 'Daylight'. Neil insisted it was 'a gloriously fun moment' but did joke that Sharon needed to be 'severely medicated' to get through it. It was the first glimpse of what would become known as Pajama Club, named for the simple fact that they usually wore PJs when they jammed together at home. (They originally called themselves Pajama Party but learned another group had claims to the name.)

A few months later, on 8 April 2010, Neil, Hart, Seymour and Sherrod played seven tracks from the upcoming Crowded House album during a show at the Auckland Town Hall. On 11 May, they were once again hosted by Jools Holland on his show *Later* . . . They played 'Saturday Sun', a subtly psychedelic glimpse of *Intriguer*, Neil sporting a pencil-thin moustache that didn't do him any favours. (A dismayed fan noted that he looked like Peter Sellers' Inspector Clouseau, not the biggest rap.) They also played 'Weather With You', Neil, in a particularly chatty mood, telling the others to head 'straight to the chorus' after the first verse, and then encouraging Hart while he played a guitar solo: 'Take it, Mark, come on.' All this was brought about by what Neil thought was the fast-approaching close of the show. 'How long we got now?' Neil asked, as the song neared its end. After a quick wrap-up from Holland they delivered a verse and chorus of 'Better Be Home Soon'—and then the closing credits rolled.

The band remained in the UK for a series of dates that culminated with a big outdoor show—billed as Hard Rock Calling—on 27 June at Hyde Park. 'We're playing as well as we ever had,' Neil said backstage. 'I think we've reconnected with the spirit we had back in the day.' Neil hoped the band was viewed as 'something more than nostalgia', citing *Time on Earth* and *Intriguer* as evidence that they were still a creative force. Crowded House were the third-to-last act on the last day of the three-day festival, appearing before Crosby, Stills & Nash and headliner Paul McCartney. And it was McCartney's name that had been raised in a BBC review of *Intriguer* when it came out in mid-June. 'Crowded House have always sounded in parts like the later solo career Paul McCartney should have had,' wrote Tom Hocknell. 'Despite the anthems being on a tight leash, repeated listens reveal this to be one of their best albums.'

Intriguer charted highly in all the usual places, reaching number 1 in Oz, number 3 in New Zealand, number 12 in the UK and even sneaking into the US Top 50. But it wasn't a big seller, despite some fine songs, and a flurry of positive reviews: 'Finn's durable songcraft never fails to enthral,' noted *Billboard*; 'classic Crowded House', decreed *Mojo*; while Neil was again ranked with Paul McCartney in *Spin*'s favourable review, which referred to his 'massive melodic gift'. The band undertook a heavy touring schedule, playing more than 80 shows worldwide in 2010, but *Intriguer* only managed to reach gold status in Australia.

The final Crowded House show of a hectic 2010 was staged at a winery in the Hunter Valley in New South Wales. Coincidentally, it took place on 20 November, exactly a year after Neil and Sharon's public debut at the Kings Arms in

Auckland. And that's exactly where Neil turned his attention next—to capturing on disc some of the music he and Sharon had made while jamming in their lounge room at Parnell.

★

Neil declared 2011 to be the year of the Pajama Club. It would be the exact opposite of a Crowded House project—small scale, very DIY, stress free, and done for no other reason than to please its makers, Neil and Sharon. And if they took it on the road, it'd be unlikely they'd be sharing a bill with Paul McCartney in Hyde Park; instead they'd be playing clubs and pubs. The time was right, too, because the Finns' big house in Parnell was suddenly very empty. Liam had recorded (and co-produced) a new solo album, titled *FOMO*, and when he took it on the road, Elroy joined him.

'We had time on our hands and a will to make a racket,' Neil explained.

With Neil back behind the drums and Sharon playing bass, 'the grooves we made caught our fancy and sort of demanded songs'. As Neil admitted, there was an interesting democracy at work with the Pajama Club: 'We're evenly placed on drums and bass; neither of us has the upper hand on the other person.'

The *Pajama Club* record would be a new sensation for Neil in a variety of ways—it would be his first complete set of recordings with Sharon, and also the first time he'd make an album 'from the bottom up', laying down drums and bass before focusing on anything else. 'I was working back to front,' explained Neil, who found this different approach exciting, even if he knew the results wouldn't be as immediately accessible as Crowded House and would probably alienate some rusted-on fans.

Groove was king for the Pajama Club, Neil citing ESG, a Bronx funk band formed in the late 1970s, as a major influence. He'd been listening to their music a lot of late. 'They made funk sound really simple and down home,' said Neil. The ESG track 'UFO' was one of the most sampled in music history, appearing in songs from The Notorious B.I.G., Public Enemy, 2Pac and more than 500 others.

Neil brought in a friend, Sean Donnelly (aka SJD), to help with the sessions, for a few different reasons. Not only was he a good musician who also understood the workings of Neil's studio, but in his past, Neil said, he'd been a psychiatric nurse and 'knew when to step into domestic disputes'. Neil's buddy Johnny Marr also helped out, his jetlag minimised by cups of white Nepalese tea. ('Very speedy,' reported Neil.) Marr played on two tracks, 'Can't Put It Down Until It Ends' and 'Go Kart', the latter's lyric inspired by a spill Neil once took when racing around the streets of Te Awamutu as a kid.

A few months prior to the record's release, in late June, Neil accepted an invitation for the Pajama Club to appear at Wilco's Solid Sound Festival, a three-day event staged in the foothills of the Berkshire Mountains in Massachusetts. The invitation was a classy bit of reciprocation from Jeff Tweedy and co., payback for Neil and Sharon being such generous hosts a few years back in New Zealand. Wilco, of course, would headline, while Liam Finn would also perform, making it quite the Finn-fest.

Neil and the group played a warm-up gig the night before in Virginia—up to this point, they'd only played live six times. Neil was pleasantly surprised that no one in the room shouted out for Crowded House songs. He had a theory about this, as he explained the following day at Solid Sound. 'That might have been because Sharon was giving them the evils.' After that warm-up gig, all the members of the band—which included Sean Donnelly and drummer Alana Skyring, formerly of indie-pop darlings The Grates—were given a gift: pyjamas, naturally. 'We're hoping for a good collection by the end of the tour,' said Neil.

Neil was clearly enjoying himself on stage. In the midst of one of their shows at New York's Bowery Ballroom, he and the band played Gary Numan's 'Are "Friends" Electric?', the most unlikely of covers, and they ended each of their six US shows with a take on ESG's 'It's Alright'. At Solid Sound, much of Wilco joined them for the encore, 'I Got You'. 'They totally nailed it,' Neil reported afterwards.

The self-titled *Pajama Club* album was released in September 2011. While a lot of the LP dabbled in the abstract, one of the standout tracks, 'From a Friend to a Friend', was more direct. It was about Neil and Sharon's relationship in this new, empty-nester phase of their lives. 'We were always good friends,' said Neil, 'but I think we're better friends than ever now as a result of jamming together.' The song was also possibly the first—certainly from Neil—to namecheck the Holden Commodore. Neil said he had a 'soft spot' for the popular Aussie family roadster; he'd spent his fair share of time squeezed into them while driving around Australia with Split Enz.

The *Pajama Club* album was never intended to be a bestseller or radio staple; it had a lot in common with the *Finn* record that Neil and Tim recorded together in 1995. It was understated, offbeat and seductive in its own subtle way. 'A welcome surprise,' declared *The Guardian* in its four-star review. Neil was very insistent it wasn't a one-off indulgence, either; he enjoyed the idea of having different outlets for his varying musical moods, and it had given him 'a new lease on life'. Sharon was pleased, too. 'I won't drop him now,' she said, laughing.

★

In late October 2011, Neil was invited to take part in *Songwriters' Circle*, a show filmed at Bush Hall in London and aired on BBC Four. It was a simple and effective concept—three musicians would be seated together on stage, swapping songs and stories. Neil was joined by Janis Ian, the highly regarded American singer and strummer best known for 1975's 'At Seventeen', and Ryan Adams, a big player in the Americana movement, first with the band Whiskeytown and then as a solo act. His 2001 album *Gold* was nominated for three Grammys.

Adams was known to have a short fuse. Early on in his solo career, he made a habit of demanding that punters who jokingly shouted out requests for 'Summer of '69', Bryan Adams' big hit, be ejected during live shows. He'd once left an angry message on the answering machine of a critic from the *Chicago Sun-Times* who dared give a concert a negative review; it was the type of move that never played out well.

Neil opened the *Songwriters' Circle* show with a stellar 'Distant Sun'. As he sang, the silver-haired Ian, who sat to Neil's left, mouthed the chorus softly. Ian was up next, playing 'At Seventeen', still potent as ever some 36 years after its release. While there was clearly a connection between Neil and Ian—she admitted to being a big fan of *Try Whistling This* and much of Neil's back catalogue—Adams seemed unwilling to play along (quite literally). Adams was still tuning as Ian finished 'At Seventeen', when he really should have been ready to play. Neil, however, tried to remain supportive. 'That was pretty magnificent,' he said when Adams finished his first song, 'Carolina Rain', which Neil followed with 'Don't Dream It's Over', where, admittedly, Adams did contribute some nice guitar lines and applauded at the end of the song.

It became plain for all to see, as the evening progressed, that Neil and Ian were willing participants in each other's songs, adding a guitar lick here, a whispered harmony there. They'd sometimes flash smiles at each other as their songs ended and the crowd applauded; they'd also join in the applause, encouraging each other. But not so Adams, who spent much of the set—when he wasn't playing—with his head resting on his guitar. Perhaps he was enjoying the song being played, but it seemed more likely that he simply wasn't engaged.

The on-stage mood seemed to briefly improve when Neil admitted to having days without 'a musical bone in my body', which inspired Adams to riff on that line and come up with a sketch of a song, proof that music was everywhere. (Adams boasted of being able to write five songs a day, a skill that Neil said he admired.)

The official broadcast ended with Neil's 'Weather With You', clearly a crowd favourite. Adams, to his credit, did help out with extra guitar, while Ian harmonised with Neil on the chorus. But there was one more song that didn't make it to air, 'Fall at Your Feet', which was intended to be the filmed show's finale. The producer wasn't happy with the first version they played and it was decided to re-record the song. But Adams didn't participate; he was busy on his phone, even though he'd joined in during rehearsal. The show that went to air—sans 'Fall at Your Feet'—closed with just Neil and Ian taking a final bow; there was no sign of Adams.

Post-show, an online sparring match broke out between Ian and Adams, in which it was revealed that Neil had snapped at Adams during 'Fall at Your Feet', asking him—with reason—why he couldn't simply sing the song as they'd rehearsed. According to a report from one onlooker, when Adams was asked to join in, he replied that Neil 'should just sing the fucking song'.

'No one was happy at that moment,' Janis Ian posted online. And it had been a long day—three hours on stage, working with a film crew, and something like seven hours all up at the venue.

In his defence, Adams posted that he had done as directed. 'We had set lists [that] actually said "COLLABORATE" for only two songs. The rest were meant to be solo. I stood by that. Clearly, they did not. My experience was we had a nice time til Neil started yelling at people on stage. THAT was when things got ugly . . . He yelld [sic] at me. And I bite back.'

Neil resisted going public with his version of events, apart from one pithy post on his Twitter account just before the show aired: 'Well songwriter circle on BBC will be interesting, watch out for lovely backing vocals on Fall at Your Feet from Ryan.' It was one of many funny tweets from Neil, who'd taken to social media like a chatty schoolkid. 'I like the idea that you can create a version of yourself,' he said of Twitter. But that one tweet was his last word on Ryan Adams, at least until a Pajama Club gig on 14 March 2012.

At Sydney's Oxford Art Factory, a version of the Pajama Club that included four Finns—Neil, Sharon, Liam and Elroy—were playing to a packed room. Between songs, Adams' name was mentioned, and Neil joked that it would have been interesting if Liam had been with him that night in London. 'He would have fucking showed him,' Elroy noted. Liam couldn't let it go; when Neil said, 'Let's do a song by a really great songwriter,' Liam shot back: 'Yeah, Ryan Adams.' Instead, they covered Bowie's 'Moonage Daydream', blowing the roof pretty much off the place.

*

Neil was a big admirer of Mercury Rev's 1998 album *Deserter's Songs*, a spooky and brilliant record, which had been created in the Catskills in upstate New York. The Pitchfork review of *Deserter's Songs* called it an 'orchestral rock landmark'. It was that album and that mysterious corner of the world that would influence the next step in Neil's musical life.

American David Fridmann had been a founding member of Mercury Rev but stepped aside to work as a producer, not just on *Deserter's Songs* but on numerous other highly regarded albums, including The Flaming Lips' *The Soft Bulletin*. He'd won a Grammy for his work on the Lips' 2006 LP *At War with the Mystics*. Neil recorded parts of his next album, which he named *Dizzy Heights*, with Fridmann at his Tarbox Road Studios, in Cassadaga in upstate New York.

'He's like a rocket scientist,' Neil said of Fridmann, 'and a lovely man.'

They worked at Tarbox during the depths of the northern winter and into the early spring of 2013. It was 'the back of beyond', Neil explained. 'There is some spookiness happening in those woods.' There may have been an explanation for that: Lily Dale, known as the witchcraft centre of America, was just a few minutes' drive from Tarbox.

Neil preferred not to describe albums such as *Dizzy Heights* as solo projects; to him they were collaborations, joint efforts, despite his name appearing in isolation on the cover. Sean Donnelly from Pajama Club contributed to *Dizzy Heights*, as did drummer Matt Chamberlain and Wilco's Glenn Kotche; the Wilco drummer sat in the studio while Neil was recording 'In My Blood', one of the highlights of the record, and tapped out a rhythm on his knees. Kotche was given a unique credit: 'Body percussion'. Sharon, Elroy and Liam also helped out.

When asked about working with his father, Liam said that Neil could be quite eccentric in the studio. 'Sometimes we get worried he's lost his mind, but then it all makes sense eventually,' he said. Liam cited one instance during the making of *Dizzy Heights* when Neil came up with an experiment: what would happen to the particular song they were working on—which Neil described as 'orange'—if everyone only ate carrots for two days? Would it benefit the track somehow? 'It didn't make the record and I hate carrots now,' Liam pointed out.

It was via Natalie Maines, one of Neil's co-writers on the stirring 'Silent House', and his surfing/singing buddy Eddie Vedder, that Neil got to meet Damien Echols, part of the so-called West Memphis Three. Echols and two other teenagers from West Memphis, Arkansas—Jessie Misskelley

Jr and Jason Baldwin—had been convicted in 1994 of the murder of three young boys, all in second grade. Echols was the only one sentenced to death.

Vedder and Maines had actively lobbied for the release of the three men, who were released in 2011 when new evidence was discovered. Vedder wrote a song called 'Satellite' as a tribute to Echols' wife Lorri Davis, while feature films and documentaries had been made about the case. Meeting Echols inspired Neil to write a song of his own, the haunting 'White Lies and Alibis', which was a new twist for Neil, who usually opted for the personal over the political. It was an attempt, as Neil described it, 'to put myself in his head, to some degree'. He even wrote the lyric in the first person, singing: 'The guilty man is home in bed/And it's me they wanna put to death.'

The flipside of that dark and heavy track was 'Recluse', in which Neil had fun namechecking such legendary hermits as Howard Hughes and Sly Stone, while pondering his own middle-aged predilection for staying home on the couch and watching *Game of Thrones* (as he mentioned in the lyric) rather than socialising. Neil revealed that he and Sharon didn't get many invites nowadays. 'We used to get invited to all the parties and never turn up.' But he did have an explanation for that: 'I think home is a lovely place to be. We have a nice place.'

'Divebomber' was a more opaque *Dizzy Heights* track. It was inspired by an old war movie that Neil caught one night on TV—he recorded the sound of planes directly from the set and used them on the recording. 'I'm a perverse bastard,' admitted Neil, 'and I thought it might freak out some of the fans, and it did.' The accompanying video was equally off-kilter, a combination of footage shot by Neil of kids jumping off a rock, and other footage he shot while travelling on aeroplanes. There were clouds. Lots of clouds.

Neil firmly believed that making the Pajama Club album with Sharon influenced *Dizzy Heights*. 'After making a lot of records you look for new angles on what you do,' he explained, 'and there was something about [the Pajama Club] that put a different emphasis in the music.' A few of the songs on the new album, which was released on 7 February 2014, came out of jams, like much of the *Pajama Club* LP.

It had become almost a given that every Neil Finn release would be showered with critical praise, and his latest continued the trend. '*Dizzy Heights* is more proof that Finn, as well as being one of the most extraordinary purveyors of melody since rock's birth, is indeed an adventurer,' stated Barnaby Smith at The Quietus. Writing for Pitchfork, Stephen M. Deusner described *Dizzy Heights* as 'a collection of sunny psychedelia and woozy pop grandeur'. Not every reviewer was sold, though. 'Maybe it's just a sign of an auteur getting older,' observed PopMatters' Zachary Houle, 'but *Dizzy Heights* seems to indicate a decline in the tuneful, off-kilter melodies that Finn is best known for.'

And Neil's take on his new collection of songs? That was something he could only fathom over time, as he explained in an interview on NZ website Stuff. 'I have no idea—and never do—how it stacks up in my overall canon of work. You don't know that for years, in a strange way.'

While preparing to tour in support of the album—he would play about 50 shows during 2014—Neil did something way out of character. He sat down and listened to his earlier solo records and the albums he'd made with Tim.

Neil, who could be his own harshest critic, was pleasantly surprised by what he heard. As he explained, 'You forget the process, so it's like, "Shit, how did I do that? That's really good. Why haven't I tried to do that again?"'

19

'Is it a flock of Finns? A festoon of Finns?'

Family was always paramount to Neil, and as he'd proved over the past few years, if he could bring family and music together, so much the better. On 27 February 2015, Neil and Tim took this to a whole new level, playing a twilight show 'in the round' at the rotunda in Auckland Zoo, alongside Liam, Elroy and Tim's children Harper and Elliot. Sharon joined in later on bass. Dick Finn, now 92—'and still rocking', noted Tim—was watching from his home in Cambridge via Skype. It was an absolute Finn-fest.

The songs flowed easily from the get-go. Neil and Tim strapped on acoustic guitars and opened with 'Angel's Heap' from the *Finn* album, followed by 'Six Months in a Leaky Boat', Neil's fiery guitar solo loud enough to wake any sleeping zoo animals. Liam, impossible to miss with his wild hair and vivid red jacket, showed off his multitasking skills during 'Nobody Takes Me Seriously', following up a manic theremin solo with an equally thunderstruck burst of guitar. 'Dirty Creature'—where Harper's vibrant piano solo inspired some freaky dancing from his father—bled into 'It's Only Natural', Neil and Tim pogo-ing in synch as the song built to its close, then 'Four Seasons in One Day' and 'Better Be Home Soon', which elicited an enthusiastic singalong from the crowd—and equally enthusiastic chirping from the birds in the surrounding trees.

Lighthearted banter was the order of the day. It felt more like a family get-together than a regular gig. 'There's keys we've never had to deal with before,' observed Neil, as they prepared to play some of Liam's songs, which often took unexpected twists and turns. Tim agreed: 'They're messing with my head, Neil.' Neil had a laugh about being old and out of touch when he sat down at a keyboard and didn't know which button to press. Nephew Harper came to his rescue. 'This is why we need our next generation,' Neil pointed out. 'They know how to change things on these machines.' Neil and Tim even joked about naming their 1995 album *Finn*. 'We were a bit stuck for a title on that one,' admitted Tim, before they began playing 'Only Talking Sense'.

As the evening set in, they eventually wound up proceedings with a triple treat: 'History Never Repeats', 'Weather With You' and 'I See Red'. By this stage there were seven Finns crowded on the small stage. 'What do they call that? Is it a flock of Finns?' asked Neil. 'A festoon of Finns?'

'A filth of Finns', suggested Liam, always the joker in the pack.

The only problem with playing on a rotunda was that it offered the Finns no escape route. After ending their set with a blistering 'I Got You', Neil looked around him and announced: 'We don't know where to go but this is the point where we hang about and hope you want another one.' The roar from the friendly and engaged crowd made it clear that was the case. Overall, the Finn family gig was a success, a great afternoon of song. 'The music was tight, the singing resplendent and Tim Finn can still dance with the best of them,' Ellen Read, a reporter for Stuff, pointed out.

Keeping with the family theme, Neil and Liam played several shows together in 2015—in LA, London, Belgium and Greece. Their set lists read like musical smorgasbords, mixing Crowded House tracks both popular and obscure ('Fall at Your Feet', 'English Trees', 'Distant Sun') with the odd Split Enz track and songs from their respective solo efforts. During a show at Shepherd's Bush in London they even threw in a cover of The Chills' 'Pink Frost', widely (and rightfully) considered a Kiwi indie classic. 'As I'm not entirely deluded—yet—I knew the people coming to those shows weren't as familiar with my work as Dad's,' said the always realistic Liam, 'but the shows seemed to flow really well.'

It was then they agreed to write and record together; that way, next time they toured they'd have their own songs to draw upon. The Finn father/son album *Lightsleeper* was born in that moment.

*

At this point in his musical life, it seemed like Neil couldn't leave his house without being granted another accolade. By 2016, Crowded House had claimed twelve ARIAs, eight APRAs, three New Zealand Music Awards and a Brit Award. Neil had won nine New Zealand Music Awards as a solo artist and, of course, had his OBE stashed away on a shelf somewhere in the house at Parnell.

Split Enz had been inducted into the ARIA Hall of Fame in 2005 and it seemed only natural that Crowded House would eventually follow them. In a gesture tailor-made for a band with a healthy sense of humour, they were inducted on 23 November 2016 by Bret McKenzie and Jemaine Clement, better known as Flight of the Conchords, New Zealand's biggest export since, well, Crowded House.

Clement and McKenzie took the stage at Sydney's Star Event Centre and read a note that they insisted came directly from the New Zealand prime minister John Key. His message was simple: 'Stop it.' Neil Finn was the property of New Zealand, not Australia (even though, weirdly, Crowded House weren't in the NZ Music Hall of Fame). And so what if Neil was the only member of the band from the Shaky Isles? 'We really need Crowded House,' pleaded Clement and McKenzie, both keeping the straightest of faces. A compromise, however, was quickly reached, as they announced: 'Crowded House are one of the greatest bands to come out of Australia . . . and New Zealand.'

All the while, Neil and Nick Seymour, plus Mark Hart and Matt Sherrod, sat near the stage, looking on as a video montage flashed back over their brilliant career. Sharon, as always, was seated alongside Neil. Seymour brushed away tears as they were called to the stage to a standing ovation.

It was Neil, in a purple suit and black shirt, his hair liberally sprinkled with grey, who stepped forward to speak. He noted that it'd been 30 years 'so there's a lot of people to thank'. Sharon was first, of course—'she's been there from the very beginning and through Split Enz, as well'. He noted that not only had Sharon inspired a lot of songs but she also 'put up with a lot of neurosis'. Neil thanked his sons, too—and Liam's son, Buddy Finn, Neil and Sharon's first grandchild.

Neil then spoke about Paul Hester who was, in his words, 'an amazing presence in our band'. Without him, Neil readily acknowledged, the group wouldn't have been anywhere near as 'engaging and amusing and wonderful as we sometimes were'. Hester's two daughters, Sunday and Olive, were in the audience and Neil made a point of thanking them for coming.

Neil acknowledged his father, Dick, who was then 94, and big brother Tim, who was also in Sydney at the time. He thanked all the people who'd worked with the band, from Tchad Blake to Mitchell Froom and Craig Hooper, who was in The Mullanes, as well as Hester's replacement, Peter Jones, who'd died of brain cancer in 2012 at the age of 49. 'He was a great drummer for us,' said Neil. 'Thank you, Peter.'

Neil paid his dues to former manager Grant Thomas—known as 'Bokkie' due to his thing for high-top Reeboks—and the band's current management, One Louder. He also thanked the group's crew. 'Anyone who's been in a band or on the road knows how important they are and how unsung they are most of the time.'

When the formalities were over and the applause died down, Missy Higgins eased into a heartfelt take of 'Fall at Your Feet', backed by a string section. Up next was Bernard Fanning, who'd won the night's Best Adult Contemporary Album gong, looking slightly awkward in a black suit. He strummed an acoustic guitar as he sang a subtly reworked

'Better Be Home Soon', which ebbed and flowed accordingly. Then, finally, it was time for Neil and the band to play, and they powered into 'Distant Sun'. It was a great moment. The standing ovation was enduring and genuine.

Afterwards, Neil spoke about the powerful connection people had with his music. 'It's a joy and a blessing,' he said. 'Music is all about empathy, although I have no answers to the mystery of it all.'

It had been a lively period for Neil and Crowded House. On the 30th anniversary of their debut LP, all of their studio albums (including the rarities set *Afterglow*) had just been released in double-CD formats, with all the usual trimmings: additional live cuts, demos, B-sides, the works. And the night after the ARIAs, Crowded House played their first of four shows at the Sydney Opera House, the scene of their emotional farewell 20 years earlier. Once again, they played on the forecourt, but this time in a far more controlled environment, with just 6000 people allowed into each show. But Neil and the band did secure an exemption to the noise-limit restrictions imposed on outdoor shows, which was a first. Tim joined in for a couple of songs, just as he'd done back in 1996.

When asked if the band had 'done a Farnesy' by making their comeback, Nick Seymour insisted that it wasn't so. He referred to the shows, with a knowing smile, as an 'encore performance'—in fact the shows were billed as 'Crowded House: Encore'. No one attending the four nights seemed to mind; their fans were simply glad to have the band back and in top form.

This time around, Neil chose to close their shows with 'Better Be Home Soon'. 'What a glorious night to be alive on the planet,' Neil said as he departed the stage on the first night, and he meant every word.

*

It would have been perfectly acceptable for Neil to slow down as he got older, but that simply wasn't in his nature. During August 2017 Neil decided to set himself what might well have been the biggest challenge of his career: to record an entire album live in his studio and stream it, while it happened, to a worldwide audience. In theory it seemed like an accident waiting to happen, but Neil was absolutely up for it, as he explained to Australian writer Michael Dwyer. 'I could've done a little acoustic album live on the internet,' Neil said. 'That would've been really easy. But I thought, "No, fuck it. If I'm gonna do it, why don't I do the most complex record that I've ever done?"'

Beginning on 4 August, The Infinity Sessions comprised three nights of live-streamed rehearsals and preparations for the ultimate recording. The peak audience for these streams was about 300,000. During these sessions, when Neil wasn't readying his new songs for the album, he fielded messages and requests from fans all around the world.

A mother and son Skyped Neil from the UK and asked which of his songs he'd be willing to give away. Without naming names, Neil replied that he'd be willing to sacrifice a few for 'genetic work', in order to be improved. Neil also related a story about catch-ups with his father in Cambridge, where they'd go to a quiet local bar for a game of snooker and a couple of songs on the piano. Dick always asked Neil to play 'Better Be Home Soon'. Neil also checked in via

Skype with Liam, who was in LA, and Nick Seymour, as well as English writer Caitlin Moran and her husband, the music critic Peter Paphides, who'd written extensively about The Finn Brothers. Jimmy Barnes Skyped in to join Neil on a computer-driven version of Split Enz's 'Shark Attack'. Neil was joined in the studio by Tim for a lovely 'Disembodied Voices', as their father's Super 8 home movies played on a screen, showing the boys kicking around a footy, horsing around on holidays, proudly posing in front of the family Zephyr and more.

The mood in Roundhead was a little more serious on 25 August, the night of the official recording session for *End of Silence*. It was a very full house: Neil was joined by about 30 musicians in all, as well as his sons (Liam had flown in from LA to help out) and Sharon. Tim would also join the gathering; it was yet another 'flock of Finns'. A mini-choir of twelve backing singers, including Don McGlashan, Eliza-Jane Barnes and Neil's nephew Harper, dressed in blue hooded capes, brought a touch of Stonehenge to the occasion.

At about 7 p.m., Neil, who was seated at a piano, got down to business, announcing: 'Out of chaos. From the bottom of the world. Out of silence. And straight to you, wherever you are . . . Welcome to all comers.' Over the next four hours, Neil was very much in charge, directing traffic, although he would often defer to the project's musical director, Victoria Kelly (who would also work on the track 'Where's My Room' for Neil and Liam's *Lightsleeper* LP). For the most part, Neil was intensely focused, although he did allow himself a smile at the end of 'Second Nature', by far the funkiest of the songs that would appear on *Out of Silence*. Tim dropped by to sing on the beautifully melancholic 'Alone', which he'd co-written with Neil with the notion of possibly using it in a musical. (Tim had successfully branched into musical theatre with the 2015 production *Ladies in Black*.) The song quoted some of the writing of Mervyn Peake, a favourite of Tim's—so much so that the late Peake (or at least his estate) got a co-writing credit.

At the close of the third take of 'I Know Different', the eleventh and last song of the night, Neil sat back, eyes closed, and let the tension drift out of his body. He'd nailed it. *They'd* nailed it. Neil then rose from his chair and began applauding loudly, walking over to each group of players—the strings, the brass, percussion, the hooded vocalists and especially Victoria Kelly—and thanking them profusely. He was deeply moved not just by the night of recording but the entire month-long experience, which he described as 'a massive experiment. I've loved every minute of it'.

Out of Silence was then mixed and released to the world on 1 September, within days of the actual recording.

Neil conducted a post-mortem on the *Out of Silence* experiment with Wallace Chapman, host of RNZ's *Sunday Morning* program. In essence, he didn't see it as too far removed from any other album—he wrote the songs, players learned the parts and then it was recorded, just like any LP (albeit an album recorded virtually in one hit, no small undertaking). Live-streaming, however, gave it a sense of occasion. 'I had big aspirations for the sound of this record,' said Neil. 'I knew that the songs that I had made for this record would really deserve the treatment, with strings and a singing group. It's something that's been brewing in my head for quite a while.' He called the whole process 'real and collaborative and communal . . . I wanted a kick-arse campfire singalong vibe'.

There was positive critical response to *Out of Silence*—'Finn's greatest gift is for melody,' noted RNZ's Nick Bollinger, 'and he lifts even the darkest of these reflections with tunes that work like an antidote to despair'—though it wasn't the type of project Neil could take on the road for any length of time. There were too many players and way too much cost and organisation involved. Neil, however, did see it as a contender for arts festivals, because, as he acknowledged, 'they have budgets'. And that's exactly how it panned out. Neil would perform *Out of Silence* several times over the next year, playing two dates at the Auckland Arts Festival, a further two nights as part of Vivid Live at the Sydney Opera House in May 2018, and another date at the Gold Coast Home of the Arts a few weeks later. He was accompanied by more than 30 musicians, including Liam, Elroy and Sharon, with Victoria Kelly again conducting the orchestra. The shows were a triumph—proof, as Neil proudly stated, that 'you can have a whim and follow it'.

★

Neil had another experiment in mind for his next project after *Out of Silence*. He wanted to play some live dates with his family, but in the less likely parts of New Zealand. The photographer and music promoter Ian Jorgensen was a family friend, and Neil and Liam came to him with a proposal: provide them with a unique experience. 'Take us places we've never been before. Show us New Zealand. We want to have a holiday and get to audiences we've never played to before.'

Jorgensen, who'd arranged some similar dates in Wellington halls for Liam in 2014, undertook two extensive reconnaissance trips, checking out pretty much every hall in which music had at some time been played, even if it was only for a wedding reception or a family booze-up. He learned that some spaces cost as little as $60 to rent for the night.

Eighteen dates were locked in for what would be essentially a grand tour of New Zealand community halls, billed as the 'Where's My Room?' Tour of Aotearoa, named after a song written by Neil and Liam for their upcoming *Lightsleeper* LP. The tour began on 3 January 2018 at Piha's Barnett Hall and continued until 27 January with a final date at the Milton Coronation Hall. During those three-and-a-bit weeks, 'the family band', as Neil dubbed them—featuring Liam, Sharon and Elroy as well as several other non-Finns—took in a great swathe of New Zealand from Kaiwaka in the North Island to Owaka in the South, visiting Warkworth, Waipu, Hawea Flat, Lake Tekapo and numerous other spots not typically seen on a Neil Finn tour itinerary.

Jorgensen made a point of not letting those who booked the halls know who would be playing, which made for quite a surprise when several buses arrived and began setting up. Another family friend, filmmaker Darryl Ward, documented the road trip, while Jorgensen photographed the tour (shots that would be published in a book called *Where's My Room: The Neil & Liam Finn Summer 2018 Tour of Aotearoa*).

Neil described it as 'the largest band I've ever had on some of the smallest stages'. Occasionally the stages were so small that Neil and the other players had to set up their amps on the floor of the hall. Nonetheless, as the tour rolled on, Neil was very pleasantly surprised by what he was encountering. He said these 'unlikely places . . . had the most amazing halls'. Kaiwaka War Memorial Hall, where Neil and co. played on 6 January, was a particular standout. 'It's a beautiful facility like you'd expect to find in a bigger city,' he noted.

The set list for each concert was the usual mix of what were now 'golden oldies' such as 'Four Seasons in One Day', 'I Got You' and 'Better Be Home Soon', plus tracks from the upcoming *Lightsleeper* album and some of Liam's solo material. But the mood on stage was just as crucial as the music being played. 'We do pride ourselves on being able to have a fun time together,' said Neil. 'It's a good time guaranteed for all when the Finns turn up.'

The off-the-beaten-track format proved so appealing that Neil and Liam embarked on a similar tour of Australia during February, playing intimate venues such as Anita's at Thirroul on the NSW South Coast as well as some more 'talk to the animals' shows, at Sydney's Taronga and the Royal Melbourne Zoo. Clearly, the Finn family gig at the Auckland Zoo wasn't a one-off. They also played a pair of gigs at the 250-seater Meeniyan Town Hall in Victoria's South Gippsland region, very much in keeping with the type of venues they'd played in New Zealand.

As for the *Lightsleeper* album, while it constituted two years of writing and studio work on the part of Neil and Liam, in reality it was 30-something years in the making. After all, Liam had been on the bus with Neil and Split Enz when he was a baby and had been a huge part of his father's musical journey. 'I've listened to Dad's music since I was in the womb,' explained Liam. 'I watched Dad have a lot of success and people love what he did—and I thought that looked pretty good.' He really had no option but to become a musician; as Liam admitted, he couldn't do much else, apart from make a decent coffee.

It was a family event that had sparked the father/son album into life. Neil composed a song called 'Island of Peace' for what Liam called his 'pagan wedding', in Greece during 2015, to his partner Janina. Neil played the song for the first time at the event, asking the guests—all dressed in white—to perform their own interpretive dance. Neil felt it was 'deeply dorkish as well as being sentimental'.

Most of the guests then jumped into the ocean together; when they emerged, they were joined by the marriage celebrant, who was stark naked. At dusk, the members of a circus visiting the town rolled up and were invited to join in. They played the bridal waltz on their trumpets—'and drank more margaritas than anybody', Neil noted. Liam, unfortunately, missed a lot of the action, having been knocked unconscious after a lively rumble with a family friend went wrong. Then he dislocated his thumb. All up, it was an event to remember, for those who could, and it also generated the perfect opening track for *Lightsleeper*, which was set for release in August 2018. But then a strange turn of events shifted Neil's focus elsewhere.

20

'Yes, I've joined Fleetwood Mac'

Since he had formed Fleetwood Mac in London in 1967, drummer and bandleader Mick Fleetwood had hired and fired and sometimes simply lost enough players to fill a football team—with ample reserves. Among them were musicians who went on to solo success, like the late Bob Welch, who had a hit in 1978 with 'Ebony Eyes', and others, such as ace blues guitarist and co-founder Peter Green, who allegedly found God after taking LSD in 1970, was diagnosed with schizophrenia and only occasionally heard from again. (He died in 2020.) Another Fleetwood Mac guitarist, Jeremy Spencer, left to join a religious cult and yet another, Danny Kirwan, suffered mental health problems. Tragedy and chaos seemed to haunt the band.

The most commercially successful line-up of the group—Mick Fleetwood, bassist John McVie, his former wife Christine McVie, Stevie Nicks and Lindsey Buckingham—crafted their career-defining album, 1977's *Rumours*, while living through a variety of break-ups, breakdowns, addictions and divorces—and then writing songs about their experiences. This was a band accustomed to high drama and huge success: by 2018 they'd sold more than 120 million records, won numerous Grammys, been inducted into the Rock & Roll Hall of Fame and maintained a huge global fan base. Their 2014–15 world tour, On With the Show, grossed almost US$200 million from 120 shows. That tour ended with two dates at Auckland's Mount Smart Stadium, each show drawing around 47,000 fans. Fleetwood Mac was big rock-and-roll business.

The next round of Mac turmoil happened in early April 2018 when it was announced that Buckingham, who'd joined the band in 1974—although he went solo between 1987 and 1996—had been fired over a disagreement about an upcoming world tour. He'd asked that it be delayed for three months so he could complete and promote a solo record, but the band voted against the delay. In an interview with podcaster Marc Maron, Buckingham explained, 'That sort of led to other things that kind of built up around that. And then it just got to the point where someone'—Stevie Nicks, according to Buckingham—'just didn't want to work with me anymore.' It was rumoured that former member Billy Burnette would rejoin; in response Burnette tweeted: 'Breaking news: Lindsey Buckingham is out but I'm not in.'

However, it was another message that set music fans into a frenzy. On 10 April 2018, Neil tweeted: 'Snow warnings for parts of the country, the mystery of Stonehenge solved and yes I've joined Fleetwood Mac.' (He wasn't the only new recruit: they'd also hired Mike Campbell, guitarist for Tom Petty's Heartbreakers, who'd worked closely with Stevie Nicks in the past.) This was followed by a formal statement on behalf of the band: 'We are thrilled to welcome the musical talents of . . . Mike Campbell and Neil Finn into the Fleetwood Mac family . . . Fleetwood Mac has always been a creative evolution. We look forward to honoring that spirit on this upcoming tour.'

Neil, at 60, was youthful by comparison with the core members of the band: Fleetwood and Nicks were 70, bassist John McVie was 72 and Christine McVie 74. Neil's fellow recruit Mike Campbell was 68 and was making a return to the stage after the sudden death of Tom Petty in October 2017. 'It feels good to be the baby again,' Neil said with a grin.

He accepted that some Mac fans would feel let down by the departure of Buckingham, which potentially made Neil something of a target. 'I'm not Lindsey but most people [will come] to see a joyful presence on stage and those songs delivered in a really powerful and meaningful way.'

The relationship between Neil and the band, in particular amiable drummer Fleetwood, dated back to 1999, when they met at the Concert for Linda at Royal Albert Hall. (It was the same night that Neil met and befriended Johnny Marr.) By his own admission, Fleetwood didn't really know Neil or his music, but during the evening he found himself seated next to him and they hit it off. 'We had a great night and broke a couple of glasses—so to speak—and then wandered off,' Fleetwood told a writer from *The Guardian*. They playfully talked about forming a band together. Fast forward some sixteen years, and Fleetwood Mac was closing their huge On With the Show tour in Auckland, when they met again at the New Zealand Music Awards.

'Do you remember me?' Neil asked Fleetwood.

'Of course I do,' replied Fleetwood. 'I'm your superfan.' He'd learned a lot about Neil's music in the interim.

During the course of that night, Fleetwood mentioned to Neil, 'If you ever need a drummer, let me know.' Neil took him up on his offer when he and Liam began their *Lightsleeper* project in 2018; Fleetwood played on three of its tracks. Fleetwood and his partner Chelsea rented a house in Auckland for six weeks and grew tight with the Finns. 'We became a very, very close family,' said Fleetwood. Neil noted that the dapper Fleetwood was 'by far the best dressed in the studio'.

Not long after, when the problems arose with Lindsey Buckingham, Fleetwood unveiled what he called his 'secret weapon', suggesting to the others that they invite Neil to Hawaii to jam with the band. Fleetwood reached Neil on the phone and asked him to join them, stressing that 'it's not really an audition'.

'Let me just take a breath,' said Neil. 'I'll phone you tomorrow.'

It was almost a replay of the situation in 1977 when Tim had called Neil from London, asking him to join Split Enz, and Neil had said he needed to think it over.

In truth, Neil was a bit stunned by the proposition of joining Fleetwood Mac and he needed some time to adjust to the idea. 'It was a delightful thing to be asked to do,' he told *Variety*, 'and enormously flattering, but it did spin me out for a few days.'

Fleetwood had begun to fear that Neil wasn't interested by the time Neil finally called back. 'I'm not worried whether this is an audition or not,' Neil said. 'Who wouldn't want to come and just play with Fleetwood Mac?' Stevie Nicks, as Neil soon learned, was also a fan. When she first heard 'Don't Dream It's Over', she'd made up her own harmonies to the song. 'Songs like that come around once in a lifetime,' said Nicks.

Neil clicked with the others in Hawaii and was duly invited to join what was the nineteenth iteration of the band. He issued a statement soon after: 'Two weeks ago, I received a wonderful invitation to be a part of a truly great band . . . It felt fresh and exciting, so many great songs, a spectacular rhythm section and two of the greatest voices ever'—meaning Stevie Nicks and Christine McVie. 'Best of all, we sounded good together. It was a natural fit. I can't wait to play.'

The 'An Evening with Fleetwood Mac' tour began on 3 October in Tulsa, Oklahoma, and continued for the next fourteen months, with 88 shows in total, spread across nine different countries. While Neil had played big shows, this was by far the largest production he'd ever been involved with. And the shows themselves were enormous: the smallest crowds, if you could call them that, were around 12,000, while on many nights of the tour the band would play for audiences of 50,000 and beyond. And most shows were full houses; they'd play to upwards of two million people during the tour. The amount of money that came through the box office was just as staggering—two nights at Madison Square Garden alone generated many million dollars.

While Neil was never so indiscreet as to reveal how much he stood to earn, though in time he did buy a substantial five-bedroom spread in LA, with a pool and library, not far from the Hollywood Bowl and the Greek Theatre, for a reported US$4.3 million. The former owners included Tim

Long, a writer for *The Simpsons*, and actor Katherine Heigl. His real estate portfolio was expanding.

But before any of that could take place, Neil had a problem: he'd already set in place dates with Liam in support of their album *Lightsleeper*. They released a video for the track 'Back to Life' in June, in which Neil posed at a piano while Liam stood nearby, cradling an ancient stringed instrument known as a lyre. Both wore layers of make-up. Behind them a cast of characters acted out what could have been a Greek tragedy. It was weird Finn business-as-usual and a teasing preview of the LP. Another track from the album, 'Hold Her Close', was 'gifted' by the Finns to New Zealand PM Jacinda Ardern upon the birth of her first child, a girl named Neve Te Aroha, on 21 June.

But as Liam told *Variety*, he was happy to step aside to let his father play with Fleetwood Mac, as was the rest of the Finn family. Liam was possibly an even bigger Fleetwood Mac fan than his father; he'd been turned on to the band by his wife Janina. 'You've got to go and do that,' Liam told Neil when he broke the news. What kind of son would refuse his father a dream gig?

The Finns did, however, manage to fit some *Lightsleeper* dates in before Neil hit the road in earnest in September, and the album was released to strong reviews. 'Move aside Lennon/McCartney,' declared Karl Puschmann at *The New Zealand Herald*, 'we've got Finn/Finn.'

*

Neil and the 'new' Fleetwood Mac made their public debut on US daytime talk show *Ellen* on 5 September 2018, performing 'The Chain' live in the studio. Neil, looking effortlessly cool in a dark suit and sneakers, stepped confidently into the spotlight, sharing the vocals with Nicks, while the *Ellen* crowd did what they always do—they went crazy.

'Don't they sound amazing?' exclaimed the ever-perky Ellen DeGeneres as she joined the band on the set. When asked to introduce the new members of the band, Nicks said, 'This is Mr Neil Finn. Vocals. Guitar. Fantastic,' before going on to introduce Mike Campbell. The audience went even crazier when DeGeneres told them they'd all scored tickets to see the band at The Forum in LA. Later in the show they returned to play 'Gypsy'.

Pre-tour, Neil said that he wouldn't presume he could play any of his own songs—this was a Fleetwood Mac tour, after all—but during their opening night in Tulsa, the stage was turned over to him twice, early on for 'I Got You' and then later in their 24-song set for 'Don't Dream It's Over'. Nicks joined him for the final verse, her eyes meeting Neil's as she sang 'counting the steps to the door of your heart', the sort of romantic—but not mushy—lyric every tunesmith dreamed of writing.

'Many years ago,' Fleetwood told the crowd at the second show, in Chicago on 6 October, 'I heard this beautiful song and it opened a lot of doors in my heart. I had no idea it would lead to such a night welcoming this gentleman to the stage.' Knowing fans in the 20,000-plus audience—and there were plenty of them—sang along heartily as Neil performed 'Don't Dream It's Over', Nicks again joining him. This became the norm for every night of the tour.

There were surprises for Mac fans, too: most nights Neil took the lead vocal on 'Hypnotized' (a Bob Welch song) and

Danny Kirwan's 'Tell Me All the Things You Do', songs the band hadn't played for many years. 'Free Fallin'', a classic by the late Tom Petty—a friend to all the band—featured among their encores.

Neil's long-time producer Mitchell Froom had worked with members of Fleetwood Mac and knew their music well. While he knew how good a player Buckingham was—'he's probably the most irreplaceable person in any band'—when Froom saw Neil play with Fleetwood Mac, he sensed a difference in the band. 'All of a sudden there was all this joy coming off the stage,' he said. 'That's not a small thing. When Lindsey was there . . . there was all this tension, there was a darker feeling.'

At one early show, Neil spotted someone in the front row wearing a Lindsey Buckingham T-shirt, who was gesturing to him, pointing at his outfit. But, as Neil reported, any tension faded quickly. 'By halfway through the show,' he told the BBC, 'they were jigging around like everyone else.'

By mid-February 2019, the tour reached New Orleans, filling the 18,000-capacity Smoothie King Center. Fleetwood by now had tweaked his nightly introduction for Neil ever so slightly, admitting that when he'd first heard 'Don't Dream It's Over', 'I had no idea who was singing it, who had written it, or the band from whence it had come. Shortly after that, of course, I did.' He continued: 'To be standing here, not only introducing the song, but the man who wrote it, is indeed a magical pleasure. Mr Neil Finn.'

'It's so good to be here with you, playing with this magnificent band,' said Neil in response, as he stepped up to the microphone. Once again, a massive audience sing-along ensued as Neil, looking dapper in black, played 'Don't Dream It's Over', which had proved to segue very neatly into

'Landslide', a signature Stevie Nicks song, in which Neil accompanied her on acoustic guitar. These were two big moments of the set, night after night. But in New Orleans, as Nicks prepared to sing 'Landslide', she had an announcement about Neil's family. 'I'd like to dedicate this next song to Neil's wife Sharon . . . she's leaving us, she's bailing for two or three weeks, because they're going to have a new grandchild. So we're dedicating "Landslide" to the new baby, to Sharon and to Neil.' Clearly, the relationship between Neil and Fleetwood Mac was about much more than business.

But business was booming, as the band filled enormous venues night after night, even though some fans went to great lengths to point out on social media that it took two musicians to replace Lindsey Buckingham. They packed New York's Madison Square Garden twice, drawing 30,000 punters each night. The North American leg of the tour, 50-odd dates, averaged US$1.8 million per show.

One concert in Belgium drew a crowd of 45,000, then 48,000 in the Netherlands and 22,000 in Berlin. They filled Wembley Stadium twice, playing to about 80,000 people each night. The returns were huge and the critical response was positive. A reviewer for their Tampa Bay, Florida, gig admitted 'that while tours like these often feel like twilight cruises, you can't help but hope that this line-up will take another victory lap'.

Neil had also learned about the benefits of being in such a popular band. In California, he was pulled over by a cop after rolling through a stop sign. When asked to show some ID, Neil produced his New Zealand licence.

'What are you doing here?' asked the cop.

'I'm in a band,' Neil replied. 'Fleetwood Mac.'

Neil was waved on his way, without a ticket. He figured that at the very least he owed Mick Fleetwood a decent bottle of pinot.

*

The birth of a second son for Liam and his wife was a huge moment for family man Neil, but sadness wasn't far away. The latest leg of the Evening with Fleetwood Mac tour wound up in Auckland on 19 September—'Finn's new gig seems to fire up his sex appeal,' stated a reviewer for Stuff—but just over two weeks later, on 5 October, Neil's father died at Waikato Hospital. He was 97. Tim posted a short, sweet message: 'Fond farewell to the best boy rider in Te Rore. Richard George Finn 1922–2019. RIP.'

Neil wrapped up his Fleetwood Mac duties with a heavy heart, playing the last of the shows in San Francisco on 20 November, a fundraiser for the UCSF Benioff Children's Hospitals. In typical Neil Finn fashion, he'd somehow found the time to write and record with various members of the band while on the road. He and Mick Fleetwood wrote a song called 'My Father Told Me So', one of a number of new song ideas they'd been exploring—and a very fitting theme, given Dick's passing.

When the tour had been in New Zealand, Neil invited Stevie Nicks and Christine McVie into Roundhead for a couple of hours, where they added vocals to a track he was recording called 'Find Your Way Back Home'. This song came with an interesting backstory. Architect Nicholas 'Nicco' Stevens was a family friend of Neil's. He was the driving force behind the Auckland City Mission's HomeGround project, a community space that was, in Neil's view, 'a major civic project that's going to do a lot of good'. Stevens asked Neil if he could possibly contribute a song to help publicise the project, hence 'Find Your Way Back Home'. Mike Campbell also helped out, as did Liam. All proceeds from downloads and sales of the song went to the City Mission. 'I'm an Aucklander at heart,' said Neil on its release in May 2020, 'so it didn't seem difficult.'

When asked about his time with Fleetwood Mac, Neil described it as 'first class all the way' and he remained open to the possibility of working with them again. Remarkably, given Fleetwood Mac's reputation for conflict, there were only three band meetings during the entire tour, which stretched for thirteen months and comprised four separate legs. By tour's end, Mick Fleetwood had a clear understanding of what Neil contributed to the group: 'Class. Understanding. It's about an emotive connection.'

*

While Crowded House wasn't now as all-encompassing as it had been for Neil during the 1980s, it remained a big part of his musical life. But in the wake of his Fleetwood Mac experience, Neil decided that some changes were in order. Neil asked himself a simple question: how could he reimagine Crowded House so that it would continue to excite him? The answer was closer than he realised.

Being in Fleetwood Mac gave Neil 'an appreciation for classic bands', Neil told the panel of Australian TV show *The Project*. 'And I thought, well, they can be reinvented and reinvigorated. And why not? It means something to me.'

Neil had thoroughly enjoyed the experience of playing music with Liam and Elroy in various guises: on the road with the Pajama Club, the 'Finn family' shows and on different recordings—and he respected them as players. (And not just Neil. 'Elroy is an incredible drummer,' said Mitchell Froom.) Neil understood that Crowded House was part of his sons' DNA. 'They grew up with Crowded House,' he said, 'it's deeply ingrained in their psyches.' Liam had toured extensively with the band in 2007, while as a boy, Elroy would stand side of stage at gigs and imitate Nick Seymour's dance moves. They both learned to play drums to the sound of 'Fall at Your Feet'.

Towards the end of the Fleetwood Mac roadshow, when Neil's thoughts again turned to Crowded House, he decided to ask his sons to join the band: Liam on guitar, keyboards and vocals, and Elroy playing drums. When Neil popped the question, they had no hesitation: they were keen to sign up. Fears that Neil's offer might be seen as a gesture of nepotism didn't resonate with them at all. 'It seemed just really exciting to me,' Liam told Music Feeds, 'because I care so much about that band and I want to protect the legacy of that band . . . I was excited at the idea of helping shape what that next journey might look like.'

This all meant yet another farewell for Mark Hart, whose lengthy involvement with Crowded House appeared to involve a series of revolving doors, as well as Matt Sherrod, who'd been with the band since 2007. Hart tweeted news of his departure in mid-August 2019. 'I feel it's time to let you all know that Neil has informed me that I will not be a part of the band's new line-up. Being a part of Crowded House for 30 years was a pleasure and a privilege.' Hart wished everyone well and hoped that fans 'enjoy the new band'. In response, Neil confirmed that it was true, and that 'I have nothing but respect and goodwill for Mark'. Politeness aside, though, it must have stung Hart to be sidelined again.

Nick Seymour would be the only member of the existing band retained by Neil. He also recruited Mitchell Froom, whose association with Crowded House dated all the way back to their breakout debut album. Neil had considered asking Froom to join the band at the time of that debut, but Froom had a baby at home, and was deeply involved in establishing himself as a producer, so it wouldn't have been possible for him. Froom hadn't been a formal member of a band since he was in his teens.

'It feels great to change things up and do something different,' Froom said of his new role, when interviewed on RNZ. '[Neil's] the bandleader, he's the songwriter, it's his thing, and I'm trying to fit into it in a way that's beneficial to me and the band. It's interesting on a lot of levels . . .'

Froom acknowledged that the recruitment of Liam and Elroy, both of whom he'd known pretty much all their lives, influenced his decision to join. He loved their energy, their enthusiasm. After one rehearsal, Froom told Neil, 'I'm in. I want to do this.'

Not all of the band's fans were thrilled about the changes to Crowded House. Some comments echoed the concerns of Fleetwood Mac's true believers when Neil and Mike Campbell had been recruited. 'This all has me feeling fairly disgusted,' read one post on the Frenz Forum. 'In one fell swoop, the concept of Crowded House has become fairly meaningless. I don't know what this band is.' A few fans weren't even convinced that the news about the altered line-up was true; some hinted that it might be Neil posting under an assumed name, winding them up. One wag posted a suggestion that Mark Hart should make a record with Lindsey Buckingham.

*

None of this mattered much to Neil. He and the 2020 version of Crowded House began rehearsals for a new album the day after he came off the road with Fleetwood Mac. Neil wanted to avoid any possibility of what he called the 'post-tour slump', so he booked studio time and got back to work. Momentum was everything.

Sessions for the record began in early 2020 at Valentine Studios in Los Angeles, a peculiar time capsule of a place, which in the past had hosted everyone from Frank Zappa to The Beach Boys and Bing Crosby. The studio, which first operated between 1963 and 1979, had been shut down when the owner, Jimmy Valentine, diversified into car restoration. When it was finally reopened in 2015, nothing had been changed in over 30 years—the equipment, the fittings, the ambience, the shag-pile carpet on the walls. Liam described it as a 'really amazing timepiece'.

But then drama struck with the outbreak of COVID-19 and the lockdown that was enforced in California during March 2020. (California was the first US state to issue a 'stay at home' order.) Neil was forced to end the sessions and returned to New Zealand in March 2020, while Liam and Elroy remained in Los Angeles, where they both now lived, as did Froom. Nick Seymour went home to Ireland. But the basic tracks for the album that would become *Dreamers Are*

Waiting—'all brimming with character and energy', reported Neil—had been cut by the time of lockdown.

So over the next few months, as the world tried to understand the scope and impact of the pandemic, Neil and the others worked from home, talking regularly, bouncing revised takes between each other via Dropbox, fine-tuning the songs.

Liam managed to see the benefits of the extra time that lockdown accidentally presented. 'We got a lot more time to work on it, which was good in a way.' This also resulted in a broader spread of writing credits on the finished album: Elroy co-wrote three tracks, as did Liam, who also composed 'Goodnight Everyone' on his own. Seymour and Froom also had co-writing credits. Neil co-wrote 'Too Good For This World' with brother Tim.

Neil's original plan—to release the record in 2020 and tour the world—was put on hold. Subsequent plans were altered, and then altered again, as the pandemic stayed put and touring became an impossibility. Neil and the band spent much of 2020 in isolation. He referred to it as 'our strangest year'.

★

Crowded House hadn't played for a paying audience since their string of dates at the Sydney Opera House during November 2016. But by early 2021, through some complicated COVID-aware planning, they were finally ready to plug in and play again. They booked a dozen dates in March in New Zealand, one of the few places on the planet where it was possible at the time to perform live. It wasn't easy—Nick Seymour had to undertake a 32-hour odyssey to join the others in Auckland, all the while fearing that one of his flights might be cancelled. As he drove to the airport from his home in Sligo, Ireland, Seymour said to himself, 'This is actually delusional.'

When Seymour did finally reach New Zealand, he was straight into a two-week quarantine, along with Mitchell Froom and various members of the band's crew. After that enforced isolation, three local cases of COVID meant that Auckland was back into Level 3 lockdown. Level 4 would have meant the tour was off. Fearing this, Neil arranged for beds to be set up in the rehearsal space of his Roundhead Studios, 'so we could all stay in the same bubble under Level 4'.

Somehow the band—Neil, Seymour, Liam, Elroy and Froom—finally managed to set up together and rehearse at Roundhead on 17 February 2021 in preparation for the tour. It had been a long time coming, especially for someone so dedicated to making music as Neil. But he'd been luckier than most musicians, who were simply unable to get out and play because of lockdowns and quarantines and vaccines and the rest of it. It was a very strange time to be a musician.

'Every morning I wake up and can't believe my luck,' Neil told a reporter from Stuff. 'We're in a remarkably fortunate position.' Not so fortunate, unfortunately, that COVID didn't mess with their plans and force the postponement of a few shows.

The To the Island New Zealand Tour 2021 belatedly began on 10 March at Christchurch—Neil sported what could best be described as 'lockdown hair', even shaggier than usual, while the band's in-house fashionista, Nick Seymour, donned a kilt. Over this and the subsequent dates of the tour, Neil and the new Crowded House struck the perfect balance of standards—'Weather With You', 'Pineapple Head', 'Don't Dream It's Over' (which, at the Christchurch show, Neil dedicated to Australian music mogul Michael Gudinski, who had died on 2 March)—with samples of *Dreamers Are Waiting*, their lockdown album. Neil even threw in a cover of David Bowie's 'Heroes' among the encores, which they'd play most nights of the tour. It all wound up with an outdoor concert at the Church Road Winery in Napier on 28 March. 'The crowds were wide-eyed and full of wonder,' said Neil, 'and we felt the same way.'

A few days later, post-tour, Neil, Liam, Froom and Seymour were in Roundhead for a new Fangradio broadcast, a blow-by-blow discussion of the *Together Alone* album. Apart from more Fangradio segments and a few US TV appearances later in the year, Neil and Crowded House wouldn't resurface until April 2022—and even then, only after Neil himself recovered from COVID.

Dreamers Are Waiting, meanwhile, fared well commercially, hitting number 2 in Australia and New Zealand and number 6 in the UK. Critics praised the record, too, best summed up by a review in *American Songwriter* magazine: '*Dreamers Are Waiting* is quality, thoughtful pop from the mind of a guy who knows his way around a terrific tune.'

More than 40 years into a musical life with more twists and turns than he ever would have imagined, Neil Finn couldn't have asked for higher praise. After all, as his mother had once told him: 'A good tune is hard to come by.'

Coda

WIN Entertainment Centre, Wollongong, New South Wales, 8 November 2022

I first saw Neil Finn play live in the winter of 1979, when he was in Split Enz. I was a seventeen-year-old 'westie' from Padstow, a far-flung, red-brick suburb of Sydney. I had to sneak into the gig, which was staged at a licensed disco in the dead (and I mean dead) heart of Sydney's CBD. It was a cold work night, and the place wasn't anywhere near full, but the gig has stayed with me ever since. For one thing, I vowed to never go near a stage when Split Enz was playing. I was shocked by how damned physical they were, slamming into each other like human pinballs, all the while pulling mad faces. The songs were great, too, dynamic and exciting—this was just before the *True Colours* LP and Neil's 'I Got You', which would be their huge breakthrough success. And the band's pointy hairdos, day-glo suits and heavy applications of Max Factor—well, you didn't see a lot of that in Padstow. It only added to the weirdness of the night that the support act was shock rockers Jimmy and the Boys, whose big finale was a simulated sex act. Again, not in Padstow.

Almost 30 years later, I found myself in a Sydney recording studio, at a listening party for Crowded House's *Time on Earth*, with Neil and Nick Seymour sitting nearby like expectant parents. I was tempted to ask Neil if he remembered that gig from all those years ago—the venue, now a 'gentlemen's club', was just a few blocks away—but thought better of it. I had a more immediate task at hand: to write the press release for the album, the band's first for some fourteen years. It was a fitting comeback, heartfelt and melodic, a poignant tribute to co-founder Paul Hester, who'd died two years earlier.

During that listening session, Neil mentioned how in 1996 the band split up without undertaking a big final lap of honour; there was no farewell/cash-in tour. 'But what about the Opera House?' I asked, referring to the Farewell to the World show that drew those several hundred thousand fans to the city, many of whom were in tears by the end of the concert. Neil shot me a look that I read as, 'Okay, smart-arse, you know what I mean.' Fair enough, I figured.

Now, on a night when the sky is illuminated by a blood-red moon, I'm standing inside the cavernous expanse of the WIN Entertainment Centre, among 5000 diehard Crowded House fans who are going absolutely nuts. Neil, resplendent in a purple velvet jacket, his hair as impressive a mop as ever, is master of ceremonies, leading the band—Elroy and Liam, Nick Seymour, Mitchell Froom—through a night of songs lifted straight from the Great Antipodean Songbook. 'Fall at Your Feet', 'Pineapple Head', 'Into Temptation', 'When

You Come', 'Private Universe', 'Something So Strong', 'Don't Dream It's Over', 'Weather With You' and more classics—including a beautiful 'Message To My Girl', performed solo by Neil at an upright piano—make up their 23-song set. Each is received with a roar and farewelled with deafening applause and cheers. Okay, so not every song is a Crowded House standard; they do sneak in snippets of Fats Domino's 'Blueberry Hill', Dolly Parton's 'I Will Always Love You' and Led Zeppelin's 'Whole Lotta Love', just to show that they haven't lost their playful spirit (nor has Nick Seymour lost his sartorial edge; his kilt tonight is jet black). On stage the band is sometimes joined by an enigmatic four-piece ensemble named Maistrato, who first met the Finns in Greece and have been invited along for this, the Dreamers Are Waiting Australian tour, Crowded House's first for twelve years. Maistrato's presence goes to show that anyone who doubted 'Weather With You' wasn't written for bouzoukis was clearly mistaken. 'I'd give a limb to write one great song,' I shout to my friend between numbers. 'This guy,' I say, pointing towards the stage and Neil, 'has written dozens. Bastard!'

As I took it all in, I kept flashing back to my first glimpse of a very young Neil Finn on that chilly Tuesday night at the Pitt Street Gardens in 1979, where he crashed into his Split Enz mates on the tiny stage, unaware that his career was about to explode. It had been a long road since then for Neil, stretching more than 40 years and too many gigs to recount—and enough highs and lows to fill several biographies—but he's now a pop statesman, arguably the best songwriter of his generation, who, as he shows tonight, can captivate an audience from the opening notes of 'Distant Sun' right through to the closing strains of 'Better

Be Home Soon' some two hours later. Tonight, Neil defers (and refers) to the leader of Maistrato as 'maestro', but in truth it is he who is the maestro. Always will be.

Acknowledgements

My heartfelt thanks go out, yet again, to Jane Palfreyman, Jenn Thurgate, Samantha Kent and all at Allen & Unwin, without whom this book would not exist. Likewise the always supportive and remarkably knowledgeable Emma Driver, and proofreader Megan Johnston. It's an honour and a pleasure to work with all of you again—this is book number six, with (hopefully) more to come. It's the closest I'll ever come to knowing what it's like to be part of a great band.

And a big thank you to the many people who've helped me bring together this portrait of Neil Finn, which is derived from my many years of listening, reading and writing. So, here's to you: Ralph Alfonso, John Babbitt, James Barton, Murray Bennett, Doug Black, Jacqui Black, Kevin Borich, Chris Bourke, Alan Brown, Murray Cammick, Jewel and Barry Coburn, Ray Columbus OBE CM, Chris Cuffaro, Joe D'Ambrosio, Doug D'Arcy, Fenella Davidson, Kerry Doole, Clayton Doughty, Michael Dwyer, Christie Eliezer, Venetta Fields, Anna Fitzgerald, Terry Fong, Rob Gordon, Roger Grierson, Claire Harvey, Bobby Huff, Todd Hunter, Catherine Jehly, Jay Joyce, Herm Kovac, Bruce Kirkland, Koji Kumada, Jennifer Lasker, Nick Launay, Debbie Levitt, Lydia Livingstone, Val MacIver, Paul McNamara, Mark Moffatt, Tony Mott, Rod (and Roddy) Murdoch, Kevin

Mueller, Anthony O'Grady (R.I.P.), Chris O'Hearn, Hugh Padgham, Martin Philbey, Mark Pringle, Jennifer Probert, Andy Purcell, Gideon Reiss, Rhianne Smith, Paul Spencer, Buster Stiggs (R.I.P.), Dean and Robyn Taylor, Peter Terry, Matthew Wiley, Tay Wilson (R.I.P. Trevor Wilson).

Special thanks to Craig Hooper and Barry Divola for their time and input, to Richard Sutton for the 'magic box', and, in particular, to Peter Green and Mark Goulding for their detailed and comprehensive read and fact check—you guys have amazing memories! Thanks also for the photos. And a special nod to Barry Hughes, wherever you are, who got me on this rollercoaster in the first place back in 1979. As always, a big thank you to Diana, Christian, Elizabeth, the blue dog, the regal cat and the other members of the clan.

Neil Finn: Ten musical moments

(Author's note: This is by no means definitive.)

'Give It a Whirl': Neil's first great song (a co-write with brother Tim, in fact) and also his first track recorded by Split Enz. From the 1979 album *Frenzy*.

'Message to My Girl': The Noel Crombie-directed, one-take video (okay, two takes, watch closely), was a classic, the perfect partner for Neil's 1984 musical valentine to his wife Sharon.

'Private Universe': In June 1994, Neil brought the log drummers to TV's *Later . . . with Jools Holland* for a mind-blowing take on the standout track from *Together Alone*.

'Better Be Home Soon': Neil's solo performance at the 1995 ARIA Awards was his poignant farewell to Paul Hester.

'She Will Have Her Way': From Neil's solo debut, *Try Whistling This*, but best heard played by Neil's 7 Worlds Collide collective, live at Auckland's St James Theatre in April 2001.

'Silent House': The standout of Crowded House's *Time on Earth* album, co-written with The Chicks. From 2007.

'Song of the Lonely Mountain': Two Kiwi kings—Neil, the music maestro, meets Peter Jackson, acclaimed film director. From the soundtrack of *The Hobbit: An Unexpected Journey*, 2012.

'Don't Dream It's Over': Perhaps the most unlikely cover of this modern classic was by Ariana Grande and Miley Cyrus at the One Love Manchester concert in June 2017, a fundraiser after the bombing that killed 23 concertgoers. And so what if they needed the autocue?

'Disembodied Voices': A standout from The Finn Brothers' LP *Everyone Is Here*, best witnessed on The Infinity Sessions, August 2017, streamed on YouTube.

'Where's My Room': A song about spending too many years wandering the hallways of anonymous hotels. Wonderful weirdness that Neil recorded with his son Liam for their 2018 LP *Lightsleeper*, with an accompanying video inspired by *The Shining*.

Selected Neil Finn discography

SPLIT ENZ STUDIO ALBUMS FEATURING NEIL FINN

DIZRYTHMIA (1977)

Bold as Brass/My Mistake/Parrot Fashion Love/Sugar and Spice/Without a Doubt/Crosswords/Charlie/Nice to Know/Jamboree

Bonus track for 2006 re-release: Another Great Divide

FRENZY (1979)

I See Red/Give It a Whirl/Master Plan/Famous People/Hermit McDermitt/Stuff and Nonsense/Marooned/Frenzy/The Roughest Toughest Game in the World/She Got Body She Got Soul/Betty/Abu Dhabi/Mind Over Matter

Bonus tracks for 2006 re-release: Semi Detached/Carried Away/Horse to Water

TRUE COLOURS (1980)

Shark Attack/I Got You/What's The Matter With You/Double Happy/I Wouldn't Dream of It/I Hope I Never/Nobody Takes Me Seriously/Missing Person/Poor Boy/How Can I Resist Her/The Choral Sea

Bonus tracks for 2006 re-release: Things/Two of a Kind

WAIATA (AKA CORROBOREE) (1981)

Hard Act to Follow/One Step Ahead/I Don't Wanna Dance/Iris/Wail/Clumsy/History Never Repeats/Walking Through the Ruins/Ships/Ghost Girl/Albert of India

Bonus track for 2006 re-release: In the Wars

TIME AND TIDE (1982)

Dirty Creature/Giant Heartbeat/Hello Sandy Allen/Never Ceases to Amaze Me/Lost for Words/Small World/Take a Walk/Pioneer/Six Months in a Leaky Boat/Haul Away/Log Cabin Fever/Make Sense of It

CONFLICTING EMOTIONS (1983)

Strait Old Line/Bullet Brain and Cactus Head/Message To My Girl/Working Up an Appetite/Our Day/No Mischief/The Devil You Know/I Wake Up Every Night/Conflicting Emotions/Bon Voyage

SEE YA 'ROUND (1984)

Breakin' My Back/I Walk Away/Doctor Love/One Mouth Is Fed/Years Go By/Voices/The Lost Cat/Adz/This Is Massive/Kia Kaha/Ninnie Knees Up

Bonus track for 2006 re-release: Next Exit

THE ROOTIN TOOTIN LUTON TAPES (2007)

CD1: Miss Haps/Home Comforts/Animal Lover/Carried Away/Semi Detached/Holy Smoke/Message Boy/Hypnotised/Late in Rome/Straight Talk/Hollow Victory/Evelyn/Best Friend/Creature Comforts/Remember When

CD2: Hermit McDermitt/Betty/I See Red/Mind Over Matter/Next Exit/She Got Body She Got Soul/So This is Love/Abu Dhabi/Famous People/I'm So Up/Marooned/Livin' It Up/Frenzy

For Split Enz live albums, anthologies, etc., see:
Wikipedia: Split Enz discography: http://en.wikipedia.org/wiki/Split_Enz_discography
Kia Kaha Enz Archives: www.kiakaha.net

CROWDED HOUSE STUDIO ALBUMS

CROWDED HOUSE (1986)

Mean to Me/World Where You Live/Now We're Getting Somewhere/Don't Dream It's Over/Love You 'Til the Day I Die/Something So Strong/Hole in the River/Can't Carry On/I Walk Away/Tombstone/That's What I Call Love

TEMPLE OF LOW MEN (1988)

I Feel Possessed/Kill Eye/Into Temptation/Mansion in the Slums/When You Come/Never Be the Same/Love This Life/Sister Madly/In the Lowlands/Better Be Home Soon

WOODFACE (1991)

Chocolate Cake/It's Only Natural/Fall at Your Feet/Tall Trees/Weather With You/Whispers and Moans/Four Seasons in One Day/There Goes God/Fame Is/All I Ask/As Sure As I Am/Italian Plastic/She Goes On/How Will You Go/I'm Still Here (hidden track)

TOGETHER ALONE (1993)

Kare Kare/In My Command/Nails in My Feet/Black and White Boy/Fingers of Love/Pineapple Head/Locked Out/Private Universe/Walking on the Spot/Distant Sun/Catherine Wheels/Skin Feeling/Together Alone

TIME ON EARTH (2007)

Nobody Wants To/Don't Stop Now/She Called Up/Say That Again/Pour Le Monde/Even a Child/Heaven That I'm Making/A Sigh/Silent House/English Trees/Walked Her Way Down/Transit Lounge/You Are the Only One to Make Me Cry/People Are Like Suns

INTRIGUER (2010)

Saturday Sun/Archer's Arrows/Amsterdam/Either Side of the World/Falling Dove/Isolation/Twice If You're Lucky/Inside Out/Even If/Elephants

DREAMERS ARE WAITING (2021)

Bad Times Good/Playing With Fire/To the Island/Sweet Tooth/Whatever You Want/Show Me the Way/Goodnight Everyone/Too Good for This World/Start of Something/Real Life Woman/Love Isn't Hard at All/Deeper Down

NEIL FINN STUDIO ALBUMS

TRY WHISTLING THIS (1998)

Last One Standing/Souvenir/King Tide/Try Whistling This/She Will Have Her Way/Sinner/Twisty Bass/Loose Tongue/Truth/Astro/Dream Date/Faster Than Light/Addicted

ONE NIL (AKA ONE ALL) (2001)

The Climber/Rest of the Day Off/Hole in the Ice/Wherever You Are/Last to Know/Don't Ask Why/Secret God/Turn and Run/Elastic Heart/Anytime/Driving Me Mad/Into the Sunset

DIZZY HEIGHTS (2014)

Impressions/Dizzy Heights/Flying in the Face of Love/Divebomber/Better than TV/Pony Ride/White Lies and Alibis/Recluse/Strangest Friends/In My Blood/Lights of New York

OUT OF SILENCE (2017)

Love is Emotional/More Than One of You/Chameleon Days/Independence Day/Alone/Widow's Peak/Second Nature/The Law is Always on Your Side/Terrorise Me/I Know Different

NEIL AND LIAM FINN STUDIO ALBUMS

LIGHTSLEEPER (2018)

Prelude—Island of Peace/Meet Me in the Air/Where's My Room/Anger Plays a Part/Listen/Any Other Way/Back to Life/Hiding Place/Ghosts/We Know What It Means/Hold Her Close

PAJAMA CLUB

PAJAMA CLUB (2011)

Tell Me What You Want/Can't Put It Down Until It Ends/These Are Conditions/From a Friend to a Friend/Golden Child/Daylight/Go Kart/Dead Leg/TNT for 2/The Game We Love to Play/Diamonds in Her Eyes

TIM AND NEIL FINN (THE FINN BROTHERS) STUDIO ALBUMS

FINN (1995)

Only Talking Sense/Eyes of the World/Mood Swinging Man/Last Day of June/Suffer Never/Angel's Heap/Niwhai/Where Is My Soul/Bullets in My Hairdo/Paradise (Wherever You Are)/Kiss the Road of Rarotonga

EVERYONE IS HERE (2004)

Won't Give In/Nothing Wrong With You/Anything Can Happen/Luckiest Man Alive/Homesick/Disembodied Voices/A Life Between Us/All God's Children/Edible Flowers/All the Colours/Part of Me, Part of You/Gentle Hum

For more Finn Brothers-related releases, see the Kia Kaha Enz Archives: www.kiakaha.net

VARIOUS ARTISTS

7 WORLDS COLLIDE: LIVE AT THE ST. JAMES (2001)*

Anytime/Take a Walk/The Climber/Loose Tongue/Down on the Corner/There is a Light That Never Goes Out/Paper Doll/Turn and Run/Angel's Heap/Edible Flowers/Stuff and Nonsense/I See Red/She Will Have Her Way/Parting Ways/Weather With You/Paradise (Wherever You Are)/Don't Dream It's Over

* Originally credited to 'Neil Finn & Friends'

THE SUN CAME OUT (2009)

Too Blue/You Never Know/Little By Little/Learn to Crawl/Girl, Make Your Own Mind Up/Hazel Black/Red Wine Bottle/Black Silk Ribbon/Run in the Dust/The Ties That Bind Us/What Could Have Been/Duxton Blues/Reptile

Selected bibliography

Adams, Cameron: 'Q&A with Neil Finn', *Herald Sun*, 4 June 1998

Adams, Cameron: 'Doing the splits', *Herald Sun*, 8 June 2006

Anon: 'ENZ—the new image', *The Sydney Morning Herald*, 2 March 1980

Anon: 'Australian rock in world class', *The Sydney Morning Herald*, 5 April 1981

Anon: 'Records', *The Sydney Morning Herald*, 10 May 1982

Anon: 'Wheel turns for the Finns', *The Sydney Morning Herald*, 12 April 1987

Anon: 'Finn finds a more mainstream sound', *Orange County Register*, 2 April 1989

Anon: 'Through thick and Finn', *The Irish Times*, 10 July 1998

Anon: 'Paul McCartney leads Linda tribute', BBC News, 11 April 1999, http://news.bbc.co.uk/

Anon: 'Something so wrong', *The Age*, 3 April 2005

Anon: 'Dream never over', Te Awamutu Online, 29 July 2008, www.teawamutu.nz

Anon: 'Crowded House *Intriguer*', *Billboard*, 6 August 2010

Anon: 'Your stories from the Crowded House farewell concert', ABC News, 25 November 2016, http://abc.net.au

Anon: 'Neil Finn encouraged to pause family side project for Fleetwood Mac', Stuff, 20 June 2018, www.stuff.co.nz

Anon: 'Neil & Liam Finn reveal "Ghosts"/"Hold Her Close"', Music.net.nz, 3 August 2018, www.muzic.net.nz

Anon: 'Neil Finn's tour of NZ town halls documented in new book', RNZ, 30 March 2019, www.rnz.co.nz

Anon: 'Take a peek inside Neil Finn's $7.2m LA home', Stuff, 29 March 2020, www.stuff.co.nz

Apter, Jeff: 'Crowded House *Time on Earth*', press release, 2007

Armstrong, Alistair: 'Finn class', *The Press*, 16 February 2001

August, Billy: '"Dad wanted it to feel like a band again": Liam Finn on the new-look Crowded House', Music Feeds, 2 June 2021, https://musicfeeds.com.au

Baillie, Russell: 'Review: Neil Finn's 7 Worlds Collide', *The New Zealand Herald*, 6 January 2009

Baker, Glenn A.: 'Split Enz come together in the name of Kiwi', *Billboard*, 8 August 1992

Bessman, Jim: 'Making room at Crowded House', *Billboard*, 13 July 1991

Blair, Iain: 'Down Under trio is hailed as great white hope of power pop', *Chicago Tribune*, 31 May 1987

Bollinger, Nick: 'Review: Neil Finn's new album *Out of Silence*', RNZ, 1 September 2017, www.rnz.co.nz

Brooks, Dave: 'Fleetwood Mac's North American tour on track to sell 1 million tickets', *Billboard*, 18 March 2019

Brown, Mark: 'Finns craft finest work yet', *Rocky Mountain News*, 14 February 2005

Carter, Shayne: *Dead People I Have Known*, Upstart Press, Auckland, 2019

Casimir, Jon: 'Split Enz realise history does repeat', *The Sydney Morning Herald*, 22 November 1989

Casimir, Jon: 'I've had sex that was less intimate: Looking back on Crowded House's iconic concert', *The Sydney Morning Herald*, 19 November 2021

Chick, Stevie: 'No more Crowded House: Neil Finn's new band, Pajama Club', *The Guardian*, 26 August 2011

Clayton-Lea, Tony: 'Yearning to be forever honest', *The Irish Times*, 7 April 2001

Clifforth, John: 'Cheeky larrikin stole the show', *The Sydney Morning Herald*, 4 April 2005

Cochrane, Peter: 'Split Enz orchestrates the hoons and the swots', *The Sydney Morning Herald*, 1 February 1997

Coupe, Stuart: 'Enz are waiting to split again', *The Sydney Morning Herald*, 29 July 1979

Coupe, Stuart: 'Split Enz Rock 'n' Roll into Sydney', *The Sydney Morning Herald*, 22 March 1981

Coupe, Stuart: 'Leaky boat ban over Falklands', *The Sydney Morning Herald*, 13 June 1982

Coupe, Stuart: 'Finn goes solo, but it's no Split to Enz', *The Sydney Morning Herald*, 3 July 1983

Coupe, Stuart: 'Enz back together after soul searching', *The Sydney Morning Herald*, 18 December 1983

Coupe, Stuart: 'Enz off road again for recording stint', *The Sydney Morning Herald*, 4 March 1984

Creswell, Toby: 'The end of an odyssey', *The Sydney Morning Herald*, 5 October 1984

Danielsen, Shane: 'No room for inspiration in this house', *The Sydney Morning Herald*, 12 August 1991

Darling, Cary: 'House rules in favour of bleakness on follow-up', *Orange County Register*, 8 July 1988

deCordova, Kirk: 'Crowded House: Farewell to the World review', Music Box Magazine, 1 September 2007, www.musicbox-online.com

DeYoung, Bill: 'Crowded House empties as band members move on', *Los Angeles Daily News*, 27 June 1996

Divola, Barry: Unpublished transcript from 7 Worlds Collide tour, 2001

Donovan, Patrick: 'Band of brothers', *The Sun-Herald*, 4 June 2006

Dowling, Stephen: 'One Nil to Neil', *The Observer*, 16 April 2001

Downie, Stephen: 'Brothers in arms', *The Daily Telegraph*, 7 July 2005

Dwyer, Michael: 'Growing up in private', *The Age*, date unknown

Dwyer, Michael: 'Neil Finn', *Rolling Stone Australia*, 1998

Dwyer, Michael: 'Not the Biggest band in the World', *Rolling Stone Australia*, 1999

Dwyer, Michael: 'Neil Finn does it the hard way with *Out of Silence*', *The Sydney Morning Herald*, 5 September 2017

Dwyer, Michael: 'The Enz of innocence', *The Age*, 19 November 2004

Elder, John: 'After a Crowded life Neil finds his own beat', *The Age*, 12 December 1998

Emerson, Bo: 'With LP, Tim Finn puts his Split Enz behind him', *The Atlanta Journal and Constitution*, 12 May 1989

Fletcher, Tony: 'Acid pop from Down Under', *Newsday*, 14 July 1991

Gee, Mike: 'Enz magic will never end', *Newcastle Herald*, 6 July 2005

Greene, Andy: 'Fleetwood Mac fires Lindsey Buckingham', *Rolling Stone*, 9 April 2018

Greenhoff, Peter: *ikon*, December 1995

Harmon, Steph: '"It's a love story really"—Mick Fleetwood

and Stevie Nicks on wooing Neil Finn', *The Guardian*, 16 August 2019

Harrington, Richard: 'The family ties of Crowded House', *The Washington Post*, 29 September 1991

Holmes, Peter: 'Finn-esse', *The Sydney Morning Herald*, 28 June 1991

Holmes, Peter: 'Neil Finn's homecoming', *The Sydney Morning Herald*, 5 February 1994

Holmes, Peter: 'Finn feels less crowded', *The Sun-Herald*, 27 November 1994

Hubbard, Michael: Andy White interview, musicOMH, 1999, www.musicomh.com

Hughley, Marty: 'Band of brothers', *The Oregonian*, 9 July 2004

Hutchison, Geoff: 'Fans mourn death of Paul Hester', ABC, 28 March 2005

Jameson, Julietta: 'Music makers with a business plan', *Business Review Weekly*, 10 July 1987

Johnson, Josh: 'Here's who Eddie Vedder calls when he's "tying one on"', ABC Audio (US), 23 March 2021

Jones, Alistair: 'Can't stop the muse', *The Sydney Morning Herald*, 11 August 2001

Jones, Bridget: 'Where Neil Finn's at', Stuff, 3 February 2014, www.stuff.co.nz.

Kerr-Lazenby, Mina: 'Saving St James: Auckland's dilapidated theatre waiting on cue for its next act', Stuff, 25 September 2021, www.stuff.co.nz.

Kim, Jae-Ha: 'Crowded House has found room to succeed in U.S.', *Chicago Sun-Times*, 11 September 1987

Kloeden, Deb: 'Neil Finn "Out of Silence" @ Sydney Opera House', Amnplify, 31 May 2018, http://amnplify.com.au

Laing, Dave: 'Never missed the beat or a laugh', *The Guardian*, 4 April 2005

Lalor, Peter: 'Face to face—Australia', *The Daily Telegraph*, 20 June 1998

Langford, Jackson: 'Crowded House announce first album in over a decade', Music Feeds, 18 February 2021, https://musicfeeds.com.au

Lanham, Tom: 'Finn brothers still making a racket with *Everyone Is Here*', *Oakland Tribune*, 9 July 2004

Lewis, Randy: 'Neil Finn's happy with the sad songs', *Los Angeles Times*, 9 March 2002

Martin, Gavin: 'Fellowship of the Finns', *The Independent*, 20 August 2004

McCarroll, Jo: 'Brotherly shove', *Sunday Star-Times*, 26 May 2002

McKenzie, Simon: 'Finn on life after House music', *Edinburgh Evening News*, 16 August 2001

Meadows, Richard: 'Crowded House's Neil Finn in New Zealand property dispute', *The Sydney Morning Herald*, 11 April 2016

Mengel, Noel: 'The vault', *The Courier-Mail*, 15 June 2006

Mengel, Noel: 'Songs that last', *The Courier-Mail*, 20 April 2002

Mushroom Records, *Dizrythmia Australian tour*, press release, 1977

O'Brien, Katrina: 'Rewind 1979', *The Sun-Herald*, 3 July 2005

O'Grady, Anthony: 'Split Enz', *RAM*, 12 July 1975

Oliver, Henry: 'A quick guide to Neil Finn's Infinity Sessions', The Spinoff, 29 August 2017, http://thespinoff.co.nz

Paphides, Peter; Odell, Michael: 'Rock of Ages interview: The Finn Brothers', *The Times*, 28 August 2004

Pareles, Jon: 'Recent releases of video cassettes; Split Enz', *The New York Times*, 21 September 1984

Parvin, Chris: 'In Finnity', *Aotearoa: The Magazine of Air New Zealand Link Network*, no. 1, June 1996

Price, Simon: 'For its finale the band breaks up', *The Independent on Sunday*, 1 April 2001

Read, Ellen: 'Long may the Finn family last', Stuff, 1 March 2015, www.stuff.co.nz

Roa, Ray: 'In Tampa, Fleetwood Mac survives a slow start and hypnotizes a sold-out Amalie Arena', CL Tampa Bay, 19 February 2019

Sadlier, Kevin: 'It's standing room only for Crowded House', *The Sun-Herald*, 31 July 1988

Savage, Mark: 'Crowded House's Neil Finn: The most debauched we got was water fights', BBC News, 11 June 2021, www.bbc.com/news.

Schembri, Jim: 'Finn philosophy wins no points for charisma', *The Sydney Morning Herald*, 18 April 1986

Scherer, Jule: 'Rocky ride for Wilco', Stuff, 20 April 2010, www.stuff.co.nz

Schulz, Chris: 'Inside Crowded House's comeback: "This is actually delusional"', Stuff, 28 February 2021, www.stuff.co.nz

Sculley, Alan: 'Road led in a new direction', *St. Louis Post-Dispatch*, 22 April 1994

Semon, Craig S.: 'Once again, Tim Finn makes songwriting look easy', *Sunday Telegram*, 19 September 1993

Semon, Craig S.: 'Woodface is a guaranteed crowd pleaser', *Sunday Telegram*, 18 August 1991

Sennett, Sean: 'One's a crowd', *The Sun-Herald*, 14 June 1998

Sennett, Sean: 'Soul sisters put a fresh spin on all songs Finn', *The Sun-Herald*, 25 September 2005

Shedden, Iain: 'A less crowded house', *The Australian*, 24 June 1998

Shedden, Iain: 'Wandering minstrel happy at home', *The Australian*, 19 May 2000

Shuster, Fred: 'Crowded House breaks new ground', *Los Angeles Daily News*, 16 March 1994

Smith, Aidan: 'Escaping the comfort zone', *The Scotsman*, 15 August 2001

Snider, Eric: 'Finding a niche with a no-frills sound', *St. Petersburg Times*, 6 May 1987

Split Enz, *The Rootin Tootin Luton Tapes*, liner notes, Rhino Records, 2007

Sutcliffe, Phil: 'The rats are crawling up my back and other seasonal thoughts courtesy of Split Enz', *Sounds*, 24 December 1977

Sutcliffe, Phil: 'The Enz justify the means', *Sounds*, 25 December 1976

Sutcliffe, Phil: 'Don't dream it's over', *Q*, July 1992

Te Koha, Nui: 'Drummer's friends and fans ask why it's over', *The Courier-Mail*, 29 March 2005

Te Koha, Nui: 'Through thick and Finn', *Sunday Herald Sun*, 22 August 2004

Teague, Marcus: 'Ryan Adams and Neil Finn fall out during TV taping', *The Sydney Morning Herald*, 26 October 2011

Verrender, Ian: 'From the archives, 1996: It's chock-a-block for Crowded House', *The Sydney Morning Herald*, 24 November 2021

Washburn, Jim: 'Down Under three's a Crowded House', *Orange County Register*, 4 September 1987

Watson, Chad: 'Far from Finnished', *Newcastle Herald*, 2 July 1998

Williams, Peter: 'Low-key Finny business', *The Mercury*, 12 February 2005

Willman, Chris: 'Split Enz leaders reunite in remodeled Crowded House', *Los Angeles Times*, 3 September 1991

Willman, Chris: 'Ryan Adams shunned by the music business and "scared," pleads for labels to rescue his career', *Variety*, 27 July 2021

Willman, Chris: 'Neil and Liam Finn premiere first father–son music video', *Variety*, 19 June 2018

Wilmoth, Peter: 'Tim Finn goes solo, so Split Enz split for a bit', *The Sydney Morning Herald*, 21 October 1983

Wynn, Kirsty: 'Famous people passed his way', *The New Zealand Herald*, 4 December 2011

Zuel, Bernard: 'The homecoming', *The Sydney Morning Herald*, 27 October 1995

Zuel, Bernard: 'Smile, you're on home video', *The Sydney Morning Herald*, 28 September 2002

SELECTED AUDIO/VIDEO

Brian Edwards (host), interview with Neil Finn, *Top o' the Morning*, RNZ, 21 December 1996

Crowded House, *Farewell to the World: 10th Anniversary Edition*, DVD, EMI, 2006

Crowded House, *Together Alone* album, filmed at Karekare, 1993 https://www.youtube.com/watch?v=mhDlyWxMqIc

Deirdre O'Donoghue (host), 'Neil and Tim Finn', *Live at KCRW SNAP*, KCRW, 28 February 1988, www.youtube.com/watch?v=OA21BJSgIyY&list=PLE6F62BAEC42844A3

Jeremy Ansell (host), *Enzology*, radio documentary series, RNZ, 2005, www.rnz.co.nz/national/programmes/enzology

Jeremy Ansell (host), interview with Phil Judd, RNZ, 26 October 2006, www.rnz.co.nz/national/programmes/nat-music/audio/2530525/phil-judd

Larry Meltzer (director/producer), *Great Australian Albums: Woodface*, Mushroom Pictures, 2007

Liane Hansen (host), interview with Neil Finn, *Weekend Edition*, NPR, 30 August 1998

Mark Ellen and David Hepworth (hosts), 'Phil Manzanera', podcast episode, *Word in Your Ear*, 26 May 2021, www.youtube.com/watch?v=Y_dhheyiwcI

Split Enz, *Spellbound*, DVD, Festival Mushroom Records, 1993

WEBSITES

Neil Finn: www.neilfinn.com
Fangradio: www.fangradio.com
Crowded House: www.crowdedhouse.com
Radio New Zealand: www.rnz.co.nz
www.kiakaha.net
setlist.fm: www.setlist.fm

ADDITIONAL READING

Apter, Jeff: *Together Alone: The Story of the Finn Brothers*, Random House, 2010

Bourke, Chris: *Crowded House: Something So Strong*, Pan Macmillan, 1997

Chunn, Mike: *Stranger Than Fiction: The Life and Times of Split Enz*, GP Publications, 1992

Dix, John: *Stranded in Paradise: New Zealand Rock and Roll, 1955 to the Modern Era*, Penguin Books, 1988